COME OUT STRONGER

STRONGER

Prepare and Respond Practically
in a Hypercompetitive, Global, 4IR World

CHRISTINE M. PEARSON

**Embrace Crisis
to Stack the Odds,
Keep People on Your Side,
and Buy Time**

Published in the United States by A.J. Kelstin
First edition, 2022

Identifiers: ISBN 9781737932321 (hardcover) | ISBN 9781737932307 (ebook) | ISBN 9781737932321 (paperback)
Subjects: Crisis management | Leadership – self-development | Crisis team | Signal detection and reporting | Learning from crises

Cover design by Pete Garceau
Content editing by Gwyn Nichols
Formatting by Polgarus Studio

www.readComeOutStronger.com

LIVE SHOOTER FATALITIES

TERRORIST ATTACK

INCONSISTENT GLOBAL RESPONSE

CONTAMINATION IN BATCH MINGLING

ENVIRONMENTAL DESTRUCTION

BOYCOTT

CYBER BREACH

EXTORTION

PANDEMIC

EXECUTIVE KIDNAPING

PRODUCT TAMPERING

ORGANIZATIONAL

CRISES

WORK-RELATED HOMICIDE

NATURAL DISASTER

Ethics Scandal

RANSOMWARE ATTACK

GLOBAL MEDIA ATTACK

WORKPLACE BOMBING

PLANT EXPLOSION

FRAUD

INCONSISTENT GLOBAL PROTOCOL

GLOBAL POLITICAL INSTABILITY

HAZ MATS SPILL

DEADLY RECOMMENDATION

EMPLOYEE ASSAULT

GLOBAL PRODUCT RECALL

for
Bryan

for
John

and for
Ian I. Mitroff

Stay loose.

\- JEM

crisis:

a low-probability, high impact event that threatens the survival of an organization, often shrouded in mystery and misgivings about cause, effect, and resolution.[1]

(Pearson and Clair, 1998)

Contents

Crisis Tools

Where To Learn More

COME OUT STRONGER

STRONGER

EMBRACE CRISIS TO STACK THE ODDS,
KEEP PEOPLE ON YOUR SIDE, AND BUY TIME

Introduction

My earliest memory of an organizational crisis is the crash of a 40-passenger commercial airplane, at a small regional airport in Kentucky that had no control tower, nor fire or rescue workers stationed at the field. After striking the ground, the plane rolled to inverted position and then slid several hundred feet until it stopped beside the runway, facing backwards. The engine nose and propeller were torn from the right wing, which later sheared off at the fuselage. The left wing also tore off, and the tail was demolished. The plane was destroyed. The human toll was inconceivable: no one was injured.

On the ground, the sole airline employee on duty was the station manager, my dad, who also fulfilled the roles of first responder/radio operator/weatherman and, eventually, eye witness during the Federal investigation of the crash. I remember him describing how eerie it was to walk on the ceiling of the fuselage, seat belts dangling from above, and how astounded and grateful he was that everyone on board had adapted to the terrifying situation so adeptly.

As Dad's career advanced, his responsibilities deepened regarding crisis preparation and response. Even as a child, I recognized his courage dealing with worst-case circumstances, days and nights at aircraft accident scenes, absorbed by care and retrieval of injured and deceased passengers and crew, their loved ones, and the other responders. As a graduate student, helping keep organizations and their stakeholders safe became a core goal for me.

One of my greatest career breaks was being an early architect of the field of Organizational Crisis Management, thanks to the education, inspiration, and job offer granted me by Ian Mitroff. What I learned with Ian and the executives who worked with us at USC's Center for Crisis Management was innovative and inspiring. Together, from diverse academic, organizational, industrial, and regulatory perspectives, we built approaches and tools that uncovered causes and consequences of crises, and established procedures to lock down order and create predictability when crises loomed. We set a foundation that is still guiding organizational crisis readiness and response for many organizations and academics.

My original plan for this book was to update and adjust applications and practices to meet the challenges brought by today's work environments. However, early in its making, I recognized that pivots were sorely needed, starting with the whole notion of "managing" a crisis.

In our hypercompetitive, global, 4IR environment, the tools, trajectories, and nature of organizational control have been transformed radically. There is nowhere left to hide. The world can know about your organization's crisis instantly, even before you do. Of equal gravity, techno-fusions are mesmerizing attention and dissolving empathy, even in crises, when astute focus and human connection are needed most.

Locking down existing traces of order, securing stability for the status quo, and drawing conclusions from afar are outmoded and inadequate practices for the complex, volatile, uncertain environments that surround organizations today. Instead, to respond effectively, leaders at all levels, titled or emergent, must be ready to embrace crisis. Achieving that agility requires aligning crisis expectations and actions with core organizational values, no matter their function, power level, or location.

I have written this book for a much broader audience than typically targeted in crisis management materials. The questions, insights, and guidance here are practical and appropriate not only for executives, but also for leaders at any level and for individual employees. I am confident that you will deepen your understanding of organizational crises and strengthen your ability to influence and assist others under crisis conditions. Above all, I hope this will be a call to action, a resource for building and reinforcing a customized repertoire of assessments, approaches, and actions so that you, your organization, and your key stakeholders will cope with crises better and come out stronger.

Prologue, Fundamental Crib Notes

Top 10 Ways to Avert and Mitigate Crises

1. Never lie.
2. Act in way that would make your role model proud.
3. Anticipate the best, prepare for the worst.
4. Abide by your core values.
5. Treat your employees right.
6. Create a superb Crisis Leadership Team.
7. Respect your competitors, adversaries, critics, and antagonists.
8. Never punish the earnest messenger of bad news.
9. Build solid relationships with key stakeholders.
10. Challenge your biases and blind spots.

While these guidelines don't guarantee you will never face a crisis, if you live by them, you will avoid self-inflicted harm and be better prepared to face any crisis with better odds of surviving and coming out stronger. These tactics are rudimentary to everyday work, but even more essential in crisis, under the characteristic extremes of threatening uncertainties and relentless time pressures.

Scale Your Priorities

When it comes to preparing for crises, many organizations do very little. This leaves them dangerously vulnerable, and puts their environments at risk. Under-preparing threatens their stakeholders, the individuals, groups, and organizations who could *affect*, or *be affected by* their organization's ability to handle a crisis, adopt decisions, and take action. (See Chapter 17, Crisis Tool #3: Stakeholder Analysis for deeper details). Ignoring the potential for crises reduces or nixes the possibility of coming out stronger. If your organization banks on improvising in any coming crisis, you will probably make a dreadful, intense, complex, uncertain situation even worse.

This concise summary of crisis priorities is based on urgency and vital needs under three conditions that typically motivate crisis improvements:

1. Wolves are at your gate.
2. Danger signs are emerging.
3. You want a solid preventive, protective foundation.

On the next pages, you will find practical one-page guides for each of these conditions. Use these to contemplate your organization's status and readiness. Distribute them for discussion. Store the pages on your devices. Make them the preface of your organization's plans.

Wolves are at Your Gate

Setting: A crisis is underway. You have no crisis preparations, or those you have are insufficient or outdated.

Strategy: *Focus on assessing, treating, notifying. For now, let go of chasing blame.* Rouse and rally diverse, expert attention and power. Invest resources immediately to understand what is happening. Confirm the level of threat and critical details with experts. Alert and activate internal and external communication lines. Weigh action based on your organization's core values. Keep sharp eyes on outcomes and fluctuating circumstances.

Guidance, when wolves are at your gate...

Immediate **Actions:**

- **Do what you can within your power to reduce, delay, or stop the crisis** (Chapters 2-10).
- **Create an interim Crisis Leadership Team (CLT) immediately.** Choose a small group of trustworthy, savvy, diversely powerful, diversely skilled/experienced employees, who are open-minded, and who live up to your organization's values consistently. At this stage, favor individual speed and responsiveness as well (Chapter 4).
- **Reply briefly and solicit knowledge from the CLT.** Focus on crisis facts and insights, best- and worst-case prospects, and foreseeable needs and availability of tools, expertise, contacts, and resources (Chapters 9, 17).
- **Review your organization's values with the CLT.** Use your authentic core values to guide your objectives for the crisis, and to weigh particularly difficult decisions (Chapter 3).
- **Prioritize essential stakeholders**. Put victims and employees at the top (Chapter 9).
- **Gather additional vital information from internal and external experts.** Maintain direct contact with those closest to the core of the crisis (Chapter 9).
- **Map immediate plans.** Start with triage-level needs. Sketch a timeline. Deliberate best- and worst-case outcomes of critical decisions and turning points. Listen fully to potential threats and feedback, especially those you do not wish to hear (Chapters 5-8).

Danger Signs are Emerging

Setting: Dark clouds are building. You are aware that a potential crisis is brewing.

Strategy: *Identify and define priorities.* Expand crisis awareness and signal detection to decipher what is going on. Set direction for essentials specific to this particular crisis, such as resources, expertise, and communication.

Guidance, when danger signs are emerging…

Actions:

- **Do what you can within your immediate power to stop or slow down the anticipated crisis** (Chapters 2-10).
- **Create an interim Crisis Leadership Team (CLT) immediately.** Choose a small group of trustworthy, savvy, diversely powerful, diversely skilled/experienced employees, who are open-minded, and who live up to your organization's values consistently. At this stage, favor individual speed/responsiveness as well (Chapter 4).
- **Collect and assess all relevant signals of danger.** Seek input directly from trusted sources across your organization. Focus on anticipated epicenter of the potential crisis (Chapter 9).
- **Sharpen signal detection and reporting expectations regarding the crisis that you are anticipating.** Take quick measures to streamline access for reporting potential signals throughout your organization. Create a direct line dedicated to the issue, and remind everyone of their responsibilities to watch for and convey signals rapidly, (Chapters 7-8).
- **Determine top priority outcomes.** Conduct cost/benefit analyses regarding this crisis. Look not only at money, but also time, human resources, the potential detrimental impact on reputation and other outcomes. Base criteria and assessment on your organization's core values. Include worst-case scenarios in your deliberations (Chapter 17, Scenarios).
- **Sketch a rough map of your approach.** Create this tool to capture the big picture and details, to convey your perspective and plans to others, and to see their input (Chapters 5-6).

You Want a Solid Protective Foundation

Setting: No organizational crisis looms that you know of, but you want to improve lead time and preparation to optimize decisions and actions under threatening circumstances.

Strategy: *Determine how to make crisis investments manageable and fitting for your organization.* Develop a foundation of powerful champions to create a systemic crisis approach over time. Prioritize objectives relative to your organization's core values. Aim to eventually inform, engage and direct all employees.

Guidance, when you want a solid protective foundation...

Actions:

- **First, build your own crisis expertise and skills.** Learn typical crisis threats, and effective practices in your industry. Broaden your understanding of how crisis norms and preparations differ among your organization's locations. Deepen your grasp of your organization's current crisis readiness. Think about capabilities and gaps, resources and scarcities across hierarchical levels and functions, at headquarters, nationally, and overseas (Chapters 2-10).
- **Identify alignments between your organization's core values and its crisis readiness.** Reflect about your organization's strengths and weaknesses in crisis preparation, resources, and expertise, especially as related to your core values (Chapter 3).
- **Recruit influential support.** Engage employees who have crisis expertise, experience, and power to create a superb Crisis Leadership Team (CLT) (Chapters 4, 7).
- **Draft an initial scope of priorities for your organization.** Work with the champions, including CLT members, to begin mapping your plans (Chapter 5).
- **Read this book.** Learn crisis preparation and response fundamentals, including the following: Create and develop a superb CLT. Map your plans, and take them on a test drive. Power up your crisis readiness. Make signal detection and reporting a core technology. Develop and practice your crisis procedures. Establish avenues for ongoing input and feedback to shape and sharpen your crisis expertise and agility, creating a learning cycle that will strengthen your corporate culture and stakeholder relationships.

Why Your Team and Your Teammates' Teams Need This Book ASAP

Crisis Management has been the domain of top executives since 1984, when Charles Perrow's *Normal Accidents: Living with High Risk Technologies* set the groundwork for the field of Organizational Crisis Management. Now, it's not enough that your executives understand how to prevent, mitigate, respond to, and recover from crises. Trends rooted inside and outside of your organization have jarred crisis control from the clench of executives.

Organizations of all sizes, and employees at every level must be prepared to act swiftly and smartly to notice and respond to threats that erupt or gain traction, even from seemingly trivial sources, and in novel ways. The persistence and reach of crises have never been greater. Your viability can lurk in signals, decisions, and actions anywhere in your organization, within its footprint, or at the remote expanse of its influence.

Even the terminology of "managing" a crisis no longer applies, nor can you expect to meet the long-standing goal of dodging or diluting crises. Rather, your organization will benefit most by preparing leaders at all levels to embrace crises, riding the wave, rather than assuming you will be able to hold back the rising tide. Environmental and organizational shifts are changing the nature of crises, jolting and obliterating crisis management processes that were once effective.

Under normal conditions, volatile, uncertain, complex and ambiguous ("VUCA") characteristics complicate decisions and actions. When dangers loom, environmental VUCA forces can fuel organizational challenges into crises and incapacitate reactions. Under hazardous circumstances, each of the four defining characteristics increases insecurities about what is occurring and what will come next, churns confusion, and complicates choosing among potential outcomes. The environmental context itself distracts attention and clouds signals, disabling decisions and actions.

Trends inside organizations are transforming crises fundamentally and disrupting the effectiveness of once-reliable approaches for handling crises. With globalization, there is nowhere left to hide, even for the most powerfully resourced organizations and leaders. The speed, breadth, and depth of information access and transmission are accelerating fundamentally. The grace period—remember when hours, days, or weeks elapsed between insider knowledge and public exposure and response? —has evaporated. Today, you could be lucky to have a few moments to prepare your response, or you might learn about your crisis after the general public does. Whether you recognize it or not, prepare or not, do the right thing or not, the potential for spotlighting mistakes, wrongdoings, and even misunderstandings and misinformation has no bounds.

In "Reframing crisis management," which Judy Clair and I published in 1998, we listed this array of organizational crises:

- Extortion
- Hostile takeover
- Product tampering
- Vehicular fatality
- Copyright infringement
- Environmental spill
- Computer tampering
- Security breach
- Executive kidnaping
- Product/service boycott
- Work-related homicide
- Malicious rumor
- Natural disaster that disrupts a major product or service
- Natural disaster that destroys organizational information base
- Natural disaster that destroys corporate headquarters
- Natural disaster that eliminates key stakeholders
- Terrorist attack
- Escape of hazardous materials

- Personnel assault
- Assault of customers
- Product recall
- Counterfeiting
- Bribery
- Information sabotage
- Workplace bombing
- Terrorist attack
- Plant explosion
- Sexual harassment

A couple decades later, many crises in these categories have been morphed, launched, or magnified by the internet: cyberattacks, ransomware, social media assaults on reputation or stock price, expanded methods for counterfeiting and copyright infringement. Even the tiniest of threats, a virus, can impact every person and organization worldwide. You no longer have the luxury of wondering whether you will ever meet a crisis. You have already been affected. Now the questions are which crisis—and when, where, why, how, and how serious—and what can you do?

The content is divided into five sections. The Prologue provided a glimpse into fundamentals: the top 10 ways to avoid and mitigate crises, and a succinct look at priorities for three levels of urgency that typically incite crisis preparations. For those in doubt, the Prologue includes reasoning behind why improvisation shouldn't be your strategy when it comes to crises, especially today. As a heads-up, if you are in a crisis at this moment, turn to "Wolves are at Your Gates" right now and start there.

The Before section details how to prepare for crisis, from emulating crisis experts, to creating a strong foundation, including a superb Crisis Leadership Team. With the basics in place, this section will direct you through mapping your crisis plans in alignment with your organizational values, and optimizing their effectiveness by taking them on a test drive.

During and After describes what to do in the heat of crisis, applying the distinctive approaches and objectives of ATNA: Assessing, Treating, Notifying, and Adapting.

Today's Crisis Accelerators dives into how current crisis accelerators, hypercompetitive, global exposure and techno-fused advances, can multiply crisis risks. You will find ample recommendations to get beyond the crisis challenges of these trends, to better prepare and respond, and come out stronger as an organization, as a team, and as an individual.

Crisis Tools section provides sample tools and explanations of how to use them to strengthen your skills and maximize your research time so you can more adeptly apply the lessons of this book.

Before

1

Why Not Just Wing It?
Key Reasons to Prepare

Organizational crises used to be extraordinary events that were manageable by savvy leaders who were often able to keep them private, at least for a while. The discipline of Organizational Crisis Management was seeded by complex system failures of advancing high-risk technologies.[2] Exxon's Valdez oil spill and Occidental's Bhopal chemical leak are infamous examples. Very large corporations with deep pockets that produced potentially dangerous products or services were prime targets. Some became crisis management exemplars, from industries like transportation, chemical, oil and gas, utilities, pharmaceutical, food manufacturing, hospitality, financial services, and government entities.

Of course, even among the best, no organization has ever been immune to crises, and then and now, preparing for a crisis that *could* happen has always seemed an extravagance. That assumption is outlandish today. Complex, intertwined, volatile forces in and around organizations can spark trauma in moments. Relatively minor incidents at remote sites or among loosely linked stakeholders can fire up organizational disasters. With the forces of social media and internet access, even individuals with little formal power and scant resources can now ignite fuses globally to derail and deplete organizations. The luxury of privacy is gone.

Inventing apt responses to crises on the fly, and then resuming operations as if nothing had happened is the stuff of fantasies. Today, forces like hypercompetition, globalization, and the techno-fusions of the Fourth Industrial Revolution can pose threats to organizations of all sizes and types, worldwide. The reach, intensity, and urgency of dangers that can impair organizations have exploded. Such changes within organizations and from external environments propel crisis vulnerabilities onto center stage. The benefits of crisis preparation are vital.

What's at stake? Start with support versus condemnation from your employees, your customers, your suppliers, your local communities. Think about protection rather than harm, or progress versus decline. At the extreme, crisis readiness and fitting responses can make the ultimate difference of life over death for your organization, its environments, or the stakeholders that it touches.

Even moderate efforts to create and improve approaches can stack the odds in your favor. Informed, coordinated crisis readiness buys time when you need it most. Crisis preparation relieves employees from having to invent responses under the duress of disaster, and keeps key stakeholders on your side. Any improvements to strategies, protocols, or collective organizational mindset for crisis decisions and actions are invaluable when responses will be sharply, inherently impaired. Each of these improvements enhances the chances of coming out stronger than you were before the crisis occurred.

WHAT DETERS ORGANIZATIONS FROM PREPARING?

Powerful impacts, exceptional circumstances and intrigue of crises quickly capture attention, while the natural fear of crises deters effective preparation. Unfortunately, the prime advantage of embracing crisis is often missed or ignored: readiness reduces the causes for fear. Consequently, many organizations ignore potential crises until the threat appears. Some wait until they are in the throes of disaster. Others prepare piecemeal, often only as driven by law.

Opportunities to avert or mitigate crises are lost when responses must be invented and coordinated ad hoc. Untested approaches, patched together under duress, worsen the struggle. When leaders choose to face into crisis blindly, naïvely, impromptu, their employees at all levels must fend for themselves. The outcomes suffer. Environments may be contaminated, stakeholders devastated, careers shattered, and occasionally, leaders may land in prison.

Over the years, I have heard many excuses from leaders who chose to prepare marginally, or not at all. You may have heard these rationales in your organization. Perhaps you buy into some of them yourself.

EXCUSES: WHY NOT PREPARE?

LACK OF RESOURCES
- We're too busy.
- Crises don't happen often enough to invest in advance.
- Crisis management is a luxury and we don't have resources to spare.

FUZZY RESPONSIBILITIES
- It's not my job.
- Headquarters handles crises.
- We'll just hire an expert.
- We prepared a manual years ago. It's in the break room, somewhere.

SIZE
- We're so big and powerful that we can handle any crisis.
- We're so small and weak, we can't afford to worry about what might happen.

UNTOUCHABLE
- We help people, no one would harm us.
- We're smart enough to keep a crisis under wraps.
- Our company is an industry leader.
- Our leaders are ethical.
- Our employees are loyal.
- We can invent responses as a crisis unfolds.

HELPLESS
- No one can prepare for the unknown.
- We don't know how to prepare.

None of these were effective excuses in the past. Now, they are indefensible. Still, many organizations do no systematic crisis preparation.

Do you know whether your organization is prepared, if it has any crisis response plans? Studies by Deloitte and Forbes Insights found that about 30 percent of the board members representing more than 300 large organizations around the world did not know. Another 20 percent believed that their firms had no crisis preparations at all. The remaining half thought that some type of crisis preparations existed in their organizations, but they did not know what the approaches entailed. Even where board members thought plans existed, only a quarter of their organizations had actually tested them.[3]

WHY NOT JUST IMPROVISE?

In crisis, there will always be a need for riffs and handoffs, but lack of preparation and practice causes ad hoc responses and impromptu efforts which waste valuable time and agitate confusion and chaos instead of coordinated, effective responses. Untested and off-the-shelf crisis plans can fool leaders into believing that they are no longer vulnerable. Sometimes, incomplete preparations sway leaders to let down their guard when trouble looms and hastily discount threatening circumstances.

Many problem-solvers believe that they already manage crises every day. They do not. Messy workplace problems might certainly feel like crises, especially in today's churn, but even in the contemporary swirl, problems and crises are not the same.

- Problem: *unpleasant, undesirable situation or condition that causes difficulties, ranging from simple problems that can be bounded, managed, tamed, to wicked, ill-structured problems for which there may be unknown elements and multiple solutions.*
- Crisis: *low-probability, high-impact event that threatens survival, with high uncertainty, and very little discretionary time.*

The confusion is understandable, especially when ugly problems and crises are in their early stages. Both command our attention. Both can deeply threaten or harm organizations, their surroundings, and their stakeholders. Both can catch organizations off guard, and highlight their deficiencies. Both can cause reliable approaches to fail, and response expectations to crumble.

THE GREAT DIFFERENTIATORS:
INTENSITY AND UNCERTAINTY

Similarities between problems and crises are useful to know, but there is an indisputable, hazardous difference: successfully leading through problems, even messy, ill-structured ones, does not assure leadership effectiveness in a crisis. Problems of any magnitude are relatively modest and restrained, while crises rage. Detecting causes, consequences, and effective responses to problems may take some sleuthing, but exposing the causes, consequences, and effective responses to crises can baffle and torment us forever. In crises, even proven experience with problem solving can flop.

On problems. When problems occur, they can have wide-reaching effects that complicate operations and disrupt productivity. They may require time and focus, raising questions, issues and soliciting varied perspectives, as well as debating the pros and cons of each alternative. Worse, if handled ineffectively, problems can drive away investors, customers, and employees.

Knowing how to solve problems is a common measure of job success. Solutions to frequent problems are part of basic training for some occupations. With practice, individuals, teams, and organizations learn how to respond to recurring problems reflexively. Even for messy problems, efforts may entail puzzle solving: applying known elements into an optimal, correct solution, for which there is general agreement among experts regarding the basic definition of the problem, specifiable courses of action, and valued outcomes.[4] Over time, individual problem solvers may develop motor skills, muscle memory, and habits to drive appropriate reactions to problems, even without conscious thought.[5]

The best problem solvers tend to stick to a limited range of alternatives and outcomes, especially when solutions must come quickly or cheaply. They lean on known fixes, ready tools, and opportunities of the moment. Effective problem solvers rely on previous decisions, intuition, existing skills, as well as their own habits and biases. They seek shortcuts. Even when problems get ugly, expert problem solvers settle, and this is appropriate.[6]

On crises. When crises loom, automatically reaching for shortcuts and settling for ready fixes can be futile and hazardous. Rather, crises must be approached for what they are, the darkest, most extraordinary challenges your organization will ever face. Crises usurp organizational power lines, slither through functions, and surge across geographic bounds. They may beckon anyone in proximity to respond, or to lead. Typically, crises exceed problems in many ways.

WHEN IS IT A CRISIS (NOT A PROBLEM)?

- Causes and remedies are more obscure.
- Decision-making is more complex.
- Threats of risk and loss are harsher.
- Costs of errors are higher.
- The need for personal engagement is greater.
- Negative emotional impact goes deeper.
- Broader circles of stakeholders are affected.
- Customary paths are less reliable.
- Fundamental assumptions, long-standing norms, and perspectives of the future are tenuous.
- Even deeply held values are tested or toppled.

The practical implications of these differences are priceless. Throwing crisis-level responses at a problem is wasteful. Drawing resources too deeply, pressing engagement too broadly, or stirring negative emotions needlessly can build a tempest from moderately agitated waters. But when leaders treat a crisis as just another problem, they leave disaster in motion. At the extreme, leaders who underestimate or ignore dangers of a potential crisis can destroy their organizations, and even lure stakeholders to their deaths.

A heartbreaking example occurred at Schlitterbahn Waterpark in Kansas City. From the beginning, designers, leaders and managers were aware of major safety problems with the park's prime attraction, the tallest waterslide on earth, "Verrückt" (German for insane). Riders, secured only by simple Velcro-type straps, descended nearly vertically in small plastic rafts, dropping 17 stories in a few seconds. Extreme signals of danger were obvious, even during testing: rafts flew off the waterslide, and sandbags simulating passengers flew off the rafts. When videos of the tests went viral, a designer of the ride and co-owner of the park assured *USA Today* that Verrückt was, "dangerous, but a safe dangerous."[7] Tragically, it was not.

Red flags were everywhere. Nonetheless, managers and leaders understated, disregarded, and hid problems. As trouble intensified, park lifeguards not only reported dangers and accidents, but also refused to participate in test runs. Riders provided photos and videos of their own catastrophic experiences and other accidents they witnessed.

Even when riders' arms and faces were smashed into equipment, management continued to treat circumstances as minor problems. As injuries intensified to ruptured disks, broken bones, and concussions, neither systematic evaluations nor corrective modifications were made. Leaders and managers continued to flout signals of crisis, until 10-year-old Caleb Schwab was decapitated. Leadership incompetence in differentiating problems from crises led not only to the tragic, preventable death of a young boy, but also to lawsuits, indictments, and the demise of the waterpark. Eventually, the Kansas state legislature, which included Caleb's father, closed the regulatory gap which had allowed amusement parks to operate with no outside inspections.[8]

WHY LEADERSHIP THROUGH PLANNED CHANGES DOES NOT PREPARE YOU FOR CRISIS LEADERSHIP

It is not unusual for managers and leaders who have successfully pulled or pushed their teams or organizations through major planned changes to believe that they will have the same success leading through crisis. Some experiences of leading planned change can be invaluable in a crisis, but dramatic differences distinguish leading planned change versus leading through crises. And the differences between winging it through a crisis—versus leading with plans and preparations—are staggering.

When crises occur, norms are dislodged by unforeseen and unpredictable conditions. New troubles ignite in bursts, in their most intense forms.

Dangerous uncertainties abound. The time needed to comprehend and address a crisis seems to evaporate, especially if there has been little or no planning or preparation. Dramatic contrasts differentiate the dynamics of (a) leading planned change, (b) reacting to crisis ad hoc, and (c) responding with crisis plans and practice.

	Planned Change	Crisis by Improvization	Crisis with Protective Foundation
Mode	Proactive	Reactive	Proactive + Reactive.
Strategy	Calculated. Stable throughout change.	Impromptu. Untested. Unanticipated.	Customized. Adaptable. Based on core values + objectives + learning.
Objective	Maximize gains.	Survive. Minimize losses.	Avert, minimize losses. Come out stronger.
Drivers	Whatever you emphasize.	Whatever crisis brings. Punctuated by opinions of media/critics'/public.	Core values + crisis objectives.
Timing	You control trigger, launch, and rollout.	Crisis starts the clock. Unanticipated urgencies. Unplanned resource acquisition, delivery.	Crisis signals start clock. Anticipated urgencies and resource needs. Accelerated analysis and response. Informed, distributed crisis leadership.
Ownership	Before crisis begins, you select champions, disarm dissidents, and build support.	Race to identify, convince, coerce help. Vital decisions must be improvised. Naïve respondents.	Responses aligned on core values + crisis objectives.
Outcomes/ Framing	You declare wins, celebrate rosiest outcomes, and harness energy to institutionalize changes.	Legacy? *Best:* dark circumstances were neutralized. *Worst:* organization, stakeholders, environment destroyed.	Responses reinforced core values + crisis objectives. Learning/ improvement is already underway to come out stronger.

VIBRANT CONTEMPORARY
INSPIRATIONS FOR IMPROVEMENT

Transformations in workplaces, their environments, and their stakeholders have put major obstacles in the path of crisis readiness and crises are happening more frequently and more intensely.[9] Unfortunately, Crisis Management approaches have not kept up with the times.

Substantial examples can be drawn from the long-standing objective of Crisis Management: *To make timely decisions based on best facts and clear thinking under extraordinary conditions.* As a general concept, the objective has endured. However, the essence of nearly every detail has been morphed by deep changes inside and outside organizations.

Timely now insinuates and has shrunk to instantaneous.

Although crisis **facts** are far easier and cheaper to access today, they can be obscured by fiction and fraud as never before. Today, the fact/fiction link can be the crisis.

Clear thinking, once the duty of top executives, is no longer effectively conceived, distributed, or controlled exclusively from on high.

Perhaps most significantly, the prevalence and intensities of the **extraordinary conditions** of organizational crises can now be created and stimulated more efficiently, and then dispersed with fewer resource investments, fewer instigators and greater devastation.

Contemporary organizational and environmental shifts not only spoil the suitability of traditional crisis management perspectives and practices, but also render all types of organizations attractive targets for intentional crises.

Within organizations, deep transformations in organizational dynamics add to the complexities. Corporate cultures are being reinvented, bringing some benefits to individuals, corporations, and societies, along with greater risks and uncertainties in the transitions, from the redistributions of organizational power and responsibility, to increased diversities among workforces and clients (whether by gender, race, disability, nationality, ethnicity, age, sexual orientation, language). In many cases, employer-employee loyalty is eroding (in both directions), while the nature of jobs and the locations from which they are performed are evolving. Changes to old norms might be welcomed by many or all participants, but they can still add risks. All change creates at least temporary complexity and uncertainty, and this is an era of dramatic corporate and societal changes. Meanwhile, contemporary environmental trends, from hypercompetition, to globalization, and techno-fusion also intensify complexity, and agitate volatility and uncertainty.

WHAT HAS CHANGED?

Hypercompetitive organizations are running on fumes, relentlessly. Belt tightening can yield substantial organizational savings, but where employees are pushed relentlessly to do more with less, quicker, cheaper, and better, the impact can be exhausting and disheartening. Employees detach from their organizations, their jobs, and their colleagues. Persistent hypercompetitive pressures can drive rash decisions and actions, which can shortcut safeguards, disrupt systems, and increase errors and accidents. Where sparse resources are the standard, vigilance, response speed, signal detection, and crisis readiness suffer.

Global expansion exacerbates exposure. Global reach can bring amazing advantages, but international integration also brings more variables, across more contexts, with widely varied languages, time zones, norms, and values, across geographically distant sites. Any of these changes can slow down the flow of information and other resources, and even introduce sharply diverse interpretations of what is right or wrong, what is acceptable or forbidden. Where local practices conflict with organizational norms and values, confusion and conflict can lead to impasses and missteps.

Techno-fusion multiplies cyber risks and shrinks privacy. Interconnected systems, blurring boundaries among physical, digital and technological worlds and the related vulnerabilities introduced by the transition can cause crises. Some established methods and processes have been weakened, others made extinct. Traditional and social media facilitate data and audience access from the first suspicions of trouble. Fact and fiction can be broadcast instantaneously, and public release of information is no longer within your control.

The grace period for response has evaporated. Executives previously depended on a minimum of 24 hours before problems known inside their organizations went public. The gap was priceless for savvy leaders to contemplate threats and implications, delve into details of what was happening, debate potential repercussions, tailor their responses, and only then, communicate their intentions. Today, if any sliver of a grace period remains, it is measurable in minutes.[10]

Privacy has vanished for organizations and their leaders. Well-resourced organizations used to prepare and respond to crises off-site, outside the reach or view of media, critics, and the public. Behind-the-scenes or off-the-record no longer exist. There are no remote sites where organizational mistakes or leaders' misconduct can be kept under wraps. Rather, internal and external environments are ripe for inexpensive, easily accessible discovery and diffusion that can stoke trouble and shine attention on organizational dysfunctions, real or contrived.

Our attention is distracted. Techno-buzz is making us stupid. When our focus is captivated by techno-tools, we short-circuit two crisis management essentials: deep thinking and intense collaboration. In turmoil, especially, when we lack the power to concentrate, we lose the finesse to innovate and adapt optimal responses, and to guide or assist others gracefully.

Our empathy has hardened. Despite the ease with which contemporary advances like online meetings and instant translation allow us to build relationships around the world, we are narrowing rather than broadening our perspectives. Today, the convenience and precision of social media connections lead many to identify, seek out, and affiliate with others whose assumptions, preferences, and values mirror their own. Unfortunately, when we gather only with people who are just like us, our ability to imagine the world from others' viewpoints withers.

When we duck into our gadgets and out of real-time encounters with people, we forfeit the nuances and skills of personal engagement and rapport. Over time, this dulls us to the human consequences of crises, and short-circuits opportunities to spot and address warning signals that surface through robust personal connections. These shifts deplete our competence for understanding and handling crises.

WHAT'S A LEADER TO DO?

The best opportunities await those who are willing to embrace crises. The advantage begins with developing the insight to differentiate crises from problems quickly, so you can address them accurately. These recommendations and questions can help you hone your insights, and begin to consider your organization's current status for handling crises.

Learn to discriminate potential crises from problems

Evaluate threats promptly. If you answer Yes to any of these questions, lean toward crisis as your preliminary assessment:

- Could the trouble put your entire organization at risk?
- Is the potential weight of the trouble likely to exceed your organization's response capabilities?
- Is the frequency of the trouble increasing, or the intensity of impacts rising?
- Are the same troubles and impacts recurring?
- Are employees reporting dangers, or behaving in ways to avert dangers, such as refusing to use the product or service?
- Are customers pointing out your safety shortcomings?
- Are employees editing or withholding their reports of problems or dangers (at will or under pressure)?

Manage expectations about crises versus problems

Although causes and consequences of problems may become clear even before fixes are underway, crises activate disbelief and confusion, which can block and derail insights about what is happening, and what should come next. These cognitive and emotional impediments are significant because they can tempt leaders to ignore or underestimate crises, allowing unresolved vulnerabilities and hazardous predicaments to fester or explode.

To embrace crises, step into the fray while causes and consequences are easiest, cheapest, and quickest to address, and make peace with these possibilities:

- Causes of problems may be evident even before you start to solve them, but it can take considerable time to uncover and verify underlying causes of crises. Sometimes, you will never uncover them.

- Although there are generally positive or neutral solutions to problems, the best routes out of crisis may be the least dreadful among nothing but dismal choices.

- There will probably be a clear sense of relief when a problem has been solved, but what marks the end of a crisis may be elusive or indeterminate.

- Solving a problem usually stirs positive energy among all involved, but momentum may dwindle during a crisis and in its aftermath. After a crisis, there may still be finger-pointing and negative accusations despite optimal outcomes.

Determine your organization's readiness for contemporary crisis realities

Recognize that crises require expanded insight and intricate approaches to make assumptions explicit, calibrate and drive a sufficient level of agreement for action around issues such as the relative importance, impacts and pros and cons of potential options. Traditional approaches to crisis detection, preparation, response, and learning lag behind today's organizational and environmental realities. As starting places for improvement, consider categories and questions like these to begin evaluating your organization's crisis status:

Your Crisis Checklist

Vulnerability awareness

- ***Do you operate under the assumption that you can dodge any crisis that may strike?***
  Organizational invulnerability is a delusion. Today, crises terrorize locations once considered safe havens, from elementary schools to socially conscientious nonprofits, landmark federal buildings, and places of worship. When crises erupt today, their impacts can be spread instantaneously, globally.

Value as beacons

- ***Do all of your employees know the links between your organization's core values and your crisis preparation and response expectations?***
  The utmost foundation for crisis response reliability will be built on your organization's authentic core values. They are the best drivers and sources of alignment to move your entire organization toward the same essential targets simultaneously. These beacons can provide guidance for every employee to find their ways through crises, even when they encounter unforeseen, bizarre, worst-case circumstances.

Organization-wide engagement

- ***Does your entire organization participate in crisis preparation, through discussions, training, and practice?***
  It is impossible today for a small segment, at the very top, in the home country, to understand an entire organization's strengths and weaknesses, resources and needs across the full spectrum of its exposure. Any member of your organization can become a vital participant in detecting, averting, or alleviating a crisis, and each of them should understand crisis fundamentals and personal expectations of them. Talking about and practicing crisis

approaches improves agile thinking, expands perspective, legitimizes grounded debate, reinforces buy-in, and powers comprehension, coordination, and confidence organization-wide.

Signal detection as core technology

- *Do employees at all levels understand their personal responsibilities and available channels for detecting and reporting signals of trouble?*
  The earlier people see/hear/smell/taste/touch the signs of a crisis, the easier and cheaper it is to alert others. The sooner people are aware of potential dangers, the better they can investigate, collaborate, identify resources and expertise, notify key stakeholders, and prepare and activate responses.

Employment cycle as crisis lever

- *Is crisis preparation embedded throughout your employment cycle?*
  Fitting employment controls, from recruitment criteria and processes, to post-departure data collection, guide and reinforce each employee's attention and action. These opportunities that unify and distinguish your organization under normal conditions are equally advantageous for crisis preparation and response.

External stakeholder engagement

- *How well does your organization inform and learn from its key outsiders?*
  Crisis effectiveness is buoyed by mutually advantageous relationships beyond your organization's borders. Today, external stakeholders have powerful opportunities to impact your ability to handle crisis, while your ability to handle a crisis will have powerful impact on them, as well. With positive relationships come prompt

insights and actions in both directions, which can speed up and facilitate crisis detection, response, and learning.

Up Next

In the next section, we will focus on how to prepare for crises. This perspective is all about action. The target is crisis readiness and effective responses from all actors, including individuals, teams, and organizations.

Specifically, the next chapter highlights the perspectives of crisis experts, choices that excellent crisis leaders make, and key approaches for crisis success that others may not automatically think about or do. We begin with determining what matters most, long before a crisis occurs. Then, we will look at effectively and efficiently leading people through crises, from how to ask better questions, to how to manage negative emotions, and how to develop processes that will help individuals and organizations come out stronger.

2

Behave Like Adept Crisis Leaders, Adopt Their Perspectives

On March 11, 2011, Japan's Fukushima I nuclear power plant at Daiichi was devastated by the Tohoku earthquake and tsunami that initiated meltdowns, explosions, and equipment failures. Many would classify the cause a force of nature, and they would be accurate about what sparked the crisis. But, Dr. Kiyoshi Kurokawa, chairman of the National Diet of Japan Fukushima Accident Independent Investigation Commission, called it a "man-made disaster" that was "made in Japan."[11] Distinctions among approaches and outcomes at Daiichi versus its sister plant at Daini underscore the extraordinary influence of crisis leadership.

At Fukushima I, hundreds of panicked workers tried to evacuate the plant. More than 30 of them died. Meanwhile, plant manager Masao Yoshida took refuge in a secure, remote, windowless office about half a mile from the plant. Yoshida spent his time teleconferencing with corporate executives at Tokyo Electric Power Company (TEPCO) headquarters.

About six miles south, at the Fukushima II plant in Daini, site superintendent Naohiro Masuda guided his employees through the crisis in person. From the shop floor, he led managers and workers to gather information inside and outside the plant. Immediately and candidly, Masuda posted all data, progress and dangers, as soon as he knew them, for every employee to see. He took part in discussions to help his organization make sense of conditions in real-time and, together, they determined adjustments. Under Masuda's guidance, the employees at Fukushima II achieved remarkable feats to re-route electrical cables and achieve cold shut down of all four plant reactors. Not one employee attempted to flee the plant.[12] Highly adept leaders follow a few basics, no matter what the nature of the crisis, the context, or the reach of their involvement.

CRISIS EXPERTS' BEHAVIORAL BENCHMARKS

- Remain calm. Maintain a steady course toward crisis goals and objectives.
- Show up where you are needed most. Relocate as needs shift.
- Think before you speak. Speak honestly, with measured candor.
- Optimize your actions with your strengths. Enlist others to compensate for your weaknesses.
- Discover problems early to solve problems early. Learn and inform promptly, throughout the crisis.
- Support and acknowledge individuals and teams whenever the thought crosses your mind.

Core traits of exceptional crisis leaders are no different than excellent leaders' traits during normal times, including trustworthiness, honesty, integrity, empathy, respect, and courage. These traits manifest in their decisions and actions. They build trust before, during, and after a crisis by connecting honestly and personally with others, no matter the size or characteristics of their audiences. They preserve a consistent, accurate sense of reality, even amid dire consequences and troubling evolutions. What makes their actions extraordinary in crisis are their abilities to retain focus and unwavering resolve despite extraordinary uncertainties and unnerving conditions. The recommendations below detail actions and approaches to reinforce and enhance solid crisis leadership, from any level.

WHAT'S A LEADER TO DO?

Know thy crisis management self

As you build crisis management expertise, stay alert to the relevant personal talents that you already possess, and how you deploy them best. Know how you maintain your attention and energy so that you will be prepared to adapt and continue those restorative habits during and after the crisis. Before a crisis occurs, look for ways to boost needed competencies that you lack, including building new perspectives, and identifying specific people and resources that can help you fill the gaps and learn from them.

As a starting point, think about the following questions. Consider discussing them with trusted superiors, colleagues, and subordinates.

- Which are my greatest leadership strengths and how might they apply in crisis?
- Which are my leadership weaknesses that could be detrimental in crisis, and how can I improve them now?
- Who can complement my crisis leadership abilities, compensating for my weaker areas, and what specific contributions do we need?
- Which resources do I control that could be essential in a crisis?

Clarify standards of utmost importance

Get clear on your essential values. They will be a vital source of direction and confidence for you as unforeseen or frightening challenges emerge in crisis. Consider how they relate to your organization's values and how you intend to align your actions with them. Create a very short list of the essential values (5 to 7 items) by thinking through these questions:

- What matters most to you?
- How do your deeply held values align with your organization's values?
- Which values will you uphold, even in crisis?

Keep a copy of your list on your computer. Save it to your phone. Share it with others, perhaps your closest colleagues or your mentor. Have it ready, within handy access, when you struggle to make a decision or take action.

Ready yourself for a marathon, plus many sprints

Effective pacing is a broad tactic for effective crisis leadership. Slow down when you can, to run all out when you must. Start to build habits for doing this. During normal times, continuously improve your agility to change gears, in preparation for much more challenging circumstances.

To achieve this, keep your senses sharp with healthy habits for eating, moving, and sleeping. Avoid excesses that push against healthy habits. You may believe that you are Wonder Woman or Superman, but even if you have the stamina to fulfill those roles, your unhealthy choices will influence others' unsustainable mimicry.

Learn to build trust quickly

Everyone works more comfortably with people they know and trust. Smoothly aligned coordination eases our interactions. Where trust exists, we can act appropriately without having to second-guess each move or comment. Under normal circumstances, we may become so accustomed to working with people we trust that we can predict their behaviors and adjust our own conduct to theirs, without even thinking about it. These relationship characteristics can facilitate rapid, synchronized crisis response.

When a crisis occurs, novel circumstances, unfamiliar stakeholders, and new risks will force us to make quick judgments. We must also convey our trustworthiness, and evaluate our trust in others. In crisis, some interaction must be achieved rapidly, often with complete strangers, sometimes with people whom we never imagined would contribute to our success or failure.

To build and preserve trust, stick to fundamentals that may seem obvious, but are challenging to sustain, especially under extreme pressures of crisis. Aim to act consistently, practicing these essential principles:

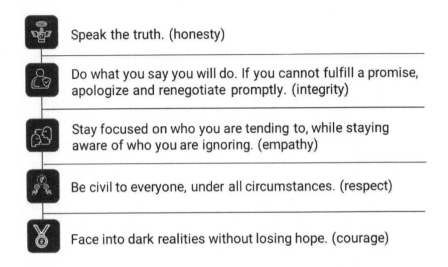

Speak the truth. (honesty)

Do what you say you will do. If you cannot fulfill a promise, apologize and renegotiate promptly. (integrity)

Stay focused on who you are tending to, while staying aware of who you are ignoring. (empathy)

Be civil to everyone, under all circumstances. (respect)

Face into dark realities without losing hope. (courage)

Ask better questions in better ways

In the novel, uncertain landscape of a crisis, drawing others' deep, candid perspectives is invaluable. Employees at all levels learn to *answer* questions well through skill development, training, and feedback. But *asking* the right questions is a skill that is strangely neglected in most organizations.[13]

Leaders at all levels are accustomed to seeking facts, often by pointedly soliciting quantitative or closed-ended (yes/no) responses. Understanding crises requires much more. Facts alone leave behind priceless insights that could be derived from broader knowledge and expertise, foundations and turning points among diverse thought processes, and gut sense. Posing questions that limit responses can miss significant aspects of the truth, including crisis causes, conditions, and consequences.

Even some of the most typical and well-meaning questions can block the flow of accurate and complete information. When a problem has occurred, it is common to ask, "Why?" or "What went wrong?" These may seem like efficient, logical places to begin, but for respondents, they may imply blame. Where fault-finding is the norm, employees at all levels build habits to justify their actions, which often includes holding back negative insights and concerns.

It is important to ask questions at every level. When gathering information in the frenzy of crisis, the insights of lower level employees are often overlooked or dismissed. Yet, these employees frequently have front-row seats to hear, see, touch, taste, and smell crisis triggers first-hand. Often, their jobs put them in direct contact with external stakeholders, such as customers and suppliers, whose feedback or actions could expose signals of trouble or sparks of crisis. To compound this problem, it is the nature of organizational power dynamics that the higher one rises in an organization, the more sheltered one becomes from the bad news below. If you don't earnestly seek input from below, you may never hear it.

The way you ask matters. Your perspective and attitude will be detectable in your tone of voice, volume, intonation, pace of questioning, and facial expressions. When you are seeking information, rather than chasing after cues that might be revealed subtly in others' vocal and nonverbal communication tells, focus on what you can control—your own behavior. To get honest answers, aim to maintain and convey an open-minded attitude. Follow these guidelines to bring forth richer, truer information:

- Ask from a perspective of curiosity, rather than criticism.
- Think about your purpose *before* asking.
  - What do you want your questions to convey?
  - What negative impacts do you want to avoid?
  - How will your tone convey support and respect?
- Do not ask a question to pin blame or punish people. Do not ask a question when a statement is more fitting. These approaches cause defensiveness, which blocks the truth and shuts down learning.
- Do not confuse *who* did something with *how* something happened. Challenge the process, not the person. It is arrogant and absurd to believe that normal workers would want to cause injury to themselves or others. During crisis, if you waste your time drilling down on underlying individual behaviors, you will miss the effects of processes that allowed failure to occur.[14]
- Aim to understand context.
  - Ask about how existing work policies or processes might have gotten in the way, or created confusion.

- o   With genuine curiosity, follow up by asking about what else was going on when trouble occurred.
- Aim to learn from everyone involved.
  - o   Do this especially when you are yanked into treacherous or unfamiliar territory.
  - o   Stay tuned to diverse and contrarian perspectives to gain insight about what you do not know, and what you may encounter next.

These categories and sample questions open conversation. They also tend to allow respondents to answer candidly.

- If you are unsure about how to start, open with traditional ice-breakers. They are easy to ask and answer, and they can convey concern, if your intent is genuine. Use your natural version of questions like these:
  - o   How are you doing today?
  - o   How are things going?
  - o   Is this a good time to talk?

If the response you receive is just a word or two, do not give up. To move more deeply, disclose more deeply. Honestly and *briefly* share your own perspective.

- If the *impact* of the crisis is your interest:
  - o   Does what happened make sense to you?
  - o   How is the situation surprising to you?
  - o   What do your knowledge and experience tell you?
- If *current status* is your interest:
  - o   What do you think might have caused this?
  - o   Which approaches have been tried so far?
  - o   What are we learning so far?
  - o   What else seems to be going on?
- If *helping* is your interest:

- o   What can I do to help clear any obstacles?
- o   Which additional resources do you need?
- o   Who else can I contact who would be helpful to you?
- o   How can my colleagues and I be of more help? How do you need us to step up?
- o   How are we getting in the way? How do you need us to step back?
- If the *anticipated future* is your interest:
  - o   Where do you think the next problem will occur?
  - o   What more do we need to know about what has happened?
  - o   What do our employees (or customers, community, suppliers, etc.) need to hear from us?

Ask better questions of yourself as well

Don't forget to turn strong questions inward, too. Tap into fundamentals for self-reflection. Make time to understand your own experiences and reactions. Consider writing your answers or discussing them with others. These questions will help you find your way through the trials and turns of crises, and they can guide personal growth afterwards:

- What matters most to me now?
- What more can I do to help? What commitments can I make now?
- What more should I prepare for?
- What am I contributing that is working well?
- How can I keep my personal values aligned with organizational values?
- How am I adding and reinforcing creative solutions to novel problems?
- Is my involvement moving at an appropriate speed?
- What is my biggest fear about the crisis now? How will I face into that fear with clear mindedness, and without losing hope?

- Which resources, assistance, and information do my employees (or colleagues, bosses, customers) need from me now? What about in the future?
- What do my employees (or colleagues, bosses, customers) need to hear from me now? And in the future?

Listen like lives depend on it

Nearly everyone thinks they are very good listeners. Most people are not.

As a crisis unfolds, listening skillfully can make the difference between failure and success. Sometimes listening adeptly is a matter of life or death.

When you tune in fully, you open the door for deeper information and feedback. People who listen carefully signal respect, and they move closer to understanding the world as the speaker knows it. Careful listening guards against failed relationships and unpleasant surprises.

Start practicing these guidelines for excellent listening before a crisis occurs. Develop skillful habits now, so that they will come naturally when you will need them most.

- After you ask a question, pause. Allow your respondent sufficient time to think, formulate, and deliver an answer.
- Move away from distractions, including phones, computers, and gadgets.
- If privacy is needed face-to-face, close your office door or find quieter, secluded space with which both of you are comfortable.
- Turn your full attention to the speaker.
  - o Stay tuned to what your speaker is saying without interrupting.
  - o Stay in the moment, rather than imagining what advice you will give, or what you will say next.
  - o Focus on what you are hearing, rather than why you agree or disagree, or what the speaker's motives might be.
- Keep an eye on alignment.

o   Does what you are hearing match what you are seeing?

o   Does something seem to be out of kilter or does something seem to be missing from what you are noticing?

o   Is there alignment among body language, tone of voice, volume, intonation, and the words spoken?

o   If you detect a misalignment, could it be the result of impacts of the crisis such as exhaustion or encounters with devastating challenges?

o   If you have any concern about potential mismatch between what you are hearing and what you are seeing or otherwise sensing, ask a gentle follow-up question such as, "Are you doing okay?"

Prepare to address dark realities without losing hope

To maneuver through tests and trials of a crisis, you must look squarely into dark possibilities with honesty and integrity. That includes admitting your own mistakes without sinking into shame. This can be very difficult for highly successful people.

Both individually and as an organization, invest the time to reflect on your previous adaptive actions in crisis. Think about and discuss questions like these to reinforce stamina and confidence for the future. They will bring to mind strategies that have worked for you in the past, and may work again in the next or current crisis.

- How have I (we) handled feelings of loss or danger effectively in the past?
- What have I (we) done to adjust successfully to exceptional challenges or deeply disrupted routines?
- How have I (we) coped when the future seemed frightening or very insecure?

Uphold realistic positive outcomes

Preparing and bracing for the worst is only half the challenge. People who are very skilled at handling crisis also aim to come out stronger, to think and act from a perspective of possibility and opportunity. This mindset is essential to effective crisis responses. But make no mistake, this does not mean exuding blind confidence or excessive cheeriness. Rather, come to a crisis with steadfast hardiness and resilience, while also keeping in mind dire realities, both actual and potential.

- Energize action by behaving consistently and demonstrating physical and psychological stamina. Practice excellent self-care, and aim to influence your team and others similarly.
- Identify realistic positive outcomes, and communicate any optimism you may genuinely feel.
- Convey credible reassurance about the future, and help others build personal perspectives of hope and growth.
- Purposefully, mindfully, slow down, as needed.

Anticipate diminished cognitive and emotional control

Remember that even with the best self-care, crises drain anyone's ability to think, act, and remain calm. Expect impaired focus and memory from others and yourself. Anticipate decision-making to be more difficult. For example, you might find it harder to assess the relevance of information or actions. You and others may experience physical tolls that manifest as muscle tension, changes in appetite, or insomnia. Be ready for waves of anger, fear, and sadness about what has happened and what could lie ahead.

It is human nature to flinch or fumble during a crisis, but leaders' glaring public missteps reveal striking lessons about what not to do. For example, former CEO of British Petroleum, Tony Hayward, while leading BP's responses to the Deepwater Horizon crisis, made comments that intensified damage to his own reputation and that of BP.[15]

- Avoid personal gushes like Hayward's: "I'd like my life back." These types of confessions draw media outrage and incense the public.
- Avoid rants among colleagues, like Hayward's: "What the hell did we do to deserve this?" Internal whining is unlikely to remain private. Even if it is not broadcast, it will only fuel complaints and negative sentiments internally, affecting team morale. Set the example.
- Refrain from making inaccurate declarations like Hayward's: "I became a villain for doing the right thing."
- Avoid condemning your own organization. Take a lesson in what not to do from Boeing's former CEO Dennis Muilenburg who, when pressed about safety decisions that cost the lives of hundreds of 737 MAX passengers, testified "We don't 'sell' safety, that's not our business model."[16]

Be slow to spew your own negative emotions

- Remain calm. Crisis management success favors composed role models.
- Do not release your frustrations publicly. Your candor will come off as insensitive and uncaring.
- Stifle any urges to compare hardships with your colleagues, your customers, the public, the media, or anyone else. In crisis, misery does not love company.

Do not flinch at others' negative emotions

Although manifestations can be managed, internal emotional reactions cannot be willed away. Pushing against anger, fear, or sadness drives negative reactions underground, where they are even more difficult to handle. Anger, left unattended, can cause employees, customers, and the public to shift their allegiance and behave in unexpected, risky ways. Left to brew, fear can overwhelm and disable followers and leaders, even those who are deeply loyal and resilient under less formidable conditions. Churning sadness can cause people to lose focus or direction, which can accelerate errors and deplete resilience, particularly if the crisis drags on.

When negative emotions are in the air, the most important thing you can do is to resist the urge to duck or hide. Instead of attempting to ignore or stifle them, summon the will to face into negative emotions, others' as well as your own. Learn the basics of managing specific negative emotions so that you can provide a well-focused response.

Anger

To successfully affect others' anger, above all, exercise discipline in controlling your own responses, your words and actions. Set the goal to avoid getting sucked into a reactive, unconstructive exchange. Instead, aim to slow down the situation. Breathe more deeply. Speak more slowly. Temper your tone of voice and volume. Model composure, without being condescending.

Fear

Help people avoid exaggerating perceived dangers. Be honest and upfront about organizational challenges, and candid about your own concerns. Help individuals gather facts and confront their concerns. Remind them of how their personal strengths are contributing to resolving the crisis. Help them avoid sliding into the victim's role, where hopelessness and unhappiness can take firm hold.

Sadness

When you encounter sadness, be present and patient. Demonstrate strength and communal concern. Start by listening empathically. Sometimes, that is the only action needed to help someone who is sad. In light of what you hear and observe, find ways to show that you are taking their specific challenges seriously. If possible, relieve them of some responsibilities so that they will have time to connect with their natural support networks, even if only temporarily.[17] Follow up by checking in with those who are sad.

Act deliberately

Know where you are heading. Keep in mind your ultimate targets for resolving the crisis, and a general sense of how you intend to reach them. Factor in time and resource constraints when you weigh alternatives. Choose the right tempos for tasks, and build your schedule accordingly.

Stay tuned to limitations that may be developing. Watch for shifts in stakeholders' perspectives, actions, and access. Stay alert to specific contextual constraints. For example, consider how expectations or approaches at any location could be affected by local laws, logistics, currencies, norms, values, and languages.

Remember that you will often be evaluating risk and benefit. Sometimes, high risk decisions and actions will be needed. As challenges and complexities mount, reassess best actions relative to the current situation, and the anticipated future.

Aim for perfection by rare exception only. Certainly, there are times when perfect is the appropriate target, for example, when formulating new drugs or disposing of lethal materials. But otherwise, try to avoid flawless as a goal. The route to perfect is dangerously time-consuming, a resource that is scarce in crisis, and it is highly unlikely that you will achieve that target. Instead, as you make crucial decisions in crisis, keep your eye on the balance between available time and the levels of certainty or perfection that are needed.

Find ways to use efficient approaches. Delegate easier decisions to save your time and energy for demands that require your peak effectiveness, your expertise, or your experience. When in doubt regarding trade-offs between time and certainty, revisit your organization's values. Then, align priorities and momentum toward the appropriate time/perfection balance according to those commitments.

Be ready to step up beyond your current position

In crisis, it is not unusual to earn an organizational version of a battlefield commission. The importance of the expertise you can bring may be greater than others' hierarchical power, for example. Links in the existing chain of command above you may break, due to others' inaccessibility, resignations, or lack of crisis competence or authority. People to whom you have turned for authority, proficiency, or resources may be injured, cut off from communication, or absorbed in other issues. When circumstances like these occur, your own authority or responsibilities may take a sudden twist or turn.

Whether your responsibilities shift, grow, diminish, or remain the same, you may have to invent new ways to move people to get the job done. This could include employees at any level, as well as external stakeholders. You may need critical information from them. You might have to motivate them to make decisions, or lead them through novel or risky actions for which plans do not exist.

You may find yourself leading people who personify a jumble of styles and objectives. People who are not members of your organization will be unlikely to follow you simply because your organization has deemed you the leader. Even longtime employees of your own organization may attempt to head out on their own paths when crisis disrupts anticipated norms, rather than go along with your preferred expectations or directives. To lead in crisis, you must find and create ways to appeal to your followers' needs and desires.[18]

This is the terrain of the hero's journey. Your best chance of success is by setting values and goals that everyone can get behind. This means identifying motives and levers that would move anyone. Nix the speeches about what you or your organization expects. Avoid pitching the nobility of individual dedication, or the call of community service. Rather, set a clear and visible measure of how your followers can achieve what matters most to them, by doing what is needed by your organization.

An outstanding, clear-cut example was set by Naohiro Masuda, the manager of Fukushima II, whose exemplary crisis leadership was featured earlier in this chapter. As in all workplace crises, Fukushima II workers wanted to go home. Instead of ignoring their desire or promising a date or time that could have proven unrealistic, Masuda set the goal of achieving cold shutdown. When that occurred, everyone could leave the plant. He added precision to the target by specifying that all reactors would have to reach temperatures below 100 degrees Celsius. These explicit targets removed any uncertainty or judgment about the finish line. They comprised a clear, common goal that would be identically measurable by everyone in the plant.

Despite intense trials that tested perseverance, creativity, and courage, employees of Fukushima II gave their all to complete the job, so that everyone could go home. Under Matsuda's superb crisis leadership, there was no meltdown, no explosion, nor a single fatality at Fukushima II.[19] For these extraordinary outcomes, Masuda was awarded numerous international honors.

The leadership process and outcomes for Yoshida at Fukushima I were quite different. During ongoing communications throughout the crisis, TEPCO's senior leaders ordered Yoshida to pump salt water into the damaged reactor. He defied the order, a stance that was initially vilified, but eventually credited as key to avoiding a nuclear fission chain reaction and additional radiation release. Ultimately, that action brought acclaim to Yoshida from TEPCO's leader and the Prime Minister of Japan.[20]

Aim to come out stronger

A crisis tests leadership, fundamentally, and at all levels. Nowhere are opportunities for leader-level learning greater. Nowhere is personal impact felt more dramatically.

As pressures lift, shift emphasis beyond survival mode. Make time and effort to evaluate and reinforce personal growth driven by the crisis and your vision of the future. Use these questions for self-assessment, and discuss them with others:

- What have you faced that tested your character or your resilience?
- How have you adhered to values (your organization's and your own) that were tested by the crisis?
- How did approaches like thinking creatively, or framing situations realistically around potential positive effects help you manage the crisis?
- What helped you most to rise to the extraordinary challenges that you faced?

A crisis provides profound opportunities for grace and gratitude. Help others appreciate how their efforts and endurance contributed to successful outcomes. Remind them of the courage and perseverance they demonstrated simply by showing up and adapting in the crisis.

It is never too early to learn and practice behaviors and characteristics that help excellent leaders succeed in a crisis. Even before a crisis looms, take some time to contemplate your own behaviors, including specific crisis-relevant strengths, as well as personal improvements you would like to achieve. Ask for feedback from people whose opinions you value most. Experiment with new behaviors and new ways of thinking that you observe in people you look up to, and envision in the person you want to become.

Improve your crisis leadership expertise before a crisis occurs, using practical techniques. Create opportunities for open discussions about major challenges and problems that your organization faces. Include employees of diverse levels and functions, inviting participants from other divisions or sites, especially if you operate internationally. Talk with leaders outside your organization and your industry about their approaches, successes, failures, and lessons learned.

Learn and practice best organizational-level crisis perspectives and practices with scenarios and cases. (See Crisis Tools.) Glean insights for your own organization's contexts and challenges, expanding your view by assessing the successes and failures of how others have handled crises in their organizations—as you, your coworkers, the media, and the public see them.

Up Next

In the next chapter, we will start to establish a solid foundation for preventing and mitigating crises. We will begin with your organization's core values, the best source for unifying your entire organization in the same direction, no matter the nature of crisis you experience, or where in your organization the troubles are centered. Recommendations for articulating values are also included, in case your organization has not yet achieved that.

We will consider another fundamental ingredient for crisis success—top leadership endorsement—including how to build early buy-in among senior executives, and how to work through any resistance they may bring. Topics, questions, and samples are included to help you begin discussing and drafting your organization's crisis objectives.

3

Establish Your Foundation

The most successful crisis approaches will come from your own organization. Your crisis preparations and responses need not be original, but they must be authentic. The resonance of your crisis objectives needs to run deep within your organization and across all sites. Other organizations' plans or generic playbooks will lack alignment with your values, your resources, your stakeholders, and your strategies. They will neither play to your organization's strengths, nor compensate for its vulnerabilities.

For a solid foundation for your organization, start by doing three things:

1. Get clear on your organization's values.
2. Secure sufficient top leadership support.
3. Draft values-based crisis objectives.

#1 GET CLEAR ON YOUR ORGANIZATION'S VALUES

The surest place to base crisis preparation and response is in your organization's core values. If the values promoted by your organization actually drive your employees' behaviors, and if decisions and actions throughout your organization measure up to your organization's claims, then you have significant advantages for handling crises. Your employees already know what matters most, they are in the habit of fitting their actions to those values, and they are rewarded for doing so. Even under threat of a crisis, this self-reinforcing cycle is invaluable for keeping your entire organization moving in the same direction, toward abiding targets.

When everyone in the organization is committed to aligning values and action, and adept at doing that, it is relatively simple to transition to crisis readiness. Begin by making your core values the cornerstone of your crisis framework, articulating connections between your shared values and your crisis priorities clearly and simply. Emphasize the importance of that link, especially when signals are increasing or difficult choices must be made, for instance, when determining which critical needs will have to be deferred or ignored.

If your organization has not identified its core values, or if behaviors do not align with and support your value claims, evaluate what is truly essential to your organization. Identify these beacons before setting crisis objectives. These questions can help guide discussions of what matters most according to the targets and practices of your organization:

- Why does our organization exist? What is its fundamental purpose?
- What drives our success internally?
- Which behaviors do we reward? Which do we ignore or admonish?
- Which stakeholders and organizational locations are most important to our organization, and why? How do we treat influencers and sites that we consider less important, and why?

A hallmark of crisis leadership, underscoring the invaluable influence of authentic values, was Johnson & Johnson (J&J)'s CEO James Burke's response to the Tylenol tampering crisis, when cyanide poisonings resulted in consumer deaths. Burke's handling of the crisis was so exceptional, it earned him the Presidential Medal of Freedom (America's highest civilian honor) and he was named one of Forbes' "10 Greatest CEOs of All Time."[21]

Key to his success was Burke's prompt decision to rely on J&J's core values. Faced with an unprecedented product tampering situation, Burke sought guidance from the Food and Drug Administration (FDA) and the Federal Bureau of Investigation (FBI), and he went in person. The FDA recommended pulling all product in the Chicago area, where the first contaminations had been found, but Burke exceeded their advice, recalling all 31 million bottles of Tylenol distributed worldwide. It was a swift $100 million bet which required great courage and resolve. This action not only curtailed the crisis, it restored Tylenol's worldwide popularity and boosted J&J's positioning among the most-admired companies. But what many do not know is that Burke's earlier actions had stacked the odds in his favor.

The year before becoming CEO, Burke had organized a process called the *Credo Challenge* to confirm whether J&J's original values (then 40 years old) still fit the emerging business era. He started at senior executive level. After deep consideration, the top leaders confirmed the endurance of J&J's values, and in doing so, renewed their individual commitment to them. Then, Burke spread the process throughout J&J.[22]

As in all successful crisis responses, luck played a hand. The insights and momentum built by the *Credo Challenge* had sharpened individual awareness and wide-spread alignment with the company's core values. One value in particular, holding consumer welfare above all else, simplified decisions and actions during the Tylenol crisis, including the board's prompt approval for funding the full recall. That is the power of aligning strong, clear, authentic organizational values and crisis objectives. J&J's outcome underscores the potency of reviewing and reconfirming values before any crisis occurs.

All organizations demonstrate their values, whether their actions match what they claim to value or not. But not all organizations have articulated them, and some that have articulated their values do not adhere to them. Rather, written or spoken values may be intended for other purposes, such as image management, marketing, or recruiting. But alignment between articulated values and values in action is essential for successful crisis preparation and response. Once you have identified what you believe to be your organization's values, test their authenticity. To do that, discuss your responses to these fundamental questions that were originally formulated by James Burke.[23]

- Are our values valid?
- If they're valid, can we live with them?
- If we can live with them, are we performing our role in seeing to it that the company lives with them?

#2 SECURE TOP LEADERSHIP SUPPORT

Organization-wide crisis preparation only works if it is driven from the very top. Top executives can power or crush crisis preparations, through even subtle actions or off-hand comments. To initiate or enhance crisis readiness that reaches across your organization, you need all top executives on your side, or you will have to at least neutralize their objections. Initially, some individuals may assume that it is impossible to prepare for crises, or that ad hoc responses will save the day. Occasionally, senior leaders even confess that they prefer taking the ostrich approach, retreating until the crisis passes.

You can best gain support by helping senior executives understand the following:

- Potential costs of crises (financial and beyond)
- Existential threats to the organization, their own reputations and livelihoods, or all of these
- The status of vulnerabilities and strengths in-house and within access
- Gaps or dangers for which major crisis improvements needed

The good news for anyone promoting crisis readiness is that it is a much easier sell these days. If senior executives seem disinterested, try any of these magic words to capture their attention: *cybercrime, terrorism, pandemic.*

If support still lags among top level leaders, galvanize your own commitment, and continue to build interest. I have worked with organizations of various sizes and industries where one well-regarded, mid-level manager succeeded in championing top executive support to initiate, shape, and institutionalize organization-wide crisis readiness. If you are that person, take heart: not everyone among your senior executive team must become a champion, and the first executives to buy in will usually help convince the others.

If you encounter resistance, focus on the rationales you are hearing. Aim to keep the conversation going, with executive engagement, candor, and additional information about approaches, costs, and benefits of preparation and improvements. Draw out diverse perspectives to help everyone in the executive group understand, test, and address challenges and concerns, and identify strengths and resources.

Customize the best criteria for convincing your senior team. Start with your organization's core values. Reassure them that the security of those values will be enhanced when plans are in place, when essential resources are primed, and when your organization is prepared to safeguard its most important stakeholders. Caution that inventing responses amid the dangers, uncertainties and time compression of a crisis can lead to panic, conflicts, delays, and rash decisions in the shorter term. Remind them that in the longer term, ad hoc responses can put your core values at risk, which could ultimately extinguish stakeholder support and threaten the viability of your organization.

If resistance prevails, facilitate a discussion of environmental challenges that threaten your organization. You might include the speed and reach of media, the powerful and erratic sway of popular opinion, the transparency of organizational errors and misjudgment, and the possibility that even *one* persistent antagonist could disrupt your organization's effectiveness.

At any point, consider raising some provocative questions, before any crisis occurs.

- Which threats keep us awake at night?
- How is our organization currently at risk?
- What kinds of vulnerabilities are we choosing to ignore?
- Which risks have been addressed locally but still persist outside headquarters or our home country?
- How does crisis readiness vary across our organization, and how could these differences derail or destroy us organization-wide?

#3 DRAFT VALUES-BASED CRISIS MANAGEMENT OBJECTIVES

Create a reciprocal relationship between your values and your crisis objectives: base your crisis objectives on your core values, and protect your core values with your crisis objectives. This orientation keeps everyone pulling in the same direction, which makes it easier to establish response parameters, accept obligations, and implement unified approaches in crises. Evaluate this balance by imagining that you are facing into a full-blown crisis. Would objectives and values be in harmony among all leaders and employees? If you asked everyone, "*What matters most throughout our organization?*" would their answers be consistent?

Start with broad discussion of your organization's desired outcomes in the event of a crisis. As you imagine circumstances, feature your key internal and external stakeholders, and their contexts. Picture what protection would look like at various power levels, in a variety of divisions or departments, and across different geographic or cultural regions where your organization operates. Consider questions like these:

- Which of our values must be upheld, no matter what the circumstances?
- What preparations and responses would be needed to protect our core business and keep fundamental operations, products, and services afloat?
- Which of our stakeholders should take priority in our decisions and actions? How do these priorities align with or undermine our core values?

It is impossible to imagine all of the precise actions needed when a crisis looms. However, it is possible to describe the direction in which you would proceed. Aim for concise targets that emerge obviously from your organization's core values. Hone your objectives until you reach consensus about broad issues. Then define, streamline, and state your crisis objectives simply. Write the objectives so clearly that everyone will understand the objectives and their intent, even under dire circumstances, even when severely stressed.

Here are samples of actual crisis objectives, from a variety of organizations and industries.

- Protect and promote the health and safety of our employees.
- Protect consumers.
- Protect the environment.

- Limit our financial liability.
- Minimize enduring damages to our reputation.
- Maintain public confidence in our products.
- Build goodwill.

Up Next

After establishing a foundation based on your core values and preliminary crisis objectives, it is time to start expanding crisis engagement and responsibility beyond the senior executive level. To begin that transition, this chapter explains how to create one of your most important resources, your Crisis Leadership Team (CLT), an expert team of employees focused on building and continuously improving crisis readiness and response throughout your organization and among your key stakeholders and environments.

The CLT will be invaluable for designing, motivating, fine-tuning, and strengthening your approaches and responses to crises. To assure that you build the best team possible, the next chapter includes specifics for team development, including how to select the best candidates, and how to forge a superb high-performance team. In alignment with today's realities, it also includes best practices for cross-cultural and virtual CLTs.

4

Create A Superb Crisis Leadership Team

When you create a Crisis Leadership Team (CLT), you must get it right. If you do, your team will be one of your most powerful levers for initiating and retaining crisis readiness, response, and learning to avert crises and optimally handle those that do occur. By design, the CLT will build in diverse experience and expertise, internal dexterity, and external coordination in crisis for your organization.

Select and build the CLT as soon as possible, in advance of any crisis. Drive every aspect of its development, planning, and execution in alignment with your organization's purpose. Prepare and poise every CLT member to protect your organization in dire situations. In crisis, their effectiveness will influence the future of your organization, your stakeholders, and your environments.[24]

SELECT CLT MEMBERS METICULOUSLY

Screen for individuals who are committed to leading through the utmost challenges that your organization will face. Base selection on candidates' expertise, responsibilities, and access to critical resources. Choose candidates who represent varied hierarchical levels, geographic locations, and job functions, including top executives who represent the best of your organization.

As top selection criteria, choose people whose behaviors align consistently with your organization's values. Gauge for individual integrity and honesty because even the best crisis management plans and approaches will be shattered by misconduct or deceit. Select for skills that will help reach down into your organization and across its internal and external borders. Prioritize candidates who confront negative outcomes realistically, and deal with new circumstances and new information receptively, calmly, and with an open mind. Consider behavioral indicators, such as listening fully, speaking with curiosity and candor, and addressing disagreements civilly. Hold all candidates to your selection criteria, even those at the highest power levels. Where essential candidates fall short on any selection criteria, invest in improving their shortcomings before bringing them on board.

Ensure diversity in as many ways as possible and relevant: gender, generation, race, location, culture, ethnicity, fluent languages, roles, shift assignments, and experiences. If your organization is multinational, this is crucial. People exactly like you may not recognize or tell what you don't know—about potential risks, current strengths and vulnerabilities, crisis signals from unfamiliar arenas, and best ways to lead or respond to stakeholders from backgrounds unlike your own.

GATHER THE TEAM

The CLT's initial meeting is prime time to build shared purpose and strengthen relationships across the team. Meet in real time. Go face-to-face if possible, gathering in person; if not, use the richest conferencing media and platforms available. Create opportunities to accelerate team development, to build a base for long-term collaboration, and to strengthen commitment among individual members.

From the first introduction, treat everyone on the CLT as colleagues. Focus icebreakers on members' crisis-relevant contexts and expertise. Ask about additional attributes and competencies useful in crisis, such as international and technological responsibilities and experience. Set the course for exceptional collaboration by confirming and modeling best practices. Listen carefully to everyone. Value everyone's opinion, especially if it does not match your own. Admit when you do not know something.

From the first meeting, initiate habits that will support optimal long-range team performance. Feature ample opportunities to connect personally through casual interactions. You might start each meeting with a rapid-fire check-in round, for instance. Confirm and model healthy practices and self-care: plenty of breaks, healthy foods/water, walks and breakout discussions in fresh air (to the extent possible), and varied meeting methods and approaches to retain engagement, focus, and energy. Start to instill these practices so that they become norms for the team and individual members, including during the toughest times, in the throes of crisis.

ORIENT THE TEAM

Help the CLT understand its charge. Describe the nature of its power, resources, and boundaries. Discuss expectations about their anticipated roles and accountability. For example, they may be responsible for staying current about shifts to strategies or operations that could affect crisis circumstances significantly, whether from within or outside your organization. The CLT may take part in devising and setting policies and approaches for preparation and response, and monitoring and enhancing crisis learning and progress.

Start to develop CLT norms about sharing relevant knowledge and information among members, and with the rest of the organization. Preview what and how members will learn about crises and handling them. Discuss intrinsic rewards for team commitment and participation, such as personal development, potential leadership opportunities, and recognition.

Affirm links between your organization's values, drafted crisis objectives, and expectations of the CLT. Work together to verify and hone alignment between drafted crisis objectives and current organizational realities, based on members' candid insights and experiences. Elicit specific examples linking core values and drafted crisis objectives, and potential misalignments. Solicit grounded opinions about potential matches and gaps between organizational values and drafted objectives, based on their experiences, insights, and observations. Together, begin to explore modifications that may be needed and goals for improvement.

With the CLT, set norms for team and individual performance. Start with the characteristics that were used for screening and selecting members. Highlight fundamental requirements of every member, such as honesty, reliability, and civility. Remind members that their responsibilities (as individuals and as a team) are critical for the long-term viability of the organization, its stakeholders, and its environments.

SHAPE A HIGH-PERFORMING TEAM

It is impossible to foresee exactly what the CLT will encounter. But, at some point they will probably bear exceptional responsibilities under threatening circumstances. Dealing with deep uncertainties and scarce time will be fundamental skills to develop. The CLT's abilities to succeed despite these strains will be stronger if they sustain two priorities: (1) take full advantage of their complementary skills and knowledge, and (2) focus on meaningful shared purpose. If members have been selected carefully and diversely, these complementary perspectives and skills will be embedded in your team. If your organization's authentic values are the drivers of its crisis objectives, both will provide meaningful common purpose for the team.

Add to this: vigilance not only about *what* the team achieves (task performance), but also *how* (approaches and processes used). For *what*, standards rest on clear targets and performance metrics to define, develop, monitor, and reinforce desired performance. For *how*, norms include devoting time and other resources to develop and work as a team, to enhance mutual understanding. These questions can be useful for checking in on what and how during various stages of team development, and after any crisis or near miss has been handled:

- How does being a part of the CLT inspire us, as a team, as individuals, and as members of our organization?
- Which strengths and weaknesses do we bring to handling complex crisis situations, individually and collectively?
- Which methods and processes for working together seem to optimize our insights?

- What reinforces our courage and tenacity to maintain our team's momentum during crisis?
- How will we continuously improve our ability to balance timeliness and careful thinking?
- Which additional resources, information, and training do we need to operate effectively, so that we can enhance crisis improvements throughout our organization?

Strengthen creative thinking

Any crisis brings unique challenges that will require innovative thinking, interpretations, and actions. To enhance agility, teach, practice and modify new ways of thinking and novel methods:

- Use *what if?* approaches. Make it a habit to discuss what *could* happen, how events *might* unfold, who *could possibly* be affected by a crisis in your organization. Include best and worst cases.
- Adopt tactics popular in design organizations like IDEO.[25] Encourage wild ideas. Defer judgment of suggestions. Build on others' energy and strengths.
- To retain engagement and maximize insights, divide meeting agendas among individual, small group, and full team discussions and activities.
- For in-person meetings, switch to new physical environments occasionally.
- During training and practice, flip conventional timing parameters:
  - When working through longer, slower planning and learning efforts, intersperse some activities and challenges with tight timeframes.
  - When speed starts to spin, interject quiet or silent breaks for deeper reflection (individually and collectively).
- Bring perspectives of a diverse array of stakeholders to CLT meetings. Balance the power of executive-level members of the CLT while still

encouraging and listening to the voices of all other team members. Consider opinions that have been voiced by competitors or adversaries. Take deeper dives to identify diverse assumptions, lessons, and actions that lie beneath exotic or contrarian perspectives. Then, cultivate potential practical insights creatively, with an open mind. Try thinking of them as "complex," rather than ridiculous.

- Introduce novel hypothetical circumstances through scenarios to test the fit and practicality of your organization's crisis norms and approaches. Practice worst-case situation and compromising responses. To build on Mike Tyson's famous response, get used to what could happen to your plans when you're punched in the mouth.[26] Imagine resources, know-how, and exceptional conditions (good and bad) and how they could be adaptable to extreme circumstances.

- *Red Team* your own approaches. Within the CLT, make a concerted effort to imagine and practice responding to oppositional views or attacks that could derail your plans. Identify ways to reinforce vulnerabilities that surface, and to find better alternatives.

Practice remaining calm and projecting composure

Venting negative feelings can damage team performance and morale. Discuss outlets for releasing negative emotions. Shy away from spewing negative sentiments, even when members believe that they are out of public view, making it a responsibility of the CLT to model adept leadership when negative emotions arise.

Reinforce best practices cross-culturally

Build cross-cultural expertise across the team. Start with grounded information and discussion about cultures represented in the CLT. Then, help members learn more about the diverse cultures represented by your organization's key locations. (See Chapter 12 for additional recommendations regarding cross-cultural approaches.)

Reinforce best practices of virtual teams

Power communication and relationships across the CLT by using the richest media available. Choose options that will facilitate instantaneous input and synchronized discussions among members, and with other experts inside and outside your organization. For the toughest decisions, employ the richest media.

Encourage everyone to participate during virtual meetings. Avoid confusion and misunderstandings by keeping accountability and progress visible to the entire team. Do not assume that silence means agreement; ask to be sure. For particularly sensitive issues, poll the CLT privately or anonymously. (See Chapter 14 for additional recommendations for virtual teaming.)

Express gratitude and demonstrate confidence in the team

Identify and create opportunities to acknowledge the value added by each member. Appreciate the skills, perseverance, and stability brought to bear by the CLT. When crises loom, lean toward the team's exceptional expertise, and support the authority that has been vested in them. Whenever feasible, follow the CLT's lead.

———————————— Up Next ————————————

Chapter 5 focuses on drafting a map to capture your crisis preparation and response plans, expectations, and targets. Here, we will describe how to work with your CLT and additional representative leaders throughout your organization who are best suited to understand and influence alignment under extraordinary circumstances. We will look at how to create a map so that reflects your organization's realities, such as resources and key stakeholders/environments, as well as how to detail your intentions and gather additional crisis insights as an ongoing way of life.

5

Map Your Crisis Plans

Your map documents your crisis plans as a customized tracking device and a prime platform for testing your assumptions, approaches, and progress. It will guide decisions and actions across your organization, and guard against missed opportunities, rash decisions, and mistakes, before, during, and after crises. The map is also a comprehensive tool for orienting, engaging, and updating key stakeholders.

Create an initial draft of the map as a group, and make your Crisis Leadership Team an integral part. If you wish to expand beyond that team, add employees from diverse functions, locations, and levels who can add their perspectives and expertise to the mapping process. The best maps are working documents, not decorative items or marketing tools. Work in creative bursts[27] and suspend simplification[28] as you improve your map continuously. Review it: annually, when crises and near misses occur, and when organizational or environmental changes may affect your ability to manage crises. Reexamine it promptly after leadership changes, acquisitions, and expansion or contraction of your organization's footprint. Your map might begin simply, on sticky notes as illustrated here.

SKETCH A PRELIMINARY MAP OF YOUR PLANS

Work as a group to create a rough mind map of the span of your plans. Start by capturing the cornerstones of your crisis approach. Anchor your map with a clear, concise list of your organization's core values. Then, name your crisis objectives. Whenever you present your map, make these alignments among values, objectives, and plans your opening talking points.

- **Start to capture your crisis orientation, guidelines, and plans graphically.** The better you can convey your message symbolically, the easier it will be for others to interpret and remember. Think basic graphics, simple figures, plain tables, and straight-forward data. As an example, this graphic depicts the essential stages for crisis leadership. Core organizational values and crisis objectives are the entry point, followed by basic sequenced processes.

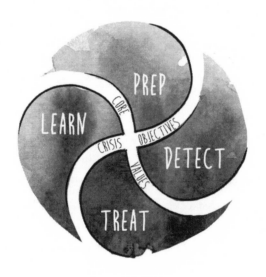

PREPARE, PLAN, TEST, PRACTICE YOUR APPROACH

- Incorporate your expectations. Note key processes and experts that can assist (or block) you in achieving your plans.
- For risks that your industry is required to control in particular ways, make sure all executives and relevant leaders receive the best

available training for addressing those risks, and that regulated requirements are trained and verified throughout your organization.

- Brainstorm a small but distinctive variety of crises that you will prepare for, creating submaps where different signals, resources or experts would be needed to address them. For example, a food product contamination, a pandemic, and a cybercrime would each involve your CLT, but their crisis signals may come from other directions, and some of the experts or resources needed to prevent, mitigate and resolve each would vary greatly.

- Include essential crisis resources already in place in your organization. Sketch in specifics and lingering issues as they occur to you, such as pending questions and decisions to be made. Use the map to keep track of what more you need to know and acquire.

- Begin to detail responsibilities and authority of the Crisis Leadership Team.

- Look ahead to key actions that are already scheduled, critical targets for your crisis preparations, and practical measures of success, and note them on the map.

DETECT, REPORT, ACT ON SIGNALS

- Specify signal detection channels and networks for distinct types of crises.

- Evaluate existing channels for crisis communication. Detail best routes for sharing information throughout your organization and with key external stakeholders.

- Identify trustworthy external stakeholders who may spot critical signals of danger early. Detail their expertise and contact information. Describe actions for building and retaining bridges to them.

- Designate systems and criteria for sensing and assessing signals. Include mechanisms and assigned responsibilities for determining the plausibility and severity of warning signals.

ASSESS, TREAT, NOTIFY, ADAPT TO CRISIS CIRCUMSTANCES

- Set guidelines for customizing content with global, national, and regional contacts across your organization. Detail best means and personnel for attaining compliance at organizational and local levels.
- Identify a range of circumstances under which top executive leadership and the CLT should be involved to assess crisis status and direct future action. Include contact information for designated representatives.
- Identify essential types of external first-responders, for instance, local law enforcement, emergency medical teams (EMTs), and victim relief services. Describe site-level expectations for building and reinforcing bridges to them.
- Describe the nature of situations under which additionally designated internal and external experts should be notified. Include contact information.
- Outline procedures for notifying government agencies, media, insurance providers, attorneys, and other authorities, with prompt attention to those for whom alerts are mandated, specifying any regulated timeframes.

LEARN, IMPROVE, SUSTAIN FOR THE FUTURE

During a crisis, track these efforts. After the crisis has ebbed, update and enhance specifics.

- Structure immediate review processes to assure compliance requirements have been met during and after the crisis.
- Gather senior leadership and the CLT promptly to assess and record significant accomplishments and shortcomings.
- Identify essential parameters for surfacing new patterns and lessons based on what is most important to your organization. Branch to specifics for revising and enhancing current plans, and add them to the map.

Tracking crisis preparation and response, both in plans and in action, can be captured graphically using common tools like Ishikawa diagrams, mind mapping and Gantt charts. Below is an excerpt of a crisis flow chart, a common tool for mapping crisis processes.

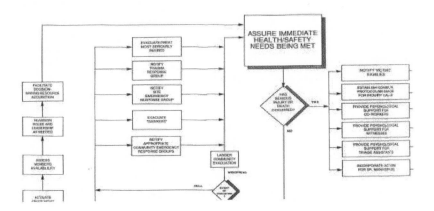

Fine-tune the Fundamentals

Once you have sketched some of the basics, take a step back to review your draft. Consider these questions and guidelines to refine it:

Does our map reinforce what matters most for our organization?

- Do our values and crisis objectives define, clarify, and direct our crisis plans?
- Do the mapped approaches secure the fundamental measures of our organization's crisis success including our values and our objectives? Are there additional elements that we must retain and protect, no matter what?
- Where are the significant gaps? What more is needed to reinforce our foundation of values and objectives?

Is the map centered on our most important stakeholders?

If you have not already done so, conduct a Stakeholder Analysis to identify individuals, groups, and organizations that are most influential for your organization. (See Crisis Tools for details.) Then, discuss your assumptions about how your key stakeholders might facilitate or impair your ability to handle a crisis. These questions can provide insightful guidance:

- According to the map, which internal and external stakeholders are we counting on when a crisis occurs?
- Which additional key stakeholders should be added to the map?
- How does the map set the course for smooth collaboration with our key internal and external stakeholders before, during, and after crises?
- According to provisions in the map, how are we protecting our key stakeholders?
- How are we planning to prioritize and choose among decisions and actions that would affect them?
- What options have we set out for sharing crisis insights with our stakeholders?

As you revise your map, be sure to include a few outlier stakeholders, whom you may not have thought of immediately, but who could severely impact your ability to manage a crisis. Incorporate a few of them as examples to broaden *What if?* discussions, to expand your thinking and improve your response agility.

What are our immediate priorities?

Keep high-level targets succinct, obvious, and easy to understand. Focus on overall guidance fitting to your organization's crisis targets, for example, "Customers first," "Keep all employees informed," or "False alarms over missed signals." Whenever you edit your map, review the priorities, recognizing that they may need revision in response to shifts in strategies, approaches, or new environmental contexts.

When major decisions or actions seem to push against your fundamental guidelines, values or objectives, make sure that the departure from your plans is warranted. Then, proceed iteratively, to allow for rapid rerouting or turning back, if assumptions, routes, or approaches prove wrong.

How can we deepen expertise about current approaches that already exist in our organization?

Collect plans across your organization. Familiarize yourselves with the quality, breadth, and status of preparations and tools that could be adopted or adapted to improve crisis readiness. Discuss how the breadth of preparations in place could accelerate your planning, as well as dangerous gaps that remain. Fold the best of your existing preparations into your map.

Who is our target audience, the people who will use the map?

Determine the best mapping formats for your organization and for users. Choose layouts and media that will be understood and readily accepted across your organization. Publish your map in a variety of forms. Consider creating digital and hard copy, in multiple languages, as appropriate to optimize accessibility and convenience throughout your organization.

How will we challenge the content of the map?

The next step will be gathering feedback and insights from employees across your organization. But before doing that, make one more critical review of your map. This time, specifically focus on potential shortcomings.

- **Look deeper into puzzling or irreconcilable implications embedded in the map.** For example, are the same individuals designated to fill too many essential roles, or to be physically present simultaneously across multiple locations? Do crucial responses rely on resources that are outside your organization's control?

- **Test assumptions that you are making about critical decisions and actions.** Build agility by flipping your expectations. Assume some of the things you are taking for granted are wrong. As an example, if you have assumed that your employees will show up for work no matter what, now assume many will not. Or select a resource that you see as a strength, and consider how it could delay or derail actions. Discuss potential impacts, and shifts that would be needed. Use this exercise to expose and reduce vulnerabilities in your map.

- **Take the perspective of your competitors, as well as a few extreme or eccentric stakeholders.** What are the worst-case scenarios that they could inflict? How does your map account for these possibilities? What additional risks do their views suggest?

- **Imagine and discuss possible impacts from secondary stakeholders.** Examine your map for specifics or implications regarding your key stakeholders' key stakeholders, for example, your employees' families and your suppliers' suppliers. In light of these additional stakeholders, where could flexibility regarding resources or additions to your plans improve the map?

- **Test and critique your plans using a few crisis scenarios.** Use brief hypotheticals (no longer than one or two pages) as common background for discussion and planning. For greater realism, customize some aspects of the scenarios to your organization's realities. After some practice with the approach, incorporate a few taboo circumstances, potential problems so scary that your organization avoids talking about them.

When we experience crises or near misses, who will log details on the map?

Track progress and setbacks during and after the events. Capture them as they occur, or promptly thereafter, when the details are still vivid and memories are fresh. Include timing parameters.

- Document and evaluate organizational strengths and weaknesses that emerged.
- Hone the performance of the CLT. Consider adjustments that may be needed to the team's structure, resources, or personnel.
- Capture questions to consider after operations advance to the next normal.
- Keep track of potential lessons for the future.
- Note ideas for improvements based on the event and how it was handled.

PREPARE TO TEST DRIVE YOUR MAP ACROSS YOUR ORGANIZATION

Identify a rich and varied sample of experience and expertise across levels, sites, and functions. Include diverse locations outside headquarters and beyond home country. Be sure to visit some particularly remote and high-risk settings.

Before collecting data, as a team, assess what you know and what you expect regarding the sites to which you will be taking the map. Discuss what you assume about their crisis readiness and responses.

- Which sites, teams, and functions do you assume will be the weakest links, and the strongest? What sorts of vulnerabilities (strengths) do you anticipate or associate with them?
- Where do you think your knowledge about local preparations might be particularly pertinent or off-base?

- How does your map compensate for anticipated challenges in connecting, evaluating, or learning from and with the weaker sites, teams, or functions?
- Which members of your team are best equipped to act as liaisons in particular sites or regions, teams, or functions?
- What key issues and questions should be explored wherever you take the map?

Up Next

Chapter 6 lays out plans for taking your map on a road trip. This expedition (in person, virtually, or in hybrid mode) will help you draw out the details of your existing states of crisis readiness across your organization, from weakest links to best practices. Details will tap how to build buy-in, identify champions, and seed compliance to initiate and enhance crisis readiness organization-wide.

6

Take Your Crisis Roadmap on a Test Drive

Your organization's readiness will only be as strong as its weakest links. Your road trip should be an eye-opener regarding the current fit and feasibility of your plans. Whether you are initiating or improving crisis practices, the test drive has deep benefits as you: (a) assess the accuracy and thoroughness of your map, (b) learn from, engage, and inform a broad sample of employees across your organization, and (c) identify and build champions who can help boost crisis readiness for your organization, its stakeholders, and its environments.

Your map is a dynamic tool for developing and maintaining an accurate picture of the quality, fit, and stability of your current crisis response plans, preparations, and practices. As you test it in diverse sites, collect field-based data through observation and discussion. Use your senses to soak up insights. Share the current perspective of values, objectives, and actions—validating the map. Seek participants' feedback, questions, answers, and observations. Create opportunities to build crisis insights collaboratively, during your visits and afterwards.

At each location you visit, aim to achieve at least three goals:

1. Learn what and where the deepest holes and greatest challenges are for advancing your organization's crisis preparations.
2. Collect clues and answers to better understand and handle weaknesses and strengths, gaps and resources.
3. Boost awareness, acceptance, momentum, and action to be ready for crises organization-wide.

EVALUATE ACTUAL PREPARATIONS ACROSS YOUR ORGANIZATION'S FOOTPRINT

To gauge the focus, quality, and consistency of fundamental crisis preparations that are already in place throughout your organization, speak with a diverse representation of site employees. The goal is respectful engagement.[29] Start at the top to legitimize your inquiry, including individuals and groups who are accountable for emergency and crisis response content and delivery. Then discuss with employees at all levels to share the map and gather insights and support from them. Discuss the fit and appropriateness of organizational approaches, as well as any accommodations that have been made for local preferences or habits. Learn from locals about how they have handled crises in the past, how they maintain crisis information and contacts, and how they keep preparations up to date. Extract essential lessons, especially, from previous shortcomings that they have experienced.

In addition to collecting data where you anticipate ample crisis response support and strong resources, sample sites where you suspect that crisis approaches, tools, or resources may be lacking or short of expectations. Across all site visits, confirm and reinforce the mandate to consistently adhere to organizational values, and crisis objectives and guidelines.

Open all discussions by reinforcing the foundation of your plans and map, that is, your organization's core values and crisis objectives. Make the connection clear among these foundations and within the content of the map. Introduce the map as a working document that will be modified as you learn more during the test drive, and as circumstances change in your organization and its environments. Explain that the purpose of taking the map on a test drive is shared learning. Behave accordingly; for example, allow sufficient time for open discussions, and listen and respond to strengthen collaborative learning. Aim to receive and support the potential value of whatever you hear, making it clear to all that their insights and responsive actions are valued.

During discussions on the road trip, build an appreciation for each site's strengths and weaknesses regarding crisis preparation and response. Gather perspectives from diverse levels, functions, and locations with questions like these:

- What instructions or preparations are provided to local employees to build their knowledge, skills, and access to resources for potentially dangerous circumstances? What additional information or resources would improve their readiness?
- How are inspections and other safety precautions kept current and effective? Which are conducted regularly? When were they last revised?
- How are lessons from actual crises, near misses, and simulations shared? How are the new ideas incorporated into existing plans?
- Sample the quality of information about key employees named in any local plans. For example, are they still working at this site? Are they still responsible for the designated role, with the same contact information and same responsibility as noted in the materials? Who are the backup contacts?
- How well does what you are hearing and seeing at this location match the expectations captured in the map? Where are there positive matches, and potentially dangerous gaps?

Where field perspectives seem at odds with the map, pay particularly close attention, ask follow-up questions with genuine curiosity, and make notes to share with your mapping teammates when you return. Stay alert to local norms, circumstances, and environments that may signal strengths or problems. Watch operations with an eye toward insufficient safety precautions, training or resource shortages, or telltale signs of deeper problems and difficulties, such as dilapidated buildings. Report and redress safety deficiencies immediately, and investigate whether other locations need to apply the same remedies.

Review local directives, such as posted safety procedures and details of contact information. Ask questions appreciatively. When you sense or learn something new or unexpected, seek examples with respectful curiosity. Where critical procedures or risky operations are likely to occur, venture a step deeper by asking individuals to describe how they are prepared to respond, including their individual roles in an emergency or crisis.

Learn about alternative products or services that could be accessed quickly if crisis conditions destroyed or delayed supply channels, causing critical shortages. Gather data about potential alternatives such as backup suppliers, or drawing finished goods from work-in-progress or inventory on hand in other locations. Discuss how much product inventory is usually stocked in local warehouses. Explore whether stockpiled products or raw materials might be available from key customers or even competitors in a crisis.

AS A TEAM, CONSOLIDATE, ASSESS, AND FORMULATE BEST PRACTICES FROM THE FIELD

After you have completed the road trips (in person or virtually), regroup as a team to compare good news, bad news, and potential next steps. Remember that the goal is not to create a final version of the map, but to improve each iteration. Go for continuous improvement, leading with solid, practical, field-based revisions.

Take a step back to look at the big picture. Include cross-cultural experts to deepen interpretations and understanding during these discussions. Begin with the good news, field insights, and actions that affirmed your organization's core values and crisis objectives. Compare readiness and resources among and across categories by location: headquarters, other major home country sites, prime international locations, remote international and domestic locations. Include general findings about site strengths and competencies and regional patterns detected.

Turn next to site and regional trends regarding dangerous, unresolved issues. Use as your guides (a) your organization's core values and crisis objectives, and (b) existing conditions as you found them. Compare these to preparations and responses captured in the map. Stick with a strong collaborative process: remain engaged to understand, appreciate, and absorb new information and novel perspectives.

Highlight what is needed now to bring any big problems you discovered into alignment with fundamental crisis plans. Discuss available assets and shortages: financial, human, or technological, for example. Focus on significant links and barriers. Consider potential impacts to procurement, training, maintenance, transportation logistics, and communication.

Evaluate what you have learned about entry and exit points into distant sites, and the countries in which they are located. Discuss local, regional, and organizational surpluses and limitations relative to the reach, accuracy, and speed of improvements needed. Assess crucial pockets of expertise and ignorance, experience and naïveté, across levels, functions, and sites. Track strengths and weaknesses among information conduits, resource access and allocation, and personnel practices. Consider asking deeper questions like these, which relate to human resource issues, in particular:

- How strong is the knowledge and expertise among employees who will be essential for reducing risk and handling crises? To whom and how do they turn when they need additional help?
- What types of training, development, or practice fall significantly short of crisis expectations, plans, or provisions, as captured in our map?
- How quickly and smoothly can internal expertise be accessed from or shared with employees at the sites where we gathered information?
- Which logistics are in place to connect virtually to a crisis scene anywhere in our organization and to relocate essential employees to the site? What more is needed to expedite employee relocations when they are needed most?
- Which logistics are in place to evacuate employees if needed? Who is accountable for the process during and after evacuation?
- How well equipped is our organization for rapid cross-cultural adaptation in crisis? How quickly and accurately can we translate across languages, norms, and cultural expectations? What practical steps could enhance the effectiveness or speed of translations in crisis?

INCORPORATE ESSENTIAL LESSONS INTO YOUR MAP NOW

As a group, take a broad perspective of lessons learned from the field. Prioritize what should be improved now, based on your organization's core values and crisis objectives. Note new action plans in your map. Include issues to address now, projected targets for improvements in the future, and lingering questions that can be answered later. Focus your perspectives with questions like these:

- In what ways do current preparations, resources, and approaches vary across these sites? What is at risk if we make no changes?
- Currently, where are the most dangerous spots, the riskiest locations, functional responsibilities, and job tasks?
- How do receptivity and preparation for crises vary across functions and power levels at the locations we visited?
  - What patterns emerge regarding diversions or delays that could seriously impair crisis response locally or organization-wide? What patterns might also apply to sites we have not yet visited?
  - What improvements must be made to ensure that crisis-relevant information and resources move swiftly up, down, and across functions and power levels at all locations?

Prioritize urgencies according to categories that are most important for your organization. For example, criteria may vary by location (local, regional, national, international) or by timing (whether to plan and execute now, this year, years from now). Feasibility is likely to play a role, whether limited by accessible funds, technologies, expertise, equipment, or personnel. Particular beneficiaries may shape your priorities, including employees, customers, investors, the public, or the natural environment. As you discuss these difficult judgments, return to your organization's core values and crisis objectives as benchmarks for decisions.

GATHER FEEDBACK BEFORE DISTRIBUTING YOUR MAP

As you work through top priorities, request feedback about proposed adjustments from representative employees who will implement the improvements. Seek their specific recommendations to tailor best local approaches for allocations and rollouts. Confirm the value of modifications that you are making and the fitness of implementation plans with these representatives, and with the Crisis Leadership Team.

Overall, aim to incorporate, apply, and adapt your team's conclusions, as well as best recommendations from local sites that you visited. As always, before distributing the revised map, be sure to make an additional editing pass simply to ensure that the notation, language, and graphics are as straightforward and clear as possible, and then reconfirm this with locals.

Up Next

The next chapter will help you understand how to expand your crisis preparations beyond corporate headquarters and home country locations. Guidance will help you prepare broadly because crises can strike anywhere in your organization, and agitate waves globally. You will find techniques to keep your entire organization informed, reinforcing buy-in and preparation and reducing push-back, while establishing crisis preparations and practicing responses.

7

Build Strength Organization-Wide

*Everybody thinks they're already skilled at and poised to
handle a crisis, but few people are.*

— Peter Drucker

Any employee in your organization could become essential for detecting and
reporting signals, and responding to a crisis. Neglecting crisis preparation is
hazardous. Restricting crisis preparation to top executives is foolish.
Employees from all levels, functions, and locations will affect the power and
weaknesses of preparations and responses, as well as your organization's ability
to avert or effectively handle a crisis.

When employees at any level lack crisis insight and capabilities, they waste
time and make mistakes, sometimes dreadful, irreversible mistakes. For those
who lack knowledge of plans and practice, signal detection and reporting will
be slower, and collaboration and response will be haphazard. By contrast,
dispersed preparation will sharpen awareness, accelerate responses, and guide
action along your organization's desirable trajectories because you weighed
them carefully and put processes in place, during calmer times, when you had
more time.

In this chapter, we will take a close look at how innumerable stakeholders,
including organizers, cyclists, crews, support staff, spectators, and the French
government, raised the bar for crisis management preparation and response
before and during the 2020 Tour de France amidst the coronavirus pandemic.
A great deal of responsibility for health and safety rested on individual racers

and their teams, with sharp accountability and severe penalties for those who violated guidelines. Compliance with COVID protocols and strict adherence to recommended guidelines yielded exceptional successes in dealing with the pandemic. Not one Tour rider tested COVID positive before, during or after the race. Across 22 teams, only a few mechanics and one team manager were sent home.

The incredible success and safety of the French race also helped pave the way for two additional Grand Tours that followed it, the Giro d'Italia (Giro) and the Vuelta a España (Vuelta). Nonetheless, cross-over riders who had also taken part in the Tour de France expressed less comfort with their overall experience of the Giro, and those who moved on from the Tour de France to the Vuelta reported even greater uncertainties about the safeguarding of their health.

Despite plans to adapt some of the Tour approaches, the Giro's bubble was widely compromised, even before the race started. Eleven positive tests across four racing teams led to disqualifying some individual favorites and two of the top teams, who were sent home. Rider and crew protections during the Vuelta were more effective. Only one cyclist and two staff were sent home before the race began, and there were no positive results among 684 tests administered the first testing day during the race. However, another group of stakeholders did not fare as well. Two days after the Vuelta ended, 46 of Spain's civil guard who had controlled traffic along the course were confirmed positive for the coronavirus.

Pushing down workplace responsibility is nothing new. Decisions once made exclusively among top executives have been delegated to senior managers, who have delegated some of their decisions to managers at middle levels. Such shifts can add efficiency to decision-making, while empowering employees to build their personal expertise and agility. Accordingly, some organizations share power all the way to the front line, and reap competitive advantages in operations, products, and service delivery. Similar improvements are needed for crisis preparation and response.

Three tactics facilitate achieving success and benefits by empowering crisis readiness at all levels:

1. Everywhere in your organization, inform, engage and prepare employees for potential involvement.
2. Keep crisis preparations and response simple and straightforward.
3. Use practical change levers to reward compliance and overcome resistance to crisis improvements.

#1 INFORM, ENGAGE, AND PREPARE YOUR EMPLOYEES AT ALL LEVELS

Help employees understand the potential impact of their roles

- **Lower-level employees** are often the first to hear about problems, for example, during their routine contact with key stakeholders such as customers and suppliers. Their vantage point is a fundamental antidote to crises. With access to appropriate information and resources, they may be able to correct a problem before it escalates into a crisis. Even if they cannot fix a problem, knowing how to report signals promptly can initiate critical response cycles and avert dire, more costly outcomes.

- **Mid-level employees** are invaluable conduits in crisis because of their customary responsibilities to transfer and translate information and resources into action up, down, and across the organization. In crisis, those connections and experiences can accelerate nimble pivots throughout your organization. Bridges they have built make mid-level employees great candidates to identify, secure, and link essential expertise and resources. Usually, employees at this level are also more accustomed to solving novel problems, which are always characteristic of crises and warning signals. Even if they are unable to fix problems themselves, their broader operational responsibility, awareness, and expertise is likely to lead them to prompt, practical stop-gap measures.

- **Top-level employees** are always among final decision makers during their organizations' most troubling times. This capacity makes executives vital to crisis responses, especially when threats or outcomes outstretch the bounds of others' reasoning or authority. These most powerful employees bring expertise for three invaluable actions in crisis: delving the depths of potential threats, securing extraordinary resources, and driving core responses into action swiftly.

Teach basic guidelines about when and how to seek and provide help

- Encourage employees throughout your organization to ask questions when in doubt about procedures or responsibilities.
- Hold supervisors and managers accountable for responding to inquiries about potential problems promptly and civilly, even when answers may seem obvious to them.
- Where effective actions require deeper insight or higher levels of authority, establish logical, easy-access paths to move information within and among appropriate power levels promptly.

#2 KEEP CRISIS INFORMATION AND APPROACHES SIMPLE

Promote crisis prevention

Keep your organization out of trouble by leading, voicing, and reinforcing rudimentary best practices:

- Do the right thing from the start.
- Never lie. Tell the truth and tell it quickly.
- Admit mistakes.

Make it easy to do the right thing

- Distill your organization's core values into basic ground rules.
- Keep expectations clear, succinct, and memorable. Frame them as behaviors, whenever possible.
- Remove unnecessary structural and procedural barriers to crisis detection, reporting and response. Leave no individuals, teams, or sites behind.

Reduce mistakes at their roots

- Fix gawky practices. Step back to imagine how awkward procedures could increase crisis vulnerability. Where problems occur repeatedly, listen, watch closely, and think practically about what is blocking smooth execution, then improve relevant structures and processes.
- Sharpen insights and actions by assessing typical constraints with questions like these:
    - Do operators have to abandon problems to report them?
    - Must employees wait too long (for permission, approval, resources) before acting?
    - Are too many approvals required?
    - What alternatives exist when the individuals or sites that must approve exceptions are inaccessible?
    - Are there time lags between reporting an active problem and receipt of the report?
- To learn specific awkward processes, ask operators how their jobs could be simplified or streamlined. Where could awkward processes be smoothed?
- Learn where excessive redundancies or complicated hurdles must be overcome regularly by operators.

In an oil and gas refinery in Latin America, thermostats for crucial operations were on one floor, but controls for adjusting temperatures were two floors away.

In addition to wasting time and energy, the awkward arrangement left operators out of touch with current temperatures when they were near the thermostat, and they were unable to reset the thermostat instantly when they saw that excessive temperature changes had occurred. One supervisor watched and listened closely to understand operators' complaints, and then convinced his boss to relocate the equipment. To overcome cultural norms about hierarchical barriers to the upward flow of negative information, the supervisor framed his request by highlighting organizational benefits, time saved, potential disasters averted. The change was approved, which improved process safety, reduced inefficiencies, and brought an end to related employee concerns and complaints.

Make simple guidelines available to the people who will use them

Break complex instructions into small, clear steps, using straight-forward language. Convey clear priorities and specific action targets. Reinforce or replace simple text with concise graphic representation that can be understood universally.

Some workplaces print small booklets of laminated safety cards containing detailed instructions in small font. Often, they are posted on the walls of production facilities and office bays. In crisis, they are unlikely to be helpful. Instead, adapt principles like those used by commercial airlines, whose emergency procedures for passengers are straightforward, often text-free, and always within reach for each passenger, in seat pockets or on tray tables right in front of them.

#3 USE PRACTICAL CHANGE LEVERS TO REWARD COMPLIANCE AND OVERCOME RESISTANCE TO CRISIS IMPROVEMENT

Most people are not keen on change. To make matters worse, crises are frightening to think about, and difficult to deal with. But if you shy away from discussing dark circumstances and potential crises, you will never be prepared to handle them. Embracing worst-case scenarios are an essential aspect of developing crisis plans and executing reactions to crises effectively.

Start by modeling and teaching an open-minded approach to novel problems, listening carefully when you encounter friction or sense trouble. Learn from concerns, rather than ignoring or pushing against them, and look for truths and lessons behind resistance. When those ideas are worthy, find ways to inform and adjust.

To reinforce desirable behaviors

- Define expectations clearly. Communicate the value of crisis preparation repeatedly, with genuine conviction and sound reasoning. Draw clear, dramatic links between crisis fitness and your organization's core values and purpose.
- Emphasize the strength of resources available to support employees, teams, divisions, and sites. Make them accessible for enhanced crisis readiness.
- Avoid surprises and gossip. Throughout your organization, inform people candidly about crisis-relevant improvements being made, why that is a corporate best practice, and what they can expect.
- Use diverse channels to invite widespread input and feedback about crisis roles, responsibilities, and concerns within your team and organization. Acknowledge all suggestions and implement the best of them.
- Help employees accept and correct any confusion or mistakes that may occur as they start to implement new crisis tools and approaches.
- Draw positive attention to important early successes. For example, highlight effective examples of signal detection and reporting.
- Recognize and reward individuals and teams who make exceptional contributions to crisis preparation.
- Reinforce and update the flow of information, including training and practice, to enhance crisis readiness and response throughout your organization.

To overcome resistance

- Emphasize the importance of supporting and advancing crisis preparations, and supply needed resources to achieve them.
- Be clear about what is expected of employees at all levels to achieve crisis improvements, and what negative consequences will befall those who create barriers.
- Integrate compliance with crisis improvements strategically. Link follow-through to high-impact levers, such as performance evaluations, resource allocations, and financial benefits. At senior levels, linking objectives to bonuses can be highly motivational.
- Enlist additional influencers such as senior leaders and members of your Crisis Leadership Team to spread the word and reinforce compliance through action, including holding subordinates accountable for adhering to new policies and procedures.

When dangers stir, ad hoc adaptations will always be necessary. Nonetheless, advance preparations buy you time when you need it most. Building organizational fitness for crises can help everyone address novel challenges and untangle threatening uncertainties. Whether attempting to contain difficult problems, address near misses, or avert or mitigate crises, employees who are aware and informed about what is at stake, what is expected, and what processes and resources are available will have deeper insights and greater confidence to power through, even when they must innovate their responses spontaneously, even under novel and frightening circumstances.

The reach and severity of the coronavirus pandemic was an unprecedented crisis for most organizations and their stakeholders. Panic buying of staples, including food, sanitizers, and toilet paper taxed grocery stores in particular. Among the most advanced crisis preparations and practices in the industry were those employed by H-E-B, a 350-store Texas grocery chain of more than 100,000 employees, based in San Antonio. H-E-B had been developing approaches, protocols, and resources for pandemics as part of their emergency readiness since 2005 (in response to the threat of H5N1/bird flu), with revisions and improvements in 2009 (in response to the threat of H1N1/swine flu).[30]

When the COVID-19 pandemic emerged, H-E-B took action smartly and swiftly, tapping into novel information and proven resources. Within just a few weeks, the company was tracing health developments and practical responses daily with their retailer contacts in China, and monitoring trends from their retailers and suppliers in Italy and Spain, where the virus was progressing a few weeks ahead of the US. By focusing on evolutions underway elsewhere, H-E-B developed insights about the progression of the outbreak and its impacts early, and they discovered new and proven methods to protect stakeholders and procure goods that would be in highest demand. The company's century-old, values-based focus on employees and customers kept H-E-B in tune and adapting quickly as stakeholder needs shifted and grew.

Throughout these coronavirus challenges, H-E-B aligned their efforts around their motto, "to do more," and their "Bold Promise" purpose of improving the lives of their employees ("partners") and customers. As with any crisis success, not all of their pandemic approaches were home runs, but H-E-B remained ahead of competitors by applying information from field-based feedback, their stores, and relationships overseas, and effectively applying tools like tabletop scenarios and simulations in their broad internal planning to reach effective decisions and actions. The value of plans and preparation were significant for H-E-B and its customers, and in December 2020, H-E-B was named "Grocer of the Year" by *Grocery Dive*, a leading industry publication.

—————————————— Up Next ——————————————

Chapter 8 is all about enhancing signal detection. Specific recommendations take advantage of how hyper-competitive goals of quicker/cheaper/better can be advantageous for detecting/warning/and adjusting earlier to save time and other resources. This chapter features tips for developing a culture of first-class noticers who know how to report potential problems promptly to activate timely responses.

8

Amplify Signal Detection

Crises never pop up out of nowhere. Signals always exist. Always. The earlier you can detect them, the better. Early detection and reporting buy you time, a priceless resource, especially in crisis.

Unfortunately, many organizations miss or toss away signal detection opportunities, even simple ones. Supervisors, managers, or executives may attempt to dodge the challenges or costs that could lie behind potential troubles being reported. Some make a habit of ignoring or stifling bad news, especially when it only affects employees who lack privilege.

More than 1,100 garment workers were killed and 2,500 others injured in 2013 when Rana Plaza, which included five factories in an eight-story building near Dhaka, Bangladesh, collapsed. From construction, signals were ignored: the structure was built for offices and shops without sufficient reinforcement for the weight and vibration of heavy machinery that would be used in garment manufacturing; upper floors were built without a permit; inspectors had discovered cracks and recommended evacuation only the day before Rana Plaza collapsed. Retailers occupying the lower levels closed immediately, but the garment workers' supervisors claimed that the building was safe and threatened to dock workers a month's wages if they did not show up to work. Within days after the deadly collapse, thousands of protesters gathered to demand safety improvements and legal repercussions, and rioting broke out.

The tragedy stirred a great deal of public attention because it affected the full spectrum of privilege. The base of the pyramid was subjected to terrible working conditions: 14-hour work days for payment of one Euro, stifling heat, lack of safeguards such as evacuation plans, fire drills, and inspections, and finally, the bosses who insisted they defy an evacuation order. Those of higher privilege were implicated when it was revealed that this factory supplied major retailers (Primark, Walmart, JC Penney) and luxury brands (Ralph Lauren, Calvin Klein).

A compelling lesson for signal detection and reporting regards the reach of organizational responsibility, which cannot be fully outsourced safely. As evidence emerged about the causes and consequences of the building's collapse, so did cover-ups at the factory level, from understaffing, to atypical positive treatment of workers during inspectors, and audit fraud. In some cases, retailers and manufacturers were unaware that their contracted work was subcontracted to others. Many had never heard of Rana Plaza, let alone audited it. Because of this crisis, many countries, including the US, moved to increase regulations for supply chain oversight, and liability insurance for injured workers has become more common, but dangerous working conditions have not been eradicated.

Throughout every supply chain, choices that each organization makes about signal detection have long-term impact on whether employees at any link in the chain will report troubles, and how their reports will be handled. Repercussions can ripple deeply from the periphery to the core, from the minor to the catastrophic, and from the present to the distant future.

The first step is awareness of vulnerabilities and strengths. And the good news is that there are many levers to amplify signal detection: making contextual improvements, developing first-class noticing, streamlining reporting, and empowering voice and responsibility throughout your organization.

PENETRATE CONTEXTUAL CHAOS

A good place to begin improvements is to think about the reach of your organization, from sourcing to product and service delivery.

Imagine being responsible for the risks, threats, and safety of passengers during one billion journeys annually, as they travel in and out of 300 stations, across 10,000 miles served by your organization. What if signs of trouble in your buzzing context were often very subtle, but ignitable into crisis in a flash? What if your enormous, complex system were accessible to anyone, any time of day or night, 365 days per year? Suppose there was no security screening, not even identification of users? How about if your customers' loyalty was scant because most of them interacted with your system only temporarily, and many used it only occasionally? What if, on top of all this, your employees were scarcely visible to your customers?

Welcome to the London Underground, "the Tube," the city's metro/subway.

Violent crises on the Tube began in 1883 when a bomb exploded near Paddington station, injuring 62 passengers. Since then, activists, dissidents, and terrorists have drawn attention to their causes with explosives, bombs, and other highly dangerous devices by making the London Underground and its passengers their victims. Some attempts have fizzled. Some were defused. Some injured a few people. Some injured hundreds. Others killed scores of victims. Sometimes, signals of danger in and around the Tube were spotted. Other times, they were missed entirely. But signals always existed.

So how does an organization manage these especially challenging threats? At the heart of responsibility for risk, threats, and safety of the Tube are the British Transport Police (BTP), a national special forces agency. In 2019, to increase system-wide vigilance, the BTP initiated a combined campaign, "See it. Say it. Sorted." This collaboration is noteworthy simply for the breadth of forces involved, from the British government, to the Metropolitan and City of London police forces, the London Underground and Transport for London organizations, to the naïve external stakeholders at the heart of the program: the Tube passengers themselves.

Bringing passengers into the campaign added millions more eyes and voices for surveillance and response. The process is poised on the thin line between putting customers on alert and scaring them away, a line which many organizations dare not cross, even for enhanced customer safety. To ease passenger compliance, the "See it. Say it. Sorted." campaign features simple guidelines and directives, which appear in multiple media, and are repeated often.

Potential signals to "See" (unattended items, suspicious activity) are described in security announcements and on posters at stations and on trains.

"Say" is achieved by reporting signs of troubles to any police officer or railway employee, in person, via phone, text, or direct Help Point buttons, as specified on signage and in ongoing announcements. The third and final step, "Sorted," assures passengers that their role is complete, and that reports made will be handled by experts.

Although some Tube passengers complained about the earworm announcements and some poster depictions of suspicious activity, the "See it. Say it. Sorted." approach includes excellent signal detection practices. Reporting of signals is separated from solutions (passengers report the signal, then security experts determine the appropriate response), and the process errs on the side of over-reporting (attracting too many unwarranted reports versus missing actual signals). Furthermore, passenger involvement is simple and reasonable, as related to their access to the system, their potential insights, and possible risks they could incur.

DON'T UNDERMINE YOUR OWN INSIGHTS

Fundamental organizational assumptions and long-established norms can smother signal detection and reporting, leaving doors open to crises. Even in workplaces filled with exceptional, dedicated employees who are adept at coordinating practices and conceiving extraordinary precautions, limiting beliefs can trigger crisis vulnerabilities. Consider these organizational characteristics. Do any of them describe your organization?

- Resource constraints keep us from thinking about problems that might happen.
- Our priorities shift abruptly and frequently.
- We operate under tight time pressures consistently.
- We rely on past successes, rather than reevaluating how sound practices might have shifted.
- Our communication about safety issues is ineffective.
- Professional opinions that differ from the norm are stifled.
- There is little or no management integration across programs.

- Our organization's formal reporting relationships and procedures are overridden by power and decision processes that have become cumbersome, unclear, or inaccessible.

Spot any similarities to your organization? If you do, you are in stellar company— with the United States National Aeronautics and Space Administration (NASA). According to a commission convened by NASA, these characteristics and norms led to the explosion of their Space Shuttle Columbia.[31] Similar causes had been previously linked to the explosion of NASA's Space Shuttle Challenger by the Rogers Commission.[32] That investigation also determined that NASA's managers were aware of the Challenger's fatal flaw (O-ring erosion, hot gas blow-by) for years prior to the deadly explosion.

Dramatic crises, lingering shortcomings (despite precise warnings), and significant signals missed or ignored—times three. It is difficult to conceive how NASA, an organization of devoted experts who achieve unparalleled accomplishments through meticulous calculation, innovation, and design, could have been so blind.

IDENTIFY LIKELY BLOCKS TO SIGNAL DETECTION

It has always been true that external contexts, the inner workings of an organization, and the behaviors of individual employees can hinder signal detection. Moreover, today the challenges and distractions of a volatile, complex, uncertain work environment can collide with internal trends, such as globalization, hypercompetition and techno-fusion, to complicate signal detection and reporting even further.

Anyone's motivation to spot and report a negative signal is influenced by their expectations about relevant costs and benefits, negative and positive consequences for doing so. When the messenger is punished for their efforts, the cost-benefit equation quickly extinguishes efforts. When reports are ignored, messengers' motivation wanes and they are less likely to report subsequent signals. If the punishment is severe, some may leave their boss or the organization.

At team and organizational levels, norms and approaches can block noticing, reporting, and responding to signs of trouble. Where profitability rules, safety precautions may be overlooked or bypassed in favor of greater short-term earnings. Where bureaucratized procedures clog communication or resource access, delays and confusion stifle prompt reporting of dangerous circumstances. Where speed dominates, time-consuming repair investments may be postponed or overlooked. Where reward systems favor immediate wins over potential long-term gains, employees may whitewash or ignore dangers that might arise in the future.

At the individual level, information overload, excessive job responsibilities, and unresolved cross-cultural confusion can deplete employees' willingness or ability to detect, report, or deal with signals. Fatigue and repeated exposure stifle anyone's ability to detect and respond promptly. Repeated exposure to signals dulls our responsiveness. Additionally, where employees do not understand the systemic effects of their work, it is more difficult for them to imagine how unreported irregularities might lead to devastating impacts. Many employees may lack skills or experience for reporting negative information upward, or they may be unaware of channels for doing so, especially across functional, divisional, or cultural borders.

Where supervisors downplay, ignore, or flare at bad news, subordinates will be less likely to report signals, especially if they are uncertain about what they are sensing or how to fix it. Under these conditions, people may turn to more comfortable alternatives. Some revert to actions totally within their direct control, such as attempting to patch, bury, or ignore irregularities rather than report them.

Sometimes, leaders themselves hide or destroy signals. Occasionally, their maneuvers even escalate to illicit actions. As Malcolm Thornton (a pseudonym) saw it, his priority #1 as operations manager was to keep the business open. His promotions seemed to confirm that the way he had always handled bad news and complaints matched corporate expectations. Therefore, when dangers surfaced, he applied his increased autonomy to bury signals, destroy evidence of accidents, and force subordinates to whitewash their records. A downward slide of mishaps and damages ensued, which consumed more and more of Thornton's time and attention.

Although inspections, maintenance, or oversight might have brought his risky approach to his superiors' attention, Thornton was the sole monitor and custodian of all accident and safety records for his site. He had no obvious accountability for reporting data, maintenance trends, or patterns of trouble. When he was inaccessible or unmoved by reports of problems, there was no one else to turn to on site, and no channels to move information up the chain of command. Even as the nature of customer injuries deepened (open wounds, herniated disks, loss of manual dexterity), Thornton continued to address them by intercepting accident reports, and coercing employees to rewrite victims' statements and omit any information about causes of injuries. Eventually, when a fatal accident happened, the police got involved.

As evidence was gathered, it became obvious that Thornton had persistently blocked any signs of trouble. He had ignored dozens of employee reports that described equipment malfunctions and failures. He had confiscated and locked away numerous injury reports from victims and medical personnel. When investigators confronted him about these transgressions and the additional thousands of daily operations reports that he had withheld, Thornton simply claimed that he was following company policy.

By ignoring and destroying signals, as accidents and injuries intensified to crisis level, Thornton had put the survival of the organization at risk. But more sophisticated understanding requires looking upward, beyond site management. Thornton's facility and the company's headquarters were both located in the same country, only hundreds of miles apart. Yet the entire situation had seemed to escape the attention of senior executives.

As problems worsened, the absence of executive impact was conspicuous. Some might argue that actions taken by Thornton at the site level, in a location outside the local view of headquarters, would not be known by top leaders. But long before the fatal straw, bizarre accidents were broadcast on national news and early morning talk shows, and videos captured by victims and witnesses went viral. Nonetheless, no indication of executive concern or follow-up surfaced. Rather, mismanagement and poor leadership seemed to permit incidents to escalate to crisis.

Thornton was indicted on charges of involuntary manslaughter, aggravated battery, aggravated endangerment, and interference with law enforcement. The site for which he held safety and operations responsibility was closed and demolished. Although the company survived, its reputation and financial footing declined sharply. (For the full story, see "When A Manager Whitewashes" case.)[33]

ORGANIZE FOR TOP-NOTCH SIGNAL DETECTION

The ability to spot and discern signs of danger is influenced by three factors: (1) the information perceived, (2) the criteria for decision-making, and (3) the observer's knowledge and experiences. Where signal detection is valued, employees are trained and rewarded for staying alert to unusual circumstances. Reporting is expected, even when messengers are not sure of the level or nature of potential danger. To prime early detection, organizations adopt practices that attend to novel circumstances, make reporting simple, and welcome false alarms over missed problems.

In organizations that value first-class noticing, individuals and teams are expected to remain open to problems, rather than conceal them. Reports of trouble are taken seriously, with prompt follow-up and investigation. Employees at all levels are trained and empowered to act, relative to their insights, expertise, and responsibilities. Throughout such organizations, people at all levels are expected to catch unusual circumstances, and their sensitivities are valued.

Rule #1: Shine attention on the unfamiliar.
The more alert to novel circumstances, the better.

When a signal is noticed by someone, the first requirement of signal detection has been met. Fortunately, everyone is primed instinctively to notice potential dangers. Our survival depends on it. We are all hard-wired to sense signals, to notice when something is different, to determine when the difference is potentially dangerous (often before being aware of the calibration), and then to decide whether to take action or not.

When a signal occurs, there are four possible outcomes. The result can be (1) a *hit*, a signal is present and someone has noticed it, (2) a *miss*, a signal is present, but no one has noticed it, (2) a *false alarm*, there is no signal, but someone believes that they sense a signal, or (4) a *correct rejection*, there is no signal and no signal is perceived. These outcomes are the foundation for a powerful prescription for averting and mitigating crises: encourage and amplify to increase *hits,* even at the expense of *false alarms.*

REPORTED?

	YES	NO
STATUS — Valid Signal	◎ Hit	⊔● Miss
Noise	⊗ False Alarm	[×] Accurate Rejection

Organizations that value signal detection work to favor the "yes" dimensions. To achieve that, they loosen criteria for reporting and reduce communication challenges so that signals of potential dangers surface and move on to appropriate experts smoothly and promptly. Another smart step some take is to hold bosses accountable when their operators do not report the signals they spot. In organizations where safety is paramount, all employees are expected to stay alert to potential interference, even when relevant decisions or actions require exceeding their designated authority. A textbook example involves a sailor who waved off a carrier landing because he had spotted a tool left on the ship's deck that was potentially within the landing path. The sailor was called immediately to the bridge by the ship's captain. Rather than being reprimanded for overriding sharp lines of military authority, as he feared, he was commended, and later, his bravery was celebrated in a formal ceremony.[34]

Rule #2: Separate signals from solutions.
The easier it is to report a potential signal, the better.

When it comes to signal detection, a *false alarm* should trump a *miss*. But where solutions must accompany problems, warnings are stifled. In such organizations, the gap between signal detection and reporting is delayed or derailed systematically. Constraints may be explicitly imposed, "I welcome problems, as long as you bring solutions, too." Or norms to squelch problems may be inferred, for example, where the people who get ahead are those who do not "make waves" with concerns about what might go wrong.

The barrier in these examples is that bundling potential problems and fitting solutions is often extremely difficult, or even impossible, when a crisis is looming. Crises are exceptional circumstances that tend to exceed quick fixes, and they often surpass the insight, expertise, or practical responses of the individual who first notices signals. Indeed, untangling what lies beneath or beyond the novelty and complexity of crises makes it extremely challenging for any individual to foresee impacts or invent adequate solutions spontaneously. For most people, initial challenges that surface with crises make it tough to even think straight.

Rule# 3: Err on the side of over-reporting.
Favor false alarms over misses.

It should not require courage to report a novel, potentially dangerous situation. If crisis preparation is your goal, reinforce the reporting of any signal someone senses as dangerous, even if the problem turns out to be a false alarm.

In best practices, reports are welcome, and employees are trained how to report potential signals, and to whom. Norms should support seeking and providing additional insight or assistance when in doubt.

Practices vary greatly among and within organizations. Approaches are anchored by two extremes: (1) Do not bring forth concerns until you are certain that they are dangerous, or (2) Report any circumstance of issues that you believe could be dangerous. Err on the side of over-reporting.

WHAT'S A LEADER TO DO?

Personally solicit a flow of diverse information

Excellent leaders know how to attract, sort, and apply valuable input in good times and bad. Nurturing your own and others' novel perspectives is an essential condition for achieving this. Recommendations here are actions that leaders can take personally, in normal and crisis situations, to help improve crisis preparations overall.

Make "thank you" your immediate response to bad news

- Do not make excuses. Do not tune out or change the topic. Rather, listen fully.
- Fight the urge to respond by attributing blame.
- Graciously accept bad news, even from people who may have contributed to the problem.

When you need additional information, get as close as possible to the problem

- Turn first to people who are in touch with the trouble.
- Stay open to what you hear.

Flip your go-to analytical lens

- If you tend to take the broad view, dig into microscopic details. Break big issues into components and fine particles.
- If you tend to focus on details, take a telescopic view. Imagine the big picture. Cluster components for broader analysis.
- Read outside your current personal interests, and beyond obvious relevance to your life and work today.
- Explore leisure activities that require attention to both big picture and details: You might learn to draw, study a foreign language, or construct puzzles.

Master the art of listening

- Listen more. Talk less.
- Identify your listening blocks and get them under control. Watch out for mind reading, placating, or judging rather than listening.[35]
- Choose communication media carefully. Know when you must use richer media than email or texts.

Trace the validity of important information

- Learn to distinguish fact from opinion, and knowledge from conjecture.
- Know the background and expertise of primary sources that you tap. As you learn from them, stay mindful to their values and biases.
- On especially critical issues and ideas, dig back to origins.

Practice approaches that stretch your viewpoint

- Make a habit of thinking through both best- and worst-case scenarios.
- Imagine situations as people you know might see them.

- Remember that one individual's error is rarely the sole cause of a crisis or near miss.
  - o What may look like the source of a crisis is often merely a symptom or consequence of systemic failures or chains of errors that have not been discovered yet.
  - o Where handoffs of tasks seemed inadequate, look deeper to determine whether the routes to appropriate experts, authorities, or resources were inaccessible, unclear or ineffective.

SUPPORT OTHERS TO SPOT AND REPORT SIGNAL DETECTION

Make it easy and safe for all employees to report signals early

- Treat messengers of bad news as first-class noticers, rather than troublemakers.
- Turn focus to reporting the problem, rather than looking for quick fixes, or ways to rationalize errors or attribute blame.
- Drive this from the top.

Never punish anyone who brings forth bad news in good faith

- Do not push back on unwelcome information. This shuts out truth.
- Support everyone who reports problems and concerns earnestly, even if their worries prove unfounded, and even if they have contributed to the problem.
- Make the value of early signal detection clear to managers and leaders throughout your organization, including their responsibilities to welcome and address bad news from anyone with earnest concerns.

- Hold managers and leaders personally accountable if their actions squelch detection or reporting.
- When signals are missed or ignored, investigate potential obstruction up the hierarchy.

Help others become first-class noticers

- Teach employees to alert bosses to potential problems, even when they are unsure of the actual level of danger or next steps to take. Make it perfectly okay to say things like, "I believe something could be seriously wrong," or "I see a potentially dangerous problem, but I don't know what to do about it."
- Gather and teach specific sources and types of signals that employees might encounter in their particular jobs.
- Teach the uses of existing tools, equipment, and documentation that could alert people to novel and potentially dangerous problems. Solicit recommendations to adapt or acquire additional tools and data that would enhance signal detection.
- Share examples of your organization's signal detection successes and failures. Learn and teach why they were successes or failures.
- Share kudos for exemplary signal detection, whether or not the problem detected proved dangerous.

Pave the path for swift and accurate reporting

- Model and reinforce honest, direct communication.
- For all employees, establish and teach parameters for reporting potential problems.
- Provide all employees with safe ways to report dangerous issues or actions. Teach them which channels are available to them. Consider establishing employee hotlines, third party ethics lines, or other reporting channels that are truly anonymous. Make it possible to jump lines of authority when potential or actual dangers loom.

- Teach everyone to consult their bosses without hesitation when problems seem to exceed their response capabilities and provide a way to elevate concerns to a higher authority if a boss is unresponsive.
- Create an environment in which questions are welcome. Make it clear that questions are essential to avert and contain complex problems, which could become crises.

Eliminate excessive pride in achievement

- Curtail arrogant or smug behaviors. They shut out contradictory information, and silence challenges to prevailing perspectives, including insights about decisions that are terribly flawed.
- Avoid using rewards that reinforce superiority over others, whether among individuals, or within or between teams. Competing for "best" can stifle competitors' willingness to reveal problems and critical insights. In some organizations that I have audited, the quest for "#1" made some people hesitant to report errors or early signs of trouble. Stigmas associated with ruining their team's record kept injured employees from seeking first aid and ill employees from taking time off to recuperate. In some settings, claims of "Days Since Injury" were deemed insurance or marketing propaganda.

Glean insights from external stakeholders

- When externals bring bad news with good intentions, thank them genuinely.
- Listen carefully to external allies. Where relationships are strong, take the additional step to seek input and feedback about problems they have encountered or know of in your organization.
- Listen carefully to critics and adversaries. These include contentious media, third-party advocacy groups, and outsiders who do not grasp your work or the limits of your responsibilities. Rather than pushing

back or closing down, practice gleaning and assessing novel information and unfamiliar perspectives based on their interpretations. Solicit others to do the same. Make it a challenge, a high-stakes game, to think and discuss, creatively and obliquely, troubles that could evolve from their viewpoints.

- Tap your organization's existing data sources for signs of trouble, for example, external ratings/rankings of your organization, and employee and customer surveys, especially complaints.

Include diverse functions and levels when you analyze crisis-relevant data

- After a crisis or near miss occurs, include diverse functions and levels to identify weak spots, potentially dangerous trends, and deeper implications. Bring functionally diverse perspectives to data interpretation.
- Involve a diverse cross-section of experience and expertise whenever red flags warrant deeper investigation.

——————————— Up Next ———————————

Chapter 9 details the cycle of core processes for performing during and after an actual crisis, to enhance crisis preparation and response, from detecting signals to establishing relevant priorities, informing stakeholders, containing damages, and advancing toward a next normal. The details provide guidance for what newcomers to crisis programs might think of when they hear the term "crisis management."

During and After

9

Reinforce the Crisis Response Cycle

The daunting challenge of getting a crisis under control must always evolve relative to the particular crisis, its contexts, and its impacts. Although there is no universally applicable playbook, there are approaches and guidelines to help smooth the journey and improve responses. These options fall into four containment stages, the ATNA sequence, **A**ssessing, **T**reating, **N**otifying, and **A**dapting.

The evolution of these stages is not necessarily sequential. Rather, stages may occur simultaneously, or stages may repeat. In some situations, sequencing among stages may flip. For example, particular regulations may dictate that notification precede treatment. Or a series of iterative assess-treat cycles may be the best approach, for instance, when administering particularly risky approaches.

If you are coming to this moment of crisis underprepared, then you also need to establish or reinforce the principles and processes explained in these During and After chapters. Involving the whole organization and amplifying signal detection will be essential here.

Establish your processes as you gather and validate diverse information. Ponder, debate, and deliberate quickly, but without rushing. Use this approach in advance of a crisis and following crisis containment. In crisis, whether you are interpreting emergent signals, prioritizing response and resource options, or identifying and treating the most threatening impacts, immediate attention, prompt decision-making, and timely action will be essential. Bear in mind, also, in the throes of crisis inherent volatility and complexity may change the game plan, increasing the urgency and the skill you will need to optimize your timing.

Once a crisis looms, even a few wasted moments can impair vital reactions. Creative thinking, grounded reasoning, and debate will still be needed in the heat of crisis, but assessment and discussions must move quickly. Prolonged pondering and long-winded discussions must be curtailed to deal promptly with dangerous uncertainties and stay on top of rapidly shifting circumstances. In light of the actual circumstances of the crisis, what is occurring in real time and what is anticipated, you may need to reevaluate existing crisis strategies and resources, while identifying or inventing new ones, and do all of this rapidly.

As you seek to get a crisis under control by assessing, treating, notifying, and making immediate adaptations, emphasize the following practical actions adaptable to most crisis circumstances.

ASSESS

Effective assessment entails evaluating what has occurred, envisioning what could lie ahead, and gauging what is needed next and in the longer term. Reference your plans and your map, noting diversions that have been made, processes missed, and adjustments needed going forward. Excellent crisis assessments reflect diverse perspectives. Best approaches protect your organization, helping you predict impacts of the crisis on stakeholders, resources, and the environment. In this stage, you will also weigh alternative response options. Use your map and procedures as guidelines to stay on track with crisis objectives and decisions made under cooler circumstances. If you have experienced similar crises in the past, move quickly to surface and apply lessons learned from those crises.

Determine the plausibility of signals

Start by weighing the credibility of presenting circumstances. Log what you know about what has occurred, including accurate accounting of the roles your organization has played. Cull facts from speculation, assumptions, and accusations. If you cannot rule out the possibility that you are heading into a crisis, err on the side of acceptance, and press promptly toward deeper insights, and actions that align with your organization's values and your crisis objectives.

It is better to investigate a false alarm than to risk ignoring a crisis. To minimize wasted resources, evaluate threats that *might* exist incrementally. Start by intensifying and accelerating your search for facts. Make inquiries close to the source of reported signals. Consult participants, victims, and experts directly.

At an international restaurant chain, a customer complained persuasively of suffering symptoms of a dangerous food-borne illness after eating at one of their border-town restaurants. If valid, the threat would require multinational emergency notification, international product recall, and with those, a high likely of product/brand degradation through widespread bad press. Interviews were promptly conducted with the customer, the manager, and workers at the restaurant site where the product had been purchased, the chain's own product development group, and the Center for Disease Control (CDC). As the data accumulated, it became clear that the timing between food consumption and the eruption of symptoms was impossible. After due diligence across stakeholders, the crisis was averted during assessment. Throughout the process, communication was grounded in facts, collected promptly and civilly, without speculating or blaming.

Alert your Crisis Leadership Team

Whenever you have reason to suspect that a crisis could be brewing, contact your CLT immediately. Their fundamental responsibilities are to remain vigilant for crises and to respond promptly. By design and training, the team's insights are strategically-focused. The CLT should know your organization's crisis readiness and vulnerabilities intimately, and be able to provide essential information. The CLT can help you evaluate what is known about the crisis you are facing, what remains to be learned, and how to gather and share essential information most efficiently and effectively. In the food-borne illness event described above, the CLT played essential roles in contacting key stakeholders (internal and external), collecting data, and applying organizational values and crisis objectives during analysis and decision-making.

To collaborate optimally with your CLT, be clear about the roles, knowledge, and resources that you seek from them, to the extent possible. Share your initial views of what has happened, and your perspectives about resources, logistics, and expertise that will be needed for this particular crisis. Connect personally with CLT members closest to the epicenter of the crisis, whether proximity is due to their geographic location, functional specialty, personal expertise, or work experience.

Deliberate on alternatives together. An effective CLT helps drive investigations and immediate responses, while also helping you monitor and manage reactions internally and externally. The team needs familiarity and experience with approaches for forecasting and calibrating pros and cons of potential actions. To optimize your discussions of alternatives, include probable, possible, and unthinkable impacts on key stakeholders, the environment, and the viability of your organization. Returning to the alleged food-borne illness situation, the possibility of a crisis was neither diminished nor discounted until information gathered independently was validated and triangulated across facts shared by the customer, the restaurant in question, relevant food disease experts inside and outside the organization, and the CDC.

Gather data from people closest to the crisis

Talk with key stakeholders who are or have been in touch with the crisis personally. Include people who detected the signal, first-responder employees, supervisors at the affected sites, bystanders, and victims. Confer with internal and external advisors with situation-relevant expertise.

Determine what information (fact and fake) is being communicated or leaking within and beyond your organization. Identify corrective steps taken since the crisis began, and organizational data that could be relevant, such as internal reports, site logs, consumer feedback, and security videos. Drill down for insights about adjacent events and surrounding circumstances that could be affecting the crisis. Consolidate diverse perspectives of what remains to be done according to the CLT, other relevant experts, and those closest to the crisis.

Gauge operational issues

Determine whether facilities or equipment must be shut down, replaced, or repaired. Determine what is needed to maintain or resume product and service delivery and who will accomplish it. Anticipate secondary effects on production and delivery that could occur in the near future. For example, will changes to delivery channels or routes be needed? Will warehoused product be needed? As you make these evaluations, include a range of probable, potential, worst-case and best-case impacts on your organization at large, as well as key internal and external stakeholders.

TREAT

Take immediate precautions

Determine what to fix, alter, isolate, decontaminate, and monitor, then redirect tasks and employees to contain and improve crisis circumstances. Modify or eliminate policies and norms that no longer apply because of crisis conditions. For example, to streamline crisis updates and directives within your organization, consider loosening relevant internal restrictions on unclassified data access.

Based on the latest data that you can obtain about the crisis and its impacts, continue to verify that decisions match your assessments. Keep attuned to what remains actionable based on available time, resources, and personnel, and eliminate options that are no longer viable. Weigh potential negative impacts, including how treatments could possibly stimulate further damages, spreading or escalating the crisis. Weigh anticipated effects of proposed treatments against your organization's values and your crisis objectives. As you compare options, account for what could be gained, lost, or missed with each alternative.

Establish and act on priorities

Determine actions and outcomes that are most urgent and possible now. Map the desirable flow of next steps, including practical provisions for known and anticipated barriers along the way.

Seek advice and assistance promptly from experts inside and outside your organization, especially if conditions include serious adverse events such as major injury, significant health threat, illness, or death, environmental contamination, or cybercrime. Establish channels to monitor and address additional short- and long-term needs as they emerge. For example, promptly designate efficient communication routes for reporting, updating, and reviewing crisis conditions.

Identify which organizational processes can continue through the crisis, and which must be interrupted to stop or slow damages. Give priority to essential procedures that must be rerouted, redesigned, or scrapped for safety reasons. Aim for a comprehensive picture of anticipated impacts, including how primary stakeholders are likely to view your organization's responsibilities and actions.

Contact external emergency response resources

If serious injuries or major damages occur or are threatening, alert external emergency response providers who serve the local crisis sites. Among the first external lines of defense and assistance, include local law enforcement, fire departments, and nearby hospitals.

Contact additional external stakeholders whose expertise is crucial to the particular crisis at hand. Common examples include regulators, attorneys, financial and insurance providers, environmental experts, local politicians, and cybersecurity experts. If the public must be notified, work with the finest media experts (internal and external) to represent your organization accurately, and to ensure clear, factual, timely communication.

Determine assistance needed

Stay in touch with locals in affected locations for confirmation and deeper assessment of the current status of the crisis and containment efforts. Map logistical paths to provide essential resources and assistance quickly and safely, starting with key stakeholders in greatest need. Identify primary internal contacts to connect your organization to its external stakeholder groups and to determine their needs and risks, and communicate your organization's relevant resources and abilities to assist.

Anticipate the types of expertise that will be needed within your organization and beyond, estimating timing for those needs, taking preparatory actions, and scheduling next steps. Determine locations where additional employees or leaders will be required now or in the future.

Put at least one powerful decision maker on site

Catastrophes that occur near headquarters or in your organization's home country tend to be easier to manage. That proximity of powerful decision makers, and their personal familiarity with local resources, norms, and regulations sharpen attention to crisis signals and impacts. Their availability and connections can improve the speed and quality of resource access, and decision-making.

Crises at international or geographically remote domestic sites complicate assessment and response. Varied time zones, physical distance, and the need to translate language or fundamental norms and values can delay and derail responses, escalating threats and damages.

To offset these impacts, devote a fitting executive to the site promptly, in person or virtually, to facilitate and accelerate decision-making and action. Their expertise, internal power networks, and vested organizational authority will make it easier to process details, communicate updates, steer decisions, and energize actions from afar. Choose a candidate who is well-positioned to move information and resources through the hierarchy and across borders. Provide solid leadership presence on behalf of your organization by selecting someone who is steady and trustworthy, optimally someone who is also cross-culturally adept.

Let people do their jobs

When a crisis occurs, it is natural and common for executives to want to step up and take charge. Although this might seem heroic, avoid it. Excessive top leadership involvement can delay and destroy the rhythm of response.

Leaders whose expertise is not specific to the need should keep their hands off. Extraneous involvement in operational tasks diverts attention and devours precious time. Unless there are no capable operators available, push back on any leader's urge to try to fix things personally. Even if they believe that they have retained their skills, they may well be out of touch with the latest approaches, technologies, or insights.

Emphasize the importance of everyone sticking to their strengths. For leaders, this usually means making the toughest decisions, accessing critical resources that are difficult to acquire, and reinforcing forward momentum relevant to their own responsibilities, networks, and resources.

NOTIFY

Provide information patiently, sincerely, and accurately

Communicate clearly, simply, objectively. Echo the core of your essential message repeatedly, using diverse media. Explain realities simply and factually, repeating what you know and explaining what is yet to be known.

Adhere strictly to these cautionary directives. Do not give voice or authority to anyone who cannot abide by them.

- Never lie.
- Do not speculate.
- Do not create or search for a scapegoat.
- Do not make misleading promises or promise more than you can do.
- Do not whitewash what lies ahead.
- Do not sell or cheerlead.

- Do not convey overly optimistic or overly pessimistic expectations about the future.
- Do not make light of any aspect of the crisis.
- Do not make off-the-cuff comments.
- Do not make flippant remarks.
- Do not whine or complain about the difficulties that you or your organization are facing.

Set clear paths for internal communication

Ensure that your messages are clear and accurate. Point out how decisions and actions align with your organization's values and provide simple and obvious avenues for updates that others can pursue and review.

Create a protocol for sharing timely information. Explain how news will be shared with employees and with external stakeholders, which media will be used, and with what frequency. Name reliable internal contacts who can answer employees' questions about the crisis and potential repercussions, and provide their contact information.

Choose best delivery modes for specific stakeholder groups. Select the best spokesperson(s) to deliver clear and convincing messages for each audience. Before distributing, test significant communications and delivery choices with a few experts. Solicit prompt feedback from relevant CLT members, managers, or employees local to the region. Work with them to ensure that content and channels convey your message accurately and appropriately. Where messages must be translated into other languages, confirm accuracy by back-translating into the original language before distributing translated information.

Do not ignore or forget any internal stakeholders

Organizations can get so caught up in communicating externally that they under-communicate internally. Employees in lower-level positions and those working overseas or at remote sites are often shorted or left out of the loop completely. Avoid leaving any of your employees in the dark. Keep employees up to date on progress with the crisis, and expectations about your organization's future. Do not leave any employees in the awkward position of not knowing what has happened, what is currently going on, or what is anticipated about the future.

When there are no options but social media for employees to learn about their own organization's crisis, leaders have relinquished their influence, and failed the crisis imperative to keep key stakeholders informed. Think practically: communication voids breed anxiety and erode loyalty and commitment, and those effects set off chains of expensive long-term consequences.

If you do not keep frontline employees informed, you are disengaging your first line of defense. Under the extreme pressures of crisis, when people do not know what is going on, rumors fill the vacuum swiftly. When employees lack information, their close contact and exchanges with customers and suppliers can exacerbate damages, even inadvertently. They will also miss the relevance of their external contacts' experiences and insights that could power and improve organizational responses and recovery.

Keep key external stakeholders well informed, as well

Success will be sharply influenced by outsiders' understanding and acceptance of what you have done, what you plan to do, and why. In the best cases, externals can bring new perspectives and resources. Sometimes, they may even open novel opportunities and ideas to refine your crisis response. Where you retain excellent relationships with externals, they may assist you in responding to the crisis, or at least, be more reluctant to turn against you.

ADAPT

We may tend to think of adapting as the actions to take once flames have been doused, hemorrhaging has stopped, and faulty elements have been repaired or replaced. You will probably recognize this transition when you sense that the intensity of time pressures and the volume of new uncertainties are decreasing.

But adapting is also essential during crisis, before the end game is apparent, before the crisis and its impacts become calmer and clearer.

Anywhere along this spectrum, adapting translates to identifying and filling gaps that remain between where you are and where you need to be. This will require evaluating, planning, and monitoring signs of danger, while adhering to the best-known practices relative to the crisis. You will want to adopt safeguards others have invented for similar crises, while considering new insights, necessities, and options to mitigate negative impacts.

The 2020 Tour de France (Tour) is a remarkable example of adapting, by balancing threats and opportunities, and innovating toward immutable crisis objectives while retaining critical success factors.[36] By all reasonable counts, the 2020 Tour probably should have been cancelled. It could have become the ultimate coronavirus super-spreader. Typically, the race not only includes about 200 riders competing within inches of each other, but also thousands of support personnel who interact within intimate space of the riders, and millions of spectators who gather in hoards and move about freely, often within arm's reach of cyclists and staff. Despite such extraordinary vulnerabilities, the Tour achieved adaptations, adjustments, and accommodations that were innovated and implemented by the Tour's leaders, the cyclists, the support staff, the French government, the media, and the public.

Prior to the Tour, the COVID-19 pandemic had already taken a toll on indoor and stadium-constrained events, with rescheduling and cancellations of the Euro Cup, Wimbledon, the French Open, and the summer Olympics. National hockey and football leagues were playing to empty arenas and adhering to stay-in-place norms between games. But the Tour is more like a traveling carnival, with riders and staff switching hotels and towns nearly every night, and incredibly widespread public exposure every day. With a route that spans more than two thousand miles, there was no way to close the bubble, no gate to lock, no way to adhere to stay-in-place norms, and the six-foot gaps of social distancing would be impossible among pelotons of racers.

But the Tour also had advantages, beyond taking place outdoors. Competitors were accustomed to race monitoring and testing (to impede cheating and deter doping scandals). Some teams were already legendary germophobes who carried their own mattresses and pillows, avoided handshakes, and used massive amounts of hand sanitizer long before COVID made it a treasured resource.

Nonetheless, adaptations to overcome exposure during the Tour were exceptional, for riders, staff, ardent fans, media, and spectators. Riders were housed in separate hotel rooms and, wherever possible, teams were housed in separate hotels, and access to their families was barred. Masks were mandatory for riders at all times, except when in the saddle. Their COVID testing would be ongoing, before, during, and after the race.

About 4500 personnel typically support the Tour cyclists, from coaches, mechanics, and team managers, to nutritionists, massage therapists, strategists, and "soigneurs," who attend to each racer's needs. But, in response to the pandemic, each team was limited to eight riders and 22 team support crew, all of whom would be sealed off from outsiders, with mandatory COVID testing throughout the race. Fans and riders would no longer intermingle for customary selfies, autographs, and face-to-face kudos.

Millions of daily spectators and roadside crowds were culled by barricading and marshalling roads and eliminating international border crossings, while French President Emmanuel Macron urged fans to watch by television, and pressed television production companies to sharpen their coverage. Media were contained behind barriers as cyclists passed, and banned from start/finish areas. Instead, interviews took place in designated tents, with mandatory masks, telescoping microphones, and personal distancing.

The measure of adaptive crisis success, with event handling and outbreak control, was remarkable. Not one Tour rider tested positive before, during, or after the race. Across 22 teams, only a few mechanics and one team manager had positive tests. Furthermore, although some riders lamented the absence of Tour enthusiasts, others reported far less stress without media and public hassles before and after each race.

The Tour's pioneering transitions started by shifting deliberate attention to longer-range changes to be achieved and sustained in the short term, prevailing throughout the race. Deep and thorough attention was devoted to details of monitoring, adjusting, and realigning resources. Stakeholder analyses and adjustments were broad and precise, fitting historic experiences of the Tour to the novel necessities, uncertainties, and urgencies brought by a pandemic.

The range of tactical channels and approaches was exceptional. Success of the Tour under pandemic conditions required stepping up to the next normal. A feasible balance was struck between retaining and resetting traditional values, while assuring that the unique demands of crisis conditions were met.

Step into stride with the next normal

Abnormal is a characteristic of crisis, which makes the ability to innovate and adapt invaluable. Moreover, after surviving a crisis, very little returns automatically to its pre-crisis state. Instead, adjustments must be made, including rebuilding and reinforcing foundations for the next normal. Energize advances by collaborating to create a sketch or loose map of your present circumstances, your organization's desired future, and foreseeable options for the journey. The sooner that you can grasp what has changed and deliver the news, the better. The sooner you can imagine a reasoned, grounded projection of future impacts from those changes, the better.

Continue to keep people well-informed

Experiencing a crisis can deepen anyone's concerns. Even as indicators confirm that crisis circumstances are improving, stakeholders still worry about how fluctuating or unknown situations could affect their futures. Where communication is not forthcoming, lingering concerns weaken and divert coping skills and adjustments.

Candidly discuss how assumptions about operations, resources, or competitive advantages are being modified, reinforced or devastated by crisis events and outcomes. Listen carefully. Listen for ways in which stakeholders' expectations or values are being jarred by the crisis. Listen for the depth and breadth of the effects they feel. Answer their questions and concerns to the best of your ability, with factual information and empathy.

Revisit your organization's values and crisis objectives again

Discuss which core values endured intact, and which were disrupted or displaced by the crisis. Reflect on your crisis objectives and discuss how you are meeting or missing them. Consider values and objectives that must be aligned with new, emerging, and post-crisis realities, and whether values or objectives might be adapted or reinvented to move into the next normal.

For major changes, dig deeper. Consider how business models or long-range strategies must be revised or replaced. Translate needed shifts into strategic adjustments to production or delivery. Consider how job functions, reporting relationships, stakeholder contact and affiliation, or employee reward structures could be improved. As you discuss the viability and merit of alternatives, return to your organization's enduring core values as your guideposts.

Actively stabilize the next normal

From the top of your organization down, develop a shared understanding of the future, then conceptualize and paint the big picture of the next normal for your organization at large. What essentials will be needed to achieve crisis objectives and advance toward your desired future? Clarify what will be different and what will remain the same. At the broadest level, introduce the significant new approaches and resources, explaining why they were chosen. Include an overview of changes and continuities driven by the crisis among your organization's major milestones, measurements, and accountabilities.

Explain what must be stabilized through additional actions. Then, begin to detail critical expectations, responsibilities, costs and benefits. As you convey the message across your organization and beyond, include examples that are specifically relevant to each audience you address. For key external stakeholders, inform them about changes that will affect them, as well as what will remain the same, and detail concrete actions you are taking to prevent another crisis.

Recognize and reinforce adaptations already made, and internal champions already acting in alignment with targeted crisis objectives, relevant responses, and future plans. Acknowledge specific actions of individuals and teams who are moving your organization toward your next normal. Express gratitude sincerely, specifically, and widely.

WHAT'S A LEADER TO DO PERSONALLY?

Achieving planned change is applauded as a formidable accomplishment for any leader, and that is appropriate. When a crisis looms, defining fitting responses and steering forward movement can be exhilarating, and success can confer leadership excellence. The processes and outcomes of leading through crises are extraordinary, and also unsettling, precarious, and grave. They test the mettle of any leader.

When leaders' reactions are inept, they unravel crisis response effectiveness, enrage key stakeholders, and intensify the devastation caused by their organization. A dreadful example was set in motion at approximately 1:30 a.m. on July 6, 2013, when 62 tank cars of an unmanned, runaway train jumped the track in the center of Lac-Mégantic, a small, tranquil town in Québec, Canada. More than 1.5 million gallons of petroleum crude oil spewed from ruptured tanks and caught fire. The train, owned by Montreal, Maine and Atlantic Railway (MMA), turned Lac-Mégantic into an inferno. Flames soared 200 feet in the air. Fireballs blasted from sewer drains, manholes, basements, and chimneys. Earthquake-like explosions rocked the town for three hours. The heart of the town was destroyed. Forty-seven townspeople were incinerated.

Decisions and actions of MMA's chairman, Edward Burkhardt, exemplify what not to do in crisis. His fundamental errors ranged from speculation, to finger-pointing (inside and outside his own organization), and cross-cultural insensitivity. Choices he made about timing, context, and communication were poor.[37]

Burkhardt was the sole spokesperson for MMA, and he chose not to go to Lac-Mégantic for five days. His arrival trailed that of the Canadian Prime Minister by three days. Even condolences sent by Queen Elizabeth and Pope Francis arrived before Burkhardt's. From his first press conference, he made the unwise choice to speculate about how local firefighters and his own employees were to blame. His interactions with media and grieving townspeople were characterized as "impromptu scrum" led by an individual cast as "the most hated man in Lac-Mégantic."[38]

Burkhardt's communication incompetencies in the face of crisis were obvious, audible, and captured in sharp video detail by the media and townspeople. He held his press conferences outdoors, near the site of the devastation, arrived informally, dressed informally, answered questions informally, and was surrounded by townspeople without translators, despite the town being 98% French-speaking. As he spoke, he smiled and chuckled occasionally, while responding defensively to questions ("But what can you do at this point?"), or attempting to make light of the situation. His insensitivities soared across YouTube, including, "How much am I worth? A whole lot less than I was on Saturday [the day of the accident]"[39]

Five months later, speaking with the Canadian Press, Burkhardt was still complaining about being, "a victim of this whole thing." Four years later, he was still trying to blame the tragedy on former employees, each of whom were acquitted of all charges.

Leaders' strategic decisions and precarious pivots get most of the attention. Less attention is paid to their attitudes and demeanor, until it is too late. Outlook and behavior are differentiators that deeply affect organizational and individual performance in crisis. They can impact stakeholder and environmental wellbeing, as well as their organization's ability to navigate into the future. None of this is an easy journey, but there are a few exceptionally powerful positive tactics.

When struggling, reflect on past, present, and future successes

Affirm your personal confidence by reflecting on successes in overcoming deep challenges in the past. Identify immediate reasons to retain hope. Recognize what is going well, even if the successes seem trivial. To strengthen your resilience, focus on your commitment to your organization, the welfare of your stakeholders, and your values. Then aim to help others do the same, so they can persevere.

Brace for the long haul

Leading through a crisis is a marathon loaded with sprints. You must pace yourself throughout the turmoil. To persevere, retain faith in the future, while also realistically weighing bleaker realities. You may be acquiring, assessing, and dispersing crisis information and resources for weeks or months. You may be directing action and tending to lingering repercussions for years.

Throughout the crisis, the best and worst of it, stay in touch with the other facets of your life. Make time to reinforce your connections to your family, your friends, and your community. As the crisis begins to ebb, increase time for your life outside work. Make time to acknowledge your gratitude. Reengage with normal problems and celebrate happy occasions with those closest to you. Aim to be fully present when you are taking any of these restorative actions.

Keep a clear head, with your negative emotions in check

Crises require calm, careful consideration. They test anyone's stability and cognitive dexterity. Remain deliberate when making decisions. Aim to bring a clear, focused mind, whether assessing situations, identifying and prioritizing responses, or executing decisions. Communicate clearly and truthfully. Stay open to new people and new ways of thinking.

Even if you are typically quite level-headed, your negative feelings may rage during crisis. Beware that uncontrolled expressions of emotion can crush success all around you. To avert that, employ strong, steady relationship fundamentals:

- Think before you speak.
- Listen before you think.
- Read context and circumstances before you listen.

Your ability to regulate negative emotional responses (others' and your own) will be tested by the extremes and novelties of crises. The toughest tests will arise when others' actions or perspectives press against your own inclinations. Remain calm and focused to avoid misreading or overreacting to words, intonation, body language, or facial expressions that do not match your expectations or preferences.

Take the high road to the best of your ability. Aim to be patient and tolerant, while recognizing that crises tend to put both of those attributes in short supply for everyone, even you. Appreciate that people around you are experiencing their own difficult situations and challenging feelings. Remember that the stresses you are experiencing are part of the human condition, not an isolated, private, personal experience.

Ooze civility

Mutual respect is vital during crises. Extend human dignity to everyone you encounter. Everyone. Even those who push forcefully against your best intentions. Even those who do not like you. Even those you do not like, or trust.

Avoid antagonizing anyone, no matter what the circumstances. Do not make derogatory or dismissive comments, no exceptions. Remain calm through the worst offenses. Set the example, knowing that modeling mutual respect will benefit you and your organization in the long run.

If you ever lose your cool, apologize without making excuses and return to the goal of keeping a clear head and positive approach. If you don't have a meditation practice, this would be a good reason to begin. There are apps and other resources to help you learn.[40]

—————————— Up Next ——————————

Chapter 10 is the final how-to chapter. Learning, the greatest post-crisis differentiator, is the focus. Recommendations for action will center on creating crucibles of crises, by optimizing individual and organizational growth from crisis experiences.

10

Learn, Improve, Sustain

At this point, although some embers may still smolder, the flames and scorching heat of the crisis have been contained. The smoke is clearing. Your employees, customers, and suppliers are settling into their new and old routines, and making adaptations to the next normal. The media are chasing other organizations' troubles. Time to move on.

Not quite.

When a crisis occurs, organizations that survive fix things. After the crisis subsides, some organizations obsess about adjusting active failures, mistakes, errors, procedural violations that were revealed by the crisis. Far fewer take advantage of the opportunities to learn and improve systematically from crisis by examining latent conditions, such as incomplete handoffs, insufficient training, poor communication lines, or inadequate operating procedures. Among the stages through which crises pass, learning is usually the least resourced, whether by time, attention, or funding. Even very wealthy, highly visible organizations tend to invest relatively little to learn broadly from the crises or near misses they experience.

When organizations miss, ignore, or fail to act on lessons, they forfeit the restorative energy and precious insights that lie just below the surface of crises. This oversight can run them smack into their next crisis, often rooted in the very same troubles. Although specific active or operational failures may be repaired during and after crises, the persistent, latent conditions that contributed to organizational dangers often remain unchanged.

The explosions of NASA's Space Shuttles Challenger and Columbia (described above) are tragic, notorious examples. The mechanical fault lines of these crises differed. But, dangerous conditions were known. NASA missed priceless opportunities to learn.

Reactions like those at NASA are common in many organizations after experiencing crises. Their costs are high, especially when potential positive influences are missed. Crises can rattle outdated assumptions, clearing channels for new thinking and action. Their force can disrupt dysfunctional aspects of old ways, undermine obsolete practices, and jar outdated assumptions and ill-fitting perspectives of reality. Such outcomes that often accompany crises can foster priceless adjustments to realign and regain pace with next normals, even those that are imposed by other challenges.

Prevailing together during and after crises can cultivate common ground, boost solidarity, and increase stakeholder commitment to their organization and to each other. When organizations make the effort to learn together from crisis, they take a significant step in institutionalizing these approaches and outcomes. At best, the lessons of crisis successes and failures reinforce shared values and objectives, and reaffirm what matters most. Nonetheless, like NASA, even exceptionally smart organizations miss and dodge opportunities to learn, to think and act differently, to come out better, because of their crisis experiences and insights.

WHAT GETS IN THE WAY OF POST-CRISIS LEARNING?

Before we even understand why, our neuro-wiring intensifies our alertness and reflexive responses in the face of danger, triggering our urges to fight, flee, or freeze, for example. Threats and damages can incite action, whether to battle our way back to what was, or to press on to what could be. These effects can drive learning. But, reflex-based surges are often short-lived. Deeper lessons and the motivation to strive for optimal, enduring changes do not surface automatically. They must be reaped and, ironically, success gets in our way.

Tight focus on breaks and errors stunts learning

When crises occur, smart employees are quick to adjust *what* went wrong and *how*. Usually, they achieve this through *single-loop learning*, adjusting systems and behaviors according to existing norms and procedures.[41] They ask the question, "Are we doing what we do right?" Single-loop is efficient, effective, and customary.

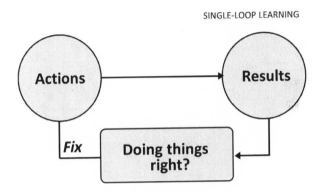

Exceptional organizations explore underlying causes, or circumstances that may have contributed to the dilemmas that they experience. They seek to overcome current limitations or patterns, to take into consideration *why* things occurred, *why* some approaches failed, and *why* others succeeded. They use *double-loop learning*[42] to surface deeper constraints, troubles, and problems. They invest in understanding novel issues and known problems in new ways. They challenge assumptions to ask, "Are we doing the right things?"

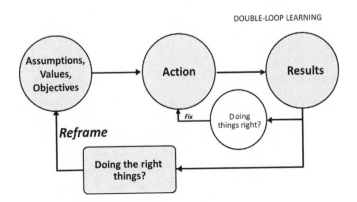

Exceptional organizations question how surrounding circumstances should affect their decisions. They ask, "How do we decide what is right?" They use *triple-loop learning*, taking context into consideration, using contextual insights to improve alignment between their actions and relevant values, goals, beliefs, and assumptions.[43] Then, they revise plans and action strategies accordingly. Facing into novelty and urgency of crises, this is the approach to use.

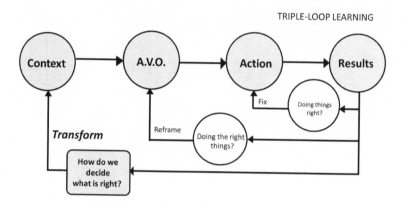

Being too "smart," running from failure

Learning from success is simple, although many people do not invest in the process. Nonetheless, when challenges have gone well, it is easy to remember positive details, such as how appropriate decisions were made. Most of us enjoy remembering, disclosing, and accepting responsibility for positive outcomes.

By contrast, learning from failure can be grueling, especially for successful organizations and smart people.[44] Lack of experience with failure is a fundamental block. For anyone, when successes rise, down go opportunities to practice, own, and rebound from mistakes and failures. Although it leaves them poorly positioned for self-correction and self-development, many smart people are unaware of this powerful cycle. Rather, individuals, teams, and organizations that lack experience with failure tend to fortify their identity as consistently smart and correct. Over time, these impacts evolve into fear of failure for some, which can cloud their judgment and warp their memories. The ever-tightening cycle squeezes out the invaluable feedback of failure.

Smart people, unaccustomed to dealing with the embarrassment or guilt that can accompany failure, try very hard to avert these painful feelings. To push the negative emotional impacts away, they may hone their defensive reasoning, hide their weaknesses, and attempt to mask or deflect their responsibilities for errors, big or small. Eventually, smart individuals/teams/organizations may become unwilling or unable to recognize their own errors. These effects deeply impair learning from crisis.

Learning can be scary

Some organizations are too stunned or overwhelmed by crises to dare unveil underlying causes, effects, and consequences. Some organizations fear that if they look more closely, worse faults will become evident, along with frightening uncertainties or impenetrable barriers that could lie ahead. Others fear that thinking or talking about the crisis will stir or recharge dreadful negative emotions. Even for organizations that take a hard look at prospects for the future, it is not surprising that their leaders may try to bury crises and the pain that came with them.

Whatever the cause, the opportunity lost by missing potential lessons is pitiful. Surging ahead obliviously jeopardizes the future. Where learning opportunities are ignored, habits of patching temporary fixes and tuning out lingering and emerging concerns are reinforced. At worst, lessons missed send wounded workplace warriors back out, fending for themselves, in a damaged, disoriented work environment.

WHAT'S A LEADER TO DO TO HELP OTHERS LEARN AND IMPROVE?

Start shifting more deliberate attention to longer-range improvements signaled by the crisis. These recommendations can help your organization uncover lessons and improve long-term from crisis experiences.

Lean toward a systems approach

Adopt a proactive approach by concentrating on working conditions and underlying influences, rather than focusing excessively on immediate effects and mistakes. Try framing errors as consequences, instead of causes. Rather than attempting to cast blame on individuals' mistakes, examine the contexts in which they occurred, with questions like these:

- Were necessary resources available?
- Were employees sufficiently trained, skilled, and experienced to use equipment and carry out designated protocols?
- Did fatigue, time pressures, or inadequate staffing affect decisions or outcomes?
- Were design features and operating procedures suitable to the tasks at hand?

Relax pressures to allow everyone to catch their breath

Focus first on restoring resilience.[45] Working through a crisis is exhausting, cognitively, physically, and emotionally. Dire circumstances, difficult decisions, long working hours, and overwhelming negative emotions deplete anyone. Even employees who always soldier on may become too tired to focus forward. But learning requires reflection and reasoning, and those processes require renewed energy and restored commitment. Otherwise, without recovery after crisis, judgment and insights will be short-circuited by fatigue. This does not suggest stepping away from commitments or lingering challenges, but finding ways for people to take some breaks.

- Eliminate unnecessary meetings. Shorten those that must occur. Let people decide for themselves whether they need to attend.
- Encourage people to shorten their working hours or take some days off.
- Remind people of the fine work they have done, and the significant, inspiring outcomes they have contributed to.

Set the stage to capture, interpret, and adapt best crisis lessons

- Secure senior executive endorsement and engagement. Feature top leaders to champion and initiate discussions and improvements post-crisis. Power up the CLT to support crisis learning, improvement, and sustained readiness.
- Allocate financial and administrative resources for crisis learning. Promptly invest resources to identify and improve potentially dangerous gaps in decisions or actions that emerged or became obvious during the crisis.
- Start planning how to capture, interpret, and adapt lessons across your organization. For example, investigate practical safeguards that were invented for the crisis. Evaluate potential advantages of integrating new processes permanently into normal operations. Bring attention to new sources that illuminated important insights about the crisis or its management.

Pay exceptional attention to the CLT

If effectively trained, resourced, and engaged, the CLT has been at the core of your organization's crisis response since signals were first detected.

- Thank them. Recognize their efforts and contributions, publicly and repeatedly.

- Appreciate and engage their perspective. Members of the CLT have had extraordinary glimpses into the belly of the beast, both of this crisis, and of your organization's operations under duress. Do not back away from that view, even if some of its perspectives are atrocious. Rather, surface and learn from it, with the CLT.
- Help the team recuperate and learn personally. Indulge their strengths and insights. They are ideal candidates to bring deep lessons from the crisis, and to spot and support crucible opportunities.
- If you are a member of the CLT, take an active role in recuperating with the team.

Revisit your organization's core values and crisis objectives anew

With open minds and careful listening, discuss which values and objectives endured intact, which were disrupted, and which were displaced by the crisis. Collectively weigh costs and benefits of potential adjustments, not only financially, but also strategically.

- Consider which values or objectives might need reinventing to put your organization in better alignment with new realities, and to get in step with the next, post-crisis normal.
- Gather a sample of cross-sectional data to determine whether/how employees were influenced by core values or organizational crisis objectives during the crisis. Solicit improvements to better align crisis responses to the values and objectives. Learn how the perspectives of significant internal and external stakeholders may have been shifted by the crisis or by your organization's response.
- Start to translate insights from the data into strategic adjustments and deep changes. Consider advantageous modifications that might be made to production/service delivery, job functions, reporting relationships, reward structures, supply chains/distribution channels.

Aim to learn from successes and failures, expectations and surprises

Hold guided discussions to share experiences and lessons of the crisis. Begin with one-on-one or small group conversations to learn key employees' particular perspectives of the way the crisis was handled, and what could be improved. Then, build on best examples with groups at large. Consider topics such as these:

- What has become clear to you about the crisis?
- During the crisis, how did novel thinking or new approaches help you (and your team, your division, your job site) respond effectively and efficiently?
- Where did you experience problems or shortcomings in crisis preparation or response personally, in your team, or across our organization?
- How did our crisis objectives (approaches, resources, tools, experts) help you manage the crisis?
- What was missing that would have made a difference?

Throughout the learning process, explore alternatives with an open mind

Bring strengths and weaknesses, capabilities and vulnerabilities to light. Help participants practice separating missteps from bad decisions, and contextual constraints from flawed plans or misdirected execution. Stay receptive to innovative perspectives, especially regarding shortcomings.

- Remind everyone to set aside spontaneous criticisms and finger-pointing, so that they can stay alert to more important lessons and deeper needs.
- Talk about surprises, good and bad.
- Explore how innovative ideas and solutions came about.

- Lead no-fault learning about actual examples. Open discussions about superb and flawed judgment calls, efficient and wasteful resource allocations, effective initiatives and false starts.

Talk with those who experienced your major crisis events and turning points first-hand

- Gather their recommendations for improving approaches and tools.
- Seek ideas about process or structural enhancements to simplify signal detection and reporting across jobs and sites.
- Visit people and places where signals were missed. Do not scratch for scapegoats. Rather, learn and improve from their experiences and insights. Discuss contexts and constraints that could masked early signs of trouble, as well as possible improvements for first-class noticing.

Engage employees in moving toward your next normal

Work with individuals and teams across your organization to customize what you are learning regarding their particular functional specialties, geographic locations, and hierarchical levels. Strengthen communication channels with open, honest, mutually respectful exchanges.

- Help people understand what will remain the same for them, and what will be changing for them, including what will not be returning to pre-crisis state. Discuss critical expectations, responsibilities, targets, metrics, and benefits related to the changes. Where possible, reveal underlying reasons candidly, especially regarding unwelcome news.
- Share information about organizational challenges that lie ahead. Explain approaches that you are taking now, including plans relevant to their future. Communicate updates on progress, shifts, and stalls candidly and promptly.

- Be frank about what is yet to be determined. Inform employees about circumstances or conditions on which new decisions and actions are still being made. Be clear about known criteria.
- Emphasize connections between the next normal and enduring organizational values.
- Establish clear accountability for the future.
- Determine any additions or substitutions needed among CLT members based on projected changes.
- Work with the CLT to identify strategic or operational changes that may be needed within the team, based on what lies ahead.
- Acknowledge adaptive successes and the people who are achieving them. Reinforce behaviors that support future plans, especially specific actions of individuals or teams that move your organization closer to the next normal.

Translate lessons into actions for all levels, globally

Identify top priorities for improvement, including how they will reinforce your organization's values and crisis objectives.

- To prioritize learning and build stronger collective buy-in for improvements, conduct post-crisis learning via synchronous, face-to-face meetings, in person or virtually.
- Create a timeline to capture useful new approaches, and to sequence best lessons that will be transformed into action.
- Start integrating targets for crisis improvement into plans, policies, and procedures.
- As you turn lessons into new ideas, approaches, and actions, keep employees informed about what has been learned. Work with their ideas, resources, and constraints to mold plans and expectations into targeted, foreseeable improvements organization-wide.

Leverage the employment cycle to hone and sustain crisis learning

- Recruit and hire people whose values and expertise align with future-facing adjustments and modifications brought on by the crisis.
- Revise orientation to reinforce lessons from the crisis, in alignment with core values.
- To spread learning throughout your organization, build training that captures improvements to strategies, approaches, and tools that emerged from the crisis.
- To retain the agility that pulled your organization through the crisis, continue to acknowledge, commend, and reinforce individual, team and organizational adaptability post-crisis.
- When employees leave your organization, seek their input about existing crisis management approaches to position the entire employment cycle toward embracing and learning from crises.

Establish accountability for implementing crisis lessons and continuous learning

- Focus first on reducing or eliminating dangers.
- Confirm and reinforce habits that improve crisis management by reinforcing continuous learning organization-wide.
- Work with the CLT to expand the network of managers and local champions throughout your organization who will help guide crisis learning organization-wide.
- Help the CLT and expanded network activate the best communication routes for collecting and sharing feedback, lessons, and new ideas.
- Provide learning champions with the appropriate skills and resources to recognize and empower people who are making exceptional contributions to crisis preparedness and learning.

- Continue to invite widespread input and feedback about crisis lessons and improvements. Act on the best of what you learn.
- Keep communication flowing about the learning process. Share lessons from the crisis up, down, and across. Communicate status and plans honestly, simply, frequently, to all employees, and to key external stakeholders.
- Enlist and reinforce champions who will help you drive changes. Increase their visibility and give them access to the power needed to energize action.
- Make peace with mistakes that will come with the learning process, including your own.
- Help individuals and teams connect lessons of the crisis to their current experiences, and their future plans.

Reinforce habits that power positive change

- Seize optimal timing. Start soon enough to engage the force of the crisis before it dissipates, but not so soon that employees will feel that they are being jerked into learning. Support recuperation organization-wide. Ease into lessons.
- Give everyone the chance to begin recuperating cognitively, emotionally, and physically, so that they can contribute at their best to compound learning and help power improvements.
- Listen rather than lecture. Discuss rather than tell.
- Soothe the most painful impacts collectively before proceeding. Tend to residual stress and exhaustion to avoid compromising concentration, darkening participants' perspectives of your organization's future, or causing people to fail at learning.
- Reinforce best suggestions with prompt follow-up action whenever possible. Focus early on improvements that will be meaningful for employees, based on what you learn from them.
- Go big on genuine positive feedback. Remind everyone that people remember criticism, but they respond to praise.

- Help employees identify how personal strengths that they demonstrated during crisis will apply in the next normal.[46]

WHAT'S A LEADER TO DO TO LEARN AND IMPROVE PERSONALLY?

Organizational crises generate rare opportunities to practice and demonstrate individual fitness under fire. Often, they evoke personal perseverance and toughness. When met with readiness and reflection, crises can become crucibles, events that draw forth deep learning and purpose from life's most challenging circumstances.[47]

When you work through ugly problems, there could be outcomes that provoke you to revamp your expertise. But when you work through a crisis, you will always encounter exceptional opportunities for personal growth. The challenge is to have the insight to spot them, and the wisdom and persistence to learn from them. The seeds are always there in crisis, but the transformation can only come from you.

Revisit your personal values

Explore them post-crisis, in writing, preferably writing by hand, to tap into your thoughts more deeply. Discuss them with family, friends, mentors, role models, or trusted colleagues. Stay tuned, especially, to tensions that arose between your values and your behaviors during the crisis. Those tensions can reveal rich opportunities for adjustment and personal growth.

- How did your deepest values drive your decisions and actions during the crisis? Did the crisis threaten your personal values at any time? What helped you remain true to your values? What events or circumstances caused you to divert from them?
- How are you different today than you were before the crisis occurred?

- What matters most to you now? How have your values changed or been strengthened because of the crisis?
- At any point during the crisis, how did your decisions or behaviors stray from your organization's values? What sorts of circumstances or contexts were influencing you at the time? How did you resolve the dilemma? Which values endured, and what can you learn about your relationship with your organization from the situation?

Do not waste the pain

- Hone your frame of mind and your behaviors for crucibles. Do not just aim to get through crises; seek to come out stronger, with better coping strategies.[48]
- Make a habit of learning from troubles. Get accustomed to embracing the lessons of hardships by practicing during moderately difficult times. Tune in and welcome learning from challenges and predicaments. Develop an appetite for creating stronger outcomes, including personal ones.
- Keep track of your perseverance through difficulties. Write about your personal perspectives of the crisis and your best contributions to managing it, or discuss them with a close friend. Round out your perspective with specific circumstances that caused your determination to rise and fall. Tap the discipline and perseverance to do this as you are working through the troubles, or as soon as possible afterwards.
- Think about the roles you filled, especially those that enhanced or impaired your efforts and endurance. Consider potential alignment between your personal strengths and these outcomes. Imagine best uses of your strengths during additional troubles in the future, as well as their potential application during normal times.
- Reflect on why you may have retreated or been derailed, for example, when confusion or negative impacts surged. Contrast

where and why you may have succumbed, versus where and why you succeeded in pushing through.

- Identify opportunities for personal growth that align with the values that matter most to you. Then make concrete plans to enhance that growth.

Initially, focus on what you did well

Own the exceptional nature of what you have accomplished. Just showing up fully and consistently during a crisis is heroic. Accept your accomplishments in crisis to replenish your personal reserve and voice your interest in learning. Embrace the positive to power up personally for what lies ahead.

Take a data-based approach to your accomplishments. Collect your thoughts in writing, then talk about them with close friends or family. Discuss themes that emerge from your crisis experiences. Others are likely to hear strengths and courage in your actions. Listen and absorb their support and insights. To get started, consider questions like these:

- What were your greatest contributions to handling the crisis?
- How did your personal values drive your decisions and actions?
- How did you adapt your role/responsibilities to what was needed most?
- How did you keep your concerns from overpowering you?
- What support did you provide to ease others' challenges?
- What life-size lessons did you learn from the crisis?
- Which of your achievements make you proud?

As you contemplate and discuss your answers, consider how the crisis reinforced your personal strengths that you were already aware of, and how it brought forth other strengths that may seem new to you.

Confront your shortcomings with grace

Personal growth requires owning up to your errors. Embrace these perspectives to make the effort easier and more rewarding.

- Wrestling honestly and openly with personal mistakes and failures is a characteristic that differentiates good leaders from great ones.
- Whether you own up to them or not, people will often find out about your shortcomings anyway. If you come forth, you will save time, energy, and distress by no longer trying to hide your flaws.
- Focus on the greater good, rather than the embarrassment or guilt that you might experience in revealing your mistakes.
- Muster the courage to step up to your own errors and failures to open the door for others to do the same. Your fearlessness and candor can generate ripples of improvement throughout your organization.
- Keep the crisis context and constraints in mind. Avoid being overly critical of others' actions or your own. Rather, focus forward for correction and improvement.

Tend lingering negative emotions kindly, including your own

Everyone deals with crises in their own ways, so recuperation will always vary by the individuals involved, and by the circumstances that they have experienced. For some people, negative emotional impact may linger for a very long time. In tragedies, the community impact will be profound.[49] In many crisis situations, offering trauma-informed counseling could be appropriate.

- Make the time needed to support learning and improvement. Speak the truth promptly to avoid communication vacuums, which are often filled by negative rumors and worst-case conjecture.

- If you want or need to gain more information from people who were dramatically affected by the crisis, for instance, victims or employees who were first responders, seek their perspectives very patiently. Anticipate poignant reactions. Keep your requests or questions simple. Regardless of the reactions you encounter, always respond with sincere gratitude for the information revealed.

Set personal learning objectives relative to the crisis

Reaffirm your personal connections and commitment to your organization's values, and to your personal values. Record personal learning goals using questions like these as starting points:

- How do your long-range goals relate to your experiences in crisis?
- What specifically do you want to learn or improve to grow personally from your experiences and observations before, during, and after the crisis?
- How could your crisis experiences and expertise enhance your day-to-day roles at work and beyond?

Regardless of how effectively you handled the crisis, contemplate what you would do differently next time

People who forge crucibles from crises approach learning in uncommon ways. They reflect with integrity, regardless of the weight of the crisis, or the shortcomings of responses (others' or their own). They contemplate the circumstances, contexts, and consequences of the crisis, and its deeper impacts. They deliberate what they wish they had said or done differently during the crisis. Ultimately, they use their experiences of crisis as grounding to examine their values, assumptions, and judgment profoundly, to identify and seek new perspectives and practices for self-improvement.

Up Next

We move now to Today's Crisis Accelerators, which details why crisis preparations are even more vital today than they were in the past. In Chapters 11-14, we explore the impacts of major environmental trends on organizational crises and crisis responses. Specifically, we look at the crisis accelerators of hypercompetition, globalization, and the techno-fusions that are often associated with the Fourth Industrial Revolution. Chapters 15 and 16 focus on how two intimate limitations of human nature, habits and biases, impact the speed, reach, and depth of contemporary crises as well as crisis responses. Each chapter centers on practical implications and action recommendations for improvements in averting and mitigating crises, including both quick hits and greater investments.

TODAY'S CRISIS ACCELERATORS

11

Running on Fumes, Relentlessly

Hypercompetitive organizations aim emphatically to do more with less, quicker, cheaper, and better. This trend plays out in strategies and approaches that are hasty, aggressive, and dynamic. Although hypercompetition can power great successes, it can also feed crises and obstruct crisis preparation and response.

Where outpacing is the primary goal, speed can eclipse quality and safety, leaving organizations more vulnerable to errors, accidents, and crises. When employees feel compelled to cut corners to save time, money or other resources no matter what, they miss and denigrate mistakes and mishaps. Whether by ignoring or burying them, this detachment stifles timely responses to crisis warning signals.

In a recent study of more than 200 organizations across 17 industries, in more than a dozen geographies, about 60% of cyber breaches were caused by carelessness or neglect on the part of employees and contractors. Even simple acts like sending a sensitive file by mistake or sending information to the wrong recipient contributed to the average cost of managing these crises and near misses, which ran from $4 million globally to $8 million in the U.S. Unraveling and addressing the breaches took months. Significant additional organizational costs ranged from lost revenue and information (employee records, customer data, trade secrets), to business disruption, and tarnished reputation.[50]

At a fundamental level, three hypercompetitively-charged scarcities contribute to dropped threads, which create holes in crisis readiness and response:

1. Efforts to squeeze time breed norms of multitasking and rushed collaborations.
2. Employment insecurity dulls allegiances and erases organizational memory.
3. Blind accountability creates systemic gaps among preparations for crisis responsiveness and leadership.

SCARCITY #1: TIME COMPRESSION

Velocity as a perpetual objective is uninspiring and disengaging. When speed is of utmost importance, peripheral vision and relationships take significant hits. When time-starved, in a permanent state of *crazybusy*, anyone may feel overworked and burned out.[51] Whether choosing to give less of themselves, or actually having less to give, employees who are continually pressured to rush forfeit attention to the nuances of their performance, to their contexts, and to their relationships.

Multitasking is a popular approach for faster: if we achieve two or more things at once, surely we must be accomplishing more, quicker, even if not quite as perfectly. Even small immediate boosts in output reinforce the appeal of splitting our attention, and achieving under pressure delivers an adrenaline rush, so there is neuro-chemical seduction, too. For habitual tasks requiring little or no thought, the approach can work just fine. However, multitasking is a lousy way to deal with extraordinary demands, which are characteristic of crises.

Dividing attention is not just exhausting, it impairs our ability to think. The damage is hard-wired. No one is immune. Everyone's sensitivity to other issues drops when they multitask. And then, subtleties like warning signals and prospects for novel solutions fall by the wayside.

To save time, we also short our attention to others intentionally, through multitasked collaborations, for example, as we check texts and messages during meetings. Here, too, the cost is missed details and subpar thinking, even when issues are critically important, even when clues to potentially dangerous circumstances surface. Furthermore, as we reduce or dismiss our attention to others, we wear down our relationships. By reciprocation, we become less able to capture or retain others' attention, even when needed urgently, even in crisis. Exhaustion, disengagement, inattention, and incivility leave little chance that teamwork or ad hoc connections will flow smoothly, or be keenly insightful. Yet these qualities are essential to comprehend and disarm crises.

SCARCITY #2: EMPLOYMENT INSECURITY, FROM BOTH SIDES NOW

Successful job performance no longer assures job security. Conversely, fair treatment no longer assures employee loyalty. Who lets go first does not really matter.

Where stability or loyalty do not count for much, it is easier for employers to terminate experienced workers, and it is easier for experienced employees to leave. With either cause of exit, out go expertise, dependable relationships, and seasoned sensitivities to trouble. When seasoned workers leave, organizational memory of past crises fades, and eventually vanishes, along with insights about what worked under extraordinary circumstances, and what did not. The hard-earned expertise of wrestling with threatening novelties disappears, too.

The anticipation and realities of shortened or truncated job tenure dull allegiances and relationships. Employees who lack long-haul perspective are disinclined to look beyond their designated duties. They also lack protection and incentive to risk bringing forth bad news or speaking truth to power, creating missing links that stifle signal detection and response severely, and erode trust, all of which can lead to crises igniting internally. And, along the way, your best employees might quit at the first whiff of serious trouble.

SCARCITY #3: SYSTEMIC GAPS IN CRISIS TRAINING AND DEVELOPMENT

Two types of workers underprepare for crisis, even in usually well-prepared organizations. This occurs because they fall outside those organizational preparations. These two very different types of workers are not privy to appropriate crisis training and development for very different reasons. Nonetheless, when an organizational crisis strikes, contingent workers and employees who have otherwise been empowered are as likely as anyone to be called to action, but they will be flying blind.

Whether through temporary or contract hiring, on-call, freelance or gig provisions, today's contingent work arrangements compound crisis threats. Once largely a stop-gap approach to fill lower-level jobs, contingent workers now take on highly-influential roles, all the way up through executive ranks. As their numbers and responsibilities have climbed dramatically, so has their potential influence in crisis.

Standard practices in many organizations reinforce the dangers. Applicants for contingent jobs are rarely screened for corporate-cultural fit to their hiring organization. Whether their interests or values align with or run counter to those of the hiring organization usually remains a mystery.

Contingent workers' onboarding usually focuses sharply on specific task fulfillment, which is often tightly defined. They are rarely taught how their contributions fit with other employees' efforts, or how the tasks they will do affect the organization more broadly. They may learn little about the organization's key stakeholders, much less which among them should command top priority if a crisis occurs. Contingent workers are often forgotten or excluded from social events and special recognition or rewards. Rather, their successful employment usually amounts to adapting rapidly to their assigned tasks, while averting or ignoring distractions.

These arrangements may sit fine with contingent workers, but during crises, the related costs and deficits, when workers lack attachment, are undeniable. They are likely to miss clues and insights about what surrounds them, blind to what is normal versus what is not. Even if they happen to be very observant individuals, who naturally spot potential threats, they receive no guidance about what to do with their suspicions. Benefits of their diverse experiences and perspectives, which could bring creative approaches to averting and responding to signals or crises are lost. Because they are out of stride with norms and context, contingent workers introduce gravely weak links, even where core employees are fastidiously prepared to deal with crises.

Contingent workers are not the only group whose perspectives of crises are myopic. Empowerment, another facet of hypercompeting, leaves some of the best full-time employees out of the loop, too. For decades, organizations have passed down authority, responsibility, information access, and decision-making from executives to upper management and, more recently, from upper to middle management.[52] Now, in the interests of hypercompeting, supervisors and line workers are also being given greater responsibilities and the tools that go with them. Faced with today's complex, volatile environment, many organizations have found that it makes sense to deeply distribute the four ingredients of empowerment: information, knowledge, power, and rewards. This is true in crisis, as well.

However, even in organizations that are well-prepared for crises, for example, where crisis leadership teams include members across the hierarchy, strategic information and skills are often still guarded among the top echelons. The dilemma is, power can shift abruptly in crisis due to urgencies and disruptions. Employees at any level may be called upon to lead. Empowered employees are likely to volunteer to step up, or be asked to, but if they lack firm awareness about higher-level intentions and priorities, they will struggle needlessly. When empowerment does not include crisis preparation specifically, when higher-level information, skills, and knowledge about their organization's crisis context, environment, and strategies have not been shared, the best efforts of people who are otherwise empowered may prolong or intensify crises, rather than resolving them. Mid-level leaders of public organizations I have worked with are often very tenuous about acting swiftly without official sign-offs, even when potential dangers linger, or when unrestricted site access for media or the public is disrupting crisis response. Without preparation for crisis exceptions, they struggle to make their way through undefined chains of command, delaying what is urgently needed.

PRACTICAL IMPLICATIONS

Apply hypercompetitive strengths to crisis preparation and response

Create opportunities to take advantage of your better/cheaper/faster modes for crisis readiness. Power up your hypercompetitive norms to strengthen your organization's responses when trouble strikes.

Quick hits

- Take stock of the crisis-relevant approaches and norms that give your organization hypercompetitive advantage. Determine ways in which they could be adopted and adapted to power up crisis preparation, response, and learning.
- Evaluate and test how potential applications of your best communication lines, technologies, and techniques can be used to smooth the flow of early warning signals and reporting.
- Evaluate and test how best approaches that enhance speed, economy, and quality in your organization might be adapted for crisis updates and logistics, and for improving the flow of resources up, down, and across your organization.
- Create or adapt your organization's leading-edge tools and techniques to spot and share insights about potential troubles and looming crises.

Greater investments

- Bring employees who rise best to hypercompetitive pressures into your Crisis Leadership Team and other crisis-relevant roles.
- Apply crisis contexts and worst-case scenarios into your leadership, teaming, and agility training occasionally.

- Provide some level of crisis training for contingent workers, to identify and align their particular strengths and expertise that could be particularly valuable in crisis.

Relax time, even a bit, to lower stress factors and increase sensitivity to early signals

To reduce errors, enhance signal detection, avoid nasty problems, and avert crises, experiment with practices that help to focus attention, and reduce stress and exhaustion. Apply some of these steps to avoid missteps, saving time and other resources in the long run.

Quick hits

- First, stop and think. Whenever you are faced with significant novelties or especially challenging circumstances, make a habit of stopping and pausing, even under intense time pressure.
- Stop consistently overscheduling yourself and your employees. Reduce a little stress day-to-day to build reserves for dark circumstances. Know what your key employees value most, and help them build reservoirs now for more difficult times ahead.
- Schedule time daily, to reflect, observe, and connect, even if only for a few moments. Champion the practice across your organization.
- Do not just speed up to go faster. Instead, stop wasting time, and respect everyone's attention. Start by shortening meetings. When they must run long, take frequent breaks and coax participants to get up and move.
- Avoid playing trivial pursuit: put the most important issues, with longer term payoffs, at the top of any meeting's agenda. Circulate the agenda in advance to stay focused and on point during the meeting. To direct and unify attention from the start, take a moment to share the focus and rationale at the beginning of

meetings. If your meetings consistently run short on time, assign a gatekeeper, set a timer, or shorten your list of agenda items. When urgently pressed for time, conduct a standing meeting.

- Eliminate mandatory attendance at meetings. Encourage individuals to decide for themselves whether attending is the best use of their time. Openly permit participants to come and go to optimize their investment individually. If you want particular people to attend for all or part of the meeting, let them know that in advance.

Greater investments

- To keep things moving productively, to improve retention of and respect for everyone's attention, build the habit of gadget-free meetings.
- Do not work to exhaustion, even during crises. Depleting energy in the present will cost efficiency and effectiveness in the future. Be a role model and champion of an investment perspective: consistently eat, move, sleep according to healthy habits.

Build bench strength for crises

Fill systematic gaps in crisis training and development. Leave no member of your organization behind.

Quick hits

- Disperse basic information about your organization's core values and crisis management objectives to everyone in your organization, including contingent workers and volunteers.
- Repeat essential information about your organization's crisis plans and experiences annually, whenever substantial changes occur within your organization or its environment, and whenever significant threats emerge.

- Commend employees at all levels who help to avert crises, for example, by bringing forth bad news quickly and earnestly. To recognize important contributions, opt for a call or face-to-face compliment, rather than a text or email message.

Greater investments

- Build executive and board support for sharpening your organization's crisis effectiveness and efficiency, including financial, resource, and developmental commitments.
- Incorporate crisis basics into everyone's training. At all levels, across functions and throughout geographic settings, integrate job-specific crisis expectations and capabilities into training, and into performance norms. Bring bottom-up recommendations for improvement to crisis approaches.
- Include relevant information and knowledge about crises and crisis responses as part of all empowerment efforts and leadership development programs.
- Customize crisis knowledge and approaches at division and site levels to support existing and anticipated roles and responsibilities.
- Teach employees at all levels when and how to step up when they sense potential dangers. Teach them how and to whom they should report problems, including alternative contacts, in case of disrupted availability. Brief all employees on the type of information that will be expected when reporting dangers. Build simple, obvious, accessible routes for reporting signs of trouble.
- Create easy access to quick approvals in problems or crisis. Use discussion and tabletop scenarios to teach employees how to determine what is fitting to their expertise and experience, and the types of situations that would warrant instantaneous expansion of their authority. Provide real examples of employees who have made reasoned decisions to step up appropriately when resources or actions were needed urgently.

- Reward top quality problem-solving and crisis responses that reinforces core values and crisis objectives.

Mitigate crisis losses to prevent accelerated turnover

From recruitment, throughout the employment cycle, keep all members aware of your organization's purpose, values, and desired outcomes when crises occur.

Quick hits

- Include your organization's core values and the essence of its crisis objectives in recruiting materials and orientation programs to provide a realistic grounding for applications and for new employees.
- When calculating turnover or retention costs, assign value for organizational memory.

Greater investments

- Discuss links between core values and norms, as related to crisis objectives and expectations. Solicit employees' examples of how their work experiences align with the core values, objectives, and expectations. Revisit the perspective with all employees from time-to-time, and whenever dangers lurk.
- Consider shadowing as a method for new hires to learn from seasoned employees what is normal relative to their jobs and contexts. Coach new members about how the core organizational values are expected to guide behavior under normal and exceptional circumstances. Include and solicit real examples.
- Link knowledge and application of key crisis objectives and techniques to professional and personal development targets.

—————————————— Up Next ——————————————

In the next chapter, we will explore how globalization affects crises and crisis preparations. A core perspective introduced in this chapter is the cross-cultural lens, an exceptional approach for identifying and creating alignment among differences. With this lens, we explore crisis challenges, costs, and benefits specific to global organizations, whether your international or cross-cultural reach involves diverse sites, employees, customers, or other stakeholders. This chapter includes short- and long-term approaches for initiating, improving and retaining preparation and response consistency throughout your organization, even across international borders and cultural diversities.

12

Nowhere Left to Hide

Expansion exacerbates exposure.[53] Although going global can bring phenomenal success to organizations that optimize complementary strengths among international sites, these additional variables, across more contexts, also bring more unknowns and less common ground. These challenges can provoke errors and open gateways to trouble. In darker times, global reach can confound, delay, and derail insights and resources that are acutely needed to respond to crises and come out stronger.

With global expansion come new cultures that can destabilize and dilute an organization's home-base perspectives. Within an organization, globalization may bring additional time zones and languages, greater physical distances among sites, and varied values, norms, and behaviors from each culture represented. Externally, being global can multiply variations in local regulations, ethical standards, and critiques and criticisms from traditional and social media. Today, global challenges do not require vast operations overseas, nor any operations overseas. Rather, workers with diverse cultural perspectives and norms may characterize single-site organizations. In crisis, global challenges, internal and external, can confound organizational insights, undermine compliance with anticipated preparations and plans, and wreck responses.

CULTURE'S COMPLICATIONS

There is not one aspect of human life that is not touched and altered by culture.
– E.T. Hall

Whether applied to an organization, a neighborhood, or a nation, culture is a way of life shared by a group of people. Values, norms, and perspectives within a culture unite its members, and differentiate their culture from others. In the global work environment, organizations become cross-cultural in many ways today, through their international sites, homeland employees working overseas, foreign employees in the organization's homeland, and similar connections among their key external stakeholders. The classical perspective below offers hints for distinguishing three intertwined layers of culture, and for appreciating the complexities that arise when work is carried on cross-culturally.[54]

Levels of Culture

Artifacts and Creations
Manifestations that can be seen, touched, heard, smelled, tasted, but their meanings may be difficult for outsiders to decipher.

Examples: art, technology, ceremonies, architecture, rituals, heroes and villains, jargon, myths, products, symbols, language, traditions.

Espoused Values
Standards and beliefs beneath what should or ought to be, which are may be decipherable by careful analysis or inference.

Examples: thought processes, feelings, rationales, knowledge, purpose, vision, mindset, worldview, strategies, philosophies.

Basic Assumptions
Perceptions, thoughts, feelings taken for granted, outside conscious awareness.

Examples: beliefs about the environment, time, space, as well as human nature, activity, and relationships.

In a homogenous culture, where norms, stories, artifacts, language, innuendoes and non-verbal communication mean the same thing to everyone, lengthy explanations are often unnecessary, even when information or circumstances are complex or unsettling, even in crisis. In multicultural organizations, such streamlined communication cannot be assumed. Rather, cross-cultural awareness is needed: members of each culture must develop an appreciation for the norms, values, and assumptions of the other cultures, to better understand and relate to one another. The value of clear communication regarding core values and crisis objectives cannot be overstated. Then, practice is needed to translate shared expectations into collaborative actions.

When achieved, this culturally conscious coordination keeps informed stakeholders throughout the organization and beyond from being overwhelmed by uncertainty, information overload, or taxing decisions—the stuff of crises. By contrast, when diverse cultures must be navigated without understanding and adapting to differences from either direction, disconnection, confusion, and conflict can brew problems into crises and baffle usually effective response teams.

To make matters worse, today's hyper-connectivity can quickly push organizational problems onto the global stage, for example, through accusations circulated by customers, the media, or the public half a world away. Seemingly questionable organizational decisions and misguided leadership actions can be spotted and broadcasted, with ease, in a flash. Juicy details made newsworthy by the familiarity of an organization can fire an ordeal into international headlines to shake brand confidence worldwide. Affected organizations may even find themselves unable to disassociate from the mistakes made by their anonymous global partners.

Production chains that link manufacturers, contractors, and sub-contractors internationally, across great distances, time zones, norms, and regulations increase crisis vulnerability. More than a decade ago, Mattel's toy recalls for lead painted products provided insights into global complications and newsworthiness, as well as a baseline that highlights the acceleration at which organizational problems and crises must be handled across borders today. Mattel's challenges initially drew global attention because of the company's reputation for high quality products, and its enormous size (the largest toy manufacturer in the world at the time).

In 2007, many of Mattel's crisis responses were exemplary. The company listened to early warning signals reported by an external stakeholder (a retailer in Europe), and reacted quickly. They began investigations overseas within days, and stopped relevant operations in China within a week. The three weeks required for Mattel to initiate the first recall (1.5 million items across 83 products, at an estimated cost of $30 million) were not unusual, and the additional weeks added for two more recalls seemed acceptable. The timing of this example certainly provides striking contrast to the "15 minute" grace period that has become popular contemporary advice.

Today, the potential speed, reach, and impact of global complexities oblige organizations with any degree of international reach to decode differences now. Anticipating cross-cultural variances in interpretations, impacts, and responses is essential before timing, intensity and media attention explode. Even organizations that are well prepared otherwise for crises should incorporate means of addressing cross-cultural contingencies in their preparations and strategies, to move with agility, at response speeds required today.

THE ULTIMATE GLOBAL TEST: HANDLING A CRISIS CROSS-CULTURALLY

Culture eats strategy for breakfast. — Peter Drucker

In normal times, inadequate cross-cultural coordination can wreck negotiations, boggle team members' understanding, and delay production. Internally, disorientations brought by crisis can breed conflict and dissention among culturally diverse employees, even those who work in the same organization, and on the same team. Externally, collisions among cultures can abruptly expose profound divides among organizational expectations and foreign stakeholders' deepest cultural roots.

Within or beyond organizational boundaries, cultural differences can distort crisis directives, even those that seem straightforward. In today's global environment, variances among cultures can cause members of the same organization to construe a situation radically differently. Take, for example, a commonly accepted crisis imperative: *Report potential warning signals promptly.*

To begin, attitudes about *reporting* are sharply affected by cultural differences. In some, shared perspectives about loyalty and power distribution will make employees reluctant to deliver bad news. Here, employees who detect signals may waste precious time attempting to cover up or fix the issue themselves, or overlook the signal, rather than risk implicating themselves (where they must save face), their teammates (where they must be loyal), or their bosses (where they must extol their wisdom or authority). On the other hand, in cultures where surfacing problems is construed as an effective avenue for learning and improvement, employees will be even more predisposed to report signs of trouble straightaway, and be seen as critical troublemakers. For newcomers to either of these cultures, the causes of behavioral differences will be disconcerting and difficult to decipher.

What is essential to remember is that each culture has a dominant profile or values orientation, as well as numerous variations. In times of change, including crises, the ordering of preferences will not be clear cut. Rather, various cultures may respond with incompatible moves, or contradictory actions, all with the genuine intention to do the right thing. At the extreme, crisis strategies and responses will please stakeholders of one culture, while enraging those of another.

When employees' perspectives and behaviors derive from cultural roots and values that are dissimilar to organizational expectations, the core question, then, is: *Which norms and values will stakeholders follow under the extraordinary, urgent, uncertain demands of a crisis?* Consider a fundamental example. Assume that your organization's culture/values/norms reinforce consistently this value: *Employees always show up for work, even and especially during difficult times.* If you rely on that assumption in crisis, you could learn that it takes a back seat to earlier cultural conditioning. If your employees are driven by another, more deeply seeded value of their original culture such as, *Family first, no matter what,* you will be surprised by unanticipated but predictable reactions from your employees—not showing up.

Without cross-cultural insights, preparations, and practice, even dramatic misalignments may be missed. Especially under duress or in unusual circumstances, behaviors can tumble out of stride with the anticipated priority of organizational values, norms, and expectations. Where cross-cultural fallout occurs, where awareness and alternative plans are lacking, the results can devastate crisis cues, responses, and learning. If your organization crosses borders, decoding cross-culturally is not an option, it is a strategic obligation.

PRACTICAL IMPLICATIONS

Learn and practice cross-culture approaches for crisis readiness now, under normal conditions

Working through crises cross-culturally requires greater patience, more limber adaptability, and sharper focus on context. Learn to interpret communication and behaviors cross-culturally and adjust your communications, behaviors, and expectations to optimize your chances of averting crises, and effectively handling those that do occur.

Quick hits

- Train and develop your organization's multicultural knowledge base, derived from broad, grounded cross-cultural research.[55]
- Build employees' personal insights and practical competence through research-based assessment tools and guidelines such as the Berlitz Cultural Orientation Indicator, Hofstede's Insights Culture Compass, and Erin Meyer's Country Mapping Tool.[56]
- Emphasize caution when applying cultural classifications. Even deeply grounded data are not reliable for predicting a particular individual's behavior. Norms within a culture vary widely and shift over time, especially in today's volatile, techno-fused environment, and in response to crisis urgencies.
- Treat cross-cultural guidance as starting points, not ultimate wisdom. Cultural classifications are always based on broad

generalizations, so they can cause differences to seem more distinctive or more influential than they actually are.

- o Treat cross-cultural insights as estimates or first guesses.
- o As employees build experiences in real situations, with actual members of new cultures, encourage them to reevaluate cultural generalizations that they may have read about.

Greater improvements

- Secure and provide resources to learn and practice crisis readiness under cross-cultural assumptions and circumstances.
- Build cross-cultural savvy into your Crisis Leadership Team.
- When working with crisis tools and approaches, identify and discuss how crisis scenarios could play out differently across your organization's foreign locations.
- Integrate local employees from your international settings to help steer crisis planning and preparations, practice, and learning appropriate to their contexts.

Differentiate your organization's fundamental crisis expectations from those that can be adjusted safely to local norms and values

Do not hesitate to insist that employees at all locations follow particular crisis approaches in exactly the same way. Also, be clear about approaches and responses that can be adapted to local norms and values.

Where *consistent* approaches or responses are needed cross-culturally:

Quick hits

- Using culture-appropriate reasoning, explain why it is necessary for everyone to follow certain principles and approaches identically.

Build from cross-cultural common ground, starting with your organization's core values.

- Keep instructions clear and simple for accurate translation and application.

Greater improvements

- Identify which universal expectations will be easier to adhere to in the particular cultures of your work, and where more guidance, reassurance, and monitoring will be needed. Allocate time, resources, and follow-up accordingly.
- Gather local input and practice local adjustments that will be necessary to meet universal organizational guidelines. Monitor and reinforce compliance in ways fitting to local affected cultures.

Where approaches and responses can be *adjusted safely to local norms and values*:

Quick hits

- Explain carefully why these are exceptions, and why they are appropriate for optimal crisis management.
- Be explicit about which responses employees can customize to their local preferences, and when and how.

Greater improvements

- Gather input about additional preferred local adjustments. Include locals who are experts on the decisions and actions that would be affected. Where they would benefit or have no ill effects on crisis preparation or response, confirm their acceptable fit to your organization's targeted crisis outcomes. Monitor, adjust, and reinforce compliance in alignment with organizational needs.

Prepare for foreseeable cross-cultural roadblocks

Quick hits

- At your international sites, recruit locals into crisis planning to improve the predictability of their sites' compliance with preparations and response expectations.
- Where available, include employees who are members of multiple relevant cultures to help broker decisions and actions across boundaries.

Greater improvements

Learn local response patterns that should be anticipated in diverse organizational sites. Start with discussions about potential impacts and anticipated needs of local stakeholders when a crisis occurs. Keep things in perspective, addressing less consequential issues after the overall organizational culture is prepared. Consider critical issues like these:

- If an organizational crisis also threatens other aspects of their lives, such as their families, homes, or local communities, how would employees' priorities shift?
- If a crisis affects their site or region, will local employees show up for work?
- What can be done to keep employees working through a crisis? What would drive employees away?
- Monitor and update crisis preparations across diverse sites periodically, and whenever your organization's global footprint shifts distinctly.

Encourage collaborative cross-cultural approaches to handling crises

Support employees at all levels to build and maintain solid relationships with colleagues from other cultures. Prepare people for difference, not similarity.

Quick hits

Add cross-cultural basics to crisis training and practice.

- Teach employees to suspend judgment cross-culturally, for example, by inserting a brief pause between others' words/actions and their reactions whenever cross-cultural confusion, misunderstandings or complications arise.
- Help them consider how alternative interpretations of what they are sensing could be valid.
- Build a norm of scanning for patterns of novel behaviors, rather than reacting to isolated unfamiliar occurrences.

Greater improvements

- Aim to match varied cultural strengths to crisis response needs. For example, teach the costs and benefits of flexible versus fixed time perspectives for crisis preparations and response.
- Teach the benefits of tolerance, especially in troubled times, including potential vital payoffs for diverse views when planning for crises or innovating urgent crisis responses.
- Practice identifying and applying meaningful measures and outcome targets appropriate for each site, rather than imposing organizational desires and home country expectations. Where possible, seek options that will bridge cultural preferences of individual employees.

INCREASE YOUR PERSONAL COMPETENCE FOR CROSS-CULTURAL DECODING

One can see culture's consequences everywhere or nowhere. – E.T. Hall

Start by learning the characteristics of your own cultures

Cultural differences go unnoticed by many people; others misattribute the impacts of cultural differences to other causes. The best place to begin cross-cultural understanding is by researching your own cultures, including your ancestral heritage, and others' cultures that may have influenced you, often where you have lived or worked for a significant time. What you learn will give you three powerful levers for practicing and learning cross-cultural differences:

1. You can personalize cross-cultural comparisons based on your own background.
2. You will have some insight into how people from other cultures will tend to generalize about your culture and you.
3. When you encounter confusion or uneasiness in diverse interactions, you can approach the situation more calmly and smartly with an understanding of the relevance of cultural roots.

Quick hits

- Learn research-based profiles of your home and ancestral cultures.[57]
- To deepen your understanding, observe, and discuss the norms and values with members of those cultures. Think about how your behaviors, norms, and values match the profiles of those cultures, and how they differ.

Stretch the boundaries of your comfort zone

Dealing effectively with uncertainty is an essential skill for effectively handling crises. Use your cross-cultural experiences to expand your tolerance for uncertainty.

Quick hits

- Learning even a little bit about local customs and a few kind words (hello, thank you, goodbye) in the foreign goes a long way in nearly every culture.
- When you cross a cultural bridge, practice staying loose about the many things that you do not understand. Accept that you may never comprehend some of them.
- Create opportunities to build and practice cross-cultural expertise first-hand with friends and acquaintances from other cultures.

Follow standard approaches for accurate crisis communication across cultures

The vital goal is to keep it simple.

Quick hits

- Avoid slang, idioms, jargon.
- Repeat essential points using different words.
- Add visuals (photos, basic graphics) to support your message succinctly.
- When working with people who are not native speakers of your language, allow time for them to catch up as they translate.
    - Speak a little more slowly. Pause more frequently.
    - Monitor your audience for their culturally relevant non-verbal behaviors. Know their signs of confusion, support, disagreement.
    - To avoid cross-cultural fatigue and retain attention, keep meetings relatively short. If long meetings are necessary, include frequent breaks.
    - In discussions, do not jump in to fill silence. Instead, allow a moment for others to translate and process what has been asked and what they want to contribute.

Experiment smartly

The more you know about another culture, the better you will understand its members. The better you understand anyone, the easier it is to build and reinforce positive relationships, which are key to handling crises successfully.

Quick hits

- Look for practical ways to bridge, blend, or compromise across diverse cultural approaches.
- Seek cultural guidance from locals. Pay attention to their behaviors, and their reactions to your behaviors. Ask for their feedback.
- If you are handling the crisis from within another culture, strive to adopt routines and rhythms of daily life as you encounter it locally.
- Find a locally-versed confidante with whom you can discuss your experiences and lingering questions about their culture. Watch, listen and follow their lead. Request recommendations for your improvement at adapting.
- When novel cross-cultural behaviors become too challenging for you, ease up on your efforts. Simply aim to avoid speaking or acting inappropriately.

Address your own cross-cultural misgivings

It is natural for anxieties to arise when entering a new culture. In crisis situations, perplexing cross-cultural interactions can cause personal frustrations to soar. When you feel the personal toll mounting, or start to feel unhappy or resentful about cross-cultural interactions, turn your focus to personal recovery, then aim to return to the new culture with restored energy and enthusiasm.

Quick hits

- If your slump is compounded by lack of sleep, jet lag, or too many experiences far outside your comfort zone, take a break, get some rest.
- If you long for your own culture or language, connect with someone from your home country or someone who speaks your native language.
- Loosen any excessive expectations that you may hold about your cross-cultural encounters or achievements.
- Acknowledge how much you are learning. Commend yourself for your cross-cultural efforts and courage.

Up Next

Chapter 13 focuses on the impacts of digital fusion and the Fourth Industrial Revolution (4IR) on crises and crisis readiness. We'll look at how to deal with sharp time compression of contemporary crisis cycles, and how to deal with the digitally powered voice of individuals, impacts that churn crises and make containing them even more difficult to achieve today. We'll look at pros and cons of 4IR advances and accelerations when it comes to crises.

13

Privacy and the Grace Period are Vanishing

Welcome to the Fourth Industrial Revolution (4IR), where technologies fused across physical, digital, and biological platforms are transforming information access, connectivity, and power distribution.[58] Among them, artificial intelligence and machine learning, augmented reality, nano- and bio-technologies, robotic process automation, and quantum computing are facilitating and enhancing adaptability and routine problem-solving. Merged technologies are also accelerating and deepening detection and comprehension of urgencies, often automatically, sometimes instantaneously, even across the world.

The 4IR benefits for handling crises are stunning, ranging from examples like autonomous vehicles that avert collisions, to advanced security systems that decipher and shut down fraud, medical devices that regulate vital organs, and other types of sensors attached to or embedded in equipment, physical structures, and our bodies to track data, detect dangerous emerging patterns, and curb disaster. When dangerous thresholds are breached today, techno-pairings instigate action to preempt harm, often without human intervention. However, despite astounding contemporary benefits, forces unleashed by 4IR also launch, expand, and escalate organizational risks and crises. For example, accelerated speed of production and delivery may improve crisis responsiveness, but hasty advances can also intensify troubles. Instantaneous connectivity can strengthen notification and response to avoid or reduce damages, yet, that same ease of connecting can power incompetent or menacing individuals to stoke organizational crises.

THE INTERLUDE BETWEEN WARNINGS AND RESPONSE IS WITHERING

As mentioned earlier, in the past, when a crisis loomed, organizations could reasonably rely on a 24-hour grace period between detecting signals and announcing a prepared crisis response, align with local or state or national media outlets to avoid the spill of negative stories or critical speculation. Many gaps lasted days, weeks, or longer, providing invaluable time during which wise leaders could contemplate what they were facing, gather data and expert opinions, delve into details of what had happened, deliberate potential repercussions, weigh their options, customize their plans, and then communicate their intentions with confidence.

Many crisis plans still count on the gap, even though it no longer exists. Rather, negative incidents and impacts are easily and quickly sensationalized today. They can become fodder for clickbait, bringing attention and profits to those who showcase them. Simple, accessible photo and video capture can easily be made viral, to shrivel or extinguish organizational control. Bad news travels fast; bad news about prominent, successful, highly esteemed or irreputable organizations accelerates the transmission. If any shard of a grace period remains when an organizational crisis occurs today, communication experts estimate that it will last no more than 15 minutes.[59] If you doubt this sobering data, check the time stamp of the next organizational crisis news that you receive.

INDIVIDUAL VOICES ARE RESOUNDING AND ORGANIZATIONAL PRIVACY IS EVAPORATING

Individual voice has been amplified by the speed and reach of communication, and its consequential traction is significant. 4IR advances have democratized spotting trouble, breaking news, sharing opinions, and gathering support. Exposing organizational problems no longer requires extraordinary personal power or prestige. Rather, armed with commonplace e-gadgets and cheap, easy access to abundant information (fact or fantasy), a determined champion with a grievance or gripe can stir suspicions, expose organizational shortcomings, and track the fault lines that lie beneath them.

Today, even one determined 4IR-powered individual who is dissatisfied by an organization's product or service can alert thousands of people through texts and tweets to solicit their attention and support. With messages that can now be tailored precisely to varied audiences, they lure recipients into joining them in spewing criticisms. With a little perseverance, a sufficiently aggravated individual might even incite an international wave of complaints, and a flood of consumer demands.

A case in point: Luo Yonghao, a Chinese school teacher/blogger had a rather basic but vexing problem: the door of his Siemens refrigerator would not stay shut, and reactions from the manufacturer's local representatives were unsatisfactory. Luo even tried airing his complaint to corporate headquarters in Munich, to no avail. Still feeling stone-walled by Siemens, Luo aired his dissatisfaction on Sina Weibo, a Chinese microblogging site. Thousands of consumers responded to his gripe, many including details of their own similar problems.

Still lacking a fitting response, Luo staged a rage, smashing malfunctioning refrigerators at the gate of Siemens' China headquarters. There was no response. Then Luo took his approach to Beijing's Haidian Theater. This time, his tirade captured more than a quarter-million views on Youku, China's top rated video and streaming. With that, Luo finally captured attention in Munich.

Within weeks, Roland Gerke, CEO of Siemens China at the time, released a video apology, pledging repair of all complainants' defective appliances. Luo's victory brought adverse attention to Siemens globally, costing the company far more than if they had responded to any of Luo's earlier complaints. Although Siemens had sufficient resources to turn the situation around, their initial inept responses created a marketing and reputational fiasco, landing them among the top 10 mishandled communications crises of the year.[60]

Neither the evaporation of the grace period, nor the individual erosion of organizational privacy have received much attention yet in the broader crisis literature, but these shifts exemplify new trends that threaten organizational vulnerability directly, as powered by 4IR advances. They draw attention to the types of techno-fused complexities and their potential impacts that must be considered when preparing for crises today.

PRACTICAL IMPLICATIONS

Losing the grace period between signal and response, and considering other techno-fused changes resets all crisis preparation and responses. The likelihood that you would need to instantaneously fend off and contend with a crisis should inspire investments in careful advance thinking and contingency planning, anchored by smart preparations, sophisticated practice, and doing the right thing to begin with.

Foster technological/cross-cultural synergy

Cross-train your Crisis Leadership Team with your technology experts.

Quick hits

- Start the conversation. Schedule one meeting to challenge your CLT to identify and expand common ground in their strategies, tactics, and tools. For example, you might try blending scenario-based training with rapid experimentation techniques.
- Track what is being said online about your company, brands/products/services, and key leaders. Consider how your latest approaches could incite crises, cause harm, and land your organization in a techno-fused Hall of Shame.[61] Even a small organization can set up free Google Alerts, and other platforms offer more powerful capabilities for understanding the conversations about your organization and productively engaging in it.
- Encourage the CLT to develop practical crisis improvements collaboratively. For instance, consider how techno-fused equipment might be customized to detect crisis warning signals earlier.

- Task them with learning how techno-fusions are shaping crises and crisis readiness and response in your industry, then consider adopting and adapting the best practices they discover.

Greater improvements

- Create crisis-oriented scenarios and simulations focused on sharpening preparation and response through 4IR approaches. Evaluate 4IR tools and technologies for any underlying crisis vulnerabilities they may add.
- Evaluate how resources your organization relies on in crisis could be altered, positively or negatively, by techno-fusions. Create ways to apply your organization's latest technologies to regulate and enhance access, connectivity, and speed in crisis.
- Build information, knowledge, authority, resources, and recognition to empower the CLT.
- Where potentially dangerous techno-gaps exist anywhere in your organization, start advancing those sites up to par with your organization's best standards.

Practice crisis approaches under time scarcity

Quick hits

- Practice by using hypothetical scenarios, or discussing actual pressing issues while they are still problems rather than crises:
  - Rapidly identify and evaluate what (and how much) you know about the issues and what it could take to resolve them.
  - Rapidly estimate how you would gather additional information, and how certain you would be about your sources and their validity.

- Rapidly determine essential connections: key internal and external stakeholders, and outliers who could influence the issue.
  - Who in your organization would initiate connections?
  - What contact information would they use? Practice finding it.
- Develop crisis agility by accelerating the evolution of scenarios and simulations. Analyze, learn from, then incorporate best practices and improve trouble spots that emerge when working very rapidly.
- Gather data about the speeds at which your organization can do the following and at what confidence levels. Evaluate the data for shortcomings to address, add a timeline for improvement projects, use 4IR to your advantage.
  - Discover and report signals.
  - Investigate, gather data, collect feedback, communicate with experts.
  - Make applicable decisions.
  - Allocate resources and authority.
  - Implement relevant actions.
  - Verify effectiveness (such as the results of a mock recall).

Embrace the elevated power of individual voice

Quick hits

- Harvest gripes and complaints. Do not diminish or ignore them. Rather, build and implement practical lessons from them.
- Learn from adversaries' and competitors' criticism. Excavate underlying truths that could be dangerous and improve. Where warranted, solve those problems.

Greater improvements

- Don't attract legitimate attacks. Do not lie. Do not take dangerous shortcuts. Treat your employees, your customers, and the public right.
- Start with the assumption that complaints are important to the people who voice them, and to the success of your organization.
  - Hire and train excellent employees to address complaints and solve customer problems while they are still small and manageable.
  - Teach these employees to gather early warning signals, collating potential patterns among complaints.
  - Encourage them to think creatively, to notice and report potentially dangerous issues that lie beneath complaints. Build on their insights to innovate and power signal detection improvements.
- Audit your organization's reputation.
  - Gather candid evaluations of your organization from your employees, your customers/consumers, other organizations and leaders within your industry, and the public.
  - Listen especially closely to criticism and recommendations for improvements.
  - Take a step further to creatively consider potential vulnerabilities of your organization's recognized strengths.

Up Next

In the next chapter, we will take a different perspective of how today's technological advances distract attention and empathy, how to prepare for and deal with the effects of growing group solidarity and the narrowing of common interests and experience, and how to retain control of our attention and harness techno-convenience to optimize readiness and response to crises.

14

Our Attention has been Snatched, Our Empathy is Hardening

While some 4IR-powered changes threaten organizations directly, others debilitate crisis capabilities through their effects on individuals and relationships, mutual understanding, and empathy. The allure and convenience of techno-fusion can delay and distort how we make sense of situations and how effectively we filter fact from fiction. The selectivity built into techno-facilitated access makes it simple to find like-minded "friends" anywhere in the world, but the results can reduce empathy, which makes it even tougher to bridge differences in crises.

TECHNO-BUZZ IS MAKING US STUPID

With techno-gadgets in hand, we cycle through rapid-paced searches and instantaneous pleasure hits aimed at our hottest personal interests and desires with stunning accuracy. Fast-churning promises of immediate gratification keep us engaged with our gadgets as they tempt us to feed our cravings. Our brains reward us neurochemically for this engagement, as we comply with prompts for simple motor responses, one more swipe or click, our attention captured.

Buzz-Doom Loop

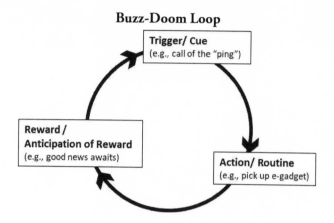

When we relinquish our attention to techno-tools, when fused technologies infatuate and stupefy us, the enduring negative impacts are outrageous. We do to ourselves what we would never let others to do to us. We allow our cognitive abilities to drift and fade. We permit our social skills to shrivel, and our self-awareness to melt away. In the clutch of techno-boosted physiological highs, we allow our personal energy and focus to dissipate.

Individually, we accept and personally reinforce all of these impairments despite the context of bold, conflicting needs that are fostered by the complexity and volatility of our contemporary environments. As we fall prey to frequent techno-interruptions, our thinking is scattered. We forfeit control over the rhythm of our work, whether by scurrying down alluring info-rich rabbit holes, or succumbing to acquaintances' and advertisers' posts on social media apps. Consenting to a short break mesmerizes us until we surface in shock that we have lost an hour or more. We tend to underestimate the length of our pursuit, and overestimate the quality.[62]

When techno-fusions command our attention, three vital ingredients for crisis success are impaired: deep thought, collaboration, and empathy. When we cede control of our attention, we permit our sensing, evaluating, and reasoning to dim. Our insights are short-circuited. When we break free and look up, we may recognize that we have missed subtle cues about what is happening, what has changed, and what may be at stake. We can miss important shifts in plain view. Losing cognitive adeptness is never a good thing, but when crises loom, interruptions and distractions can be deadly.

HOMOGENEOUS SELECTIVITY IS RISING, WHILE EMPATHY IS FADING

Since prehistoric times, groups have formed based primarily on co-location, mostly with people who live or work nearby. As they bridged their diverse viewpoints, the range of acceptable perspectives broadened for the group and its members. Today, techno-fusion is altering the nature of belonging.

Shared objectives, common interests, and tightly aligned values and preferences are overtaking proximity as fundamental criteria for group formation and identity. Techno-tailored information outlets and tightly honed search capabilities make it simple to find and connect with people who see the world exactly as we do. Now, homogeneously affiliated groups, across countless shared purposes or interests, are but a few clicks away, no matter where their members may be located.

This transition of selection criteria has intrinsic appeal: the more homogeneous a group, the smoother its interactions. Among those with shared perspectives, there is rarely strong disagreement, and little friction. In groups that self-select based on common ground, members understand each other from the start. But there is a significant downside. Homogeneous convergence blocks understanding and empathy, and this 4IR-facilitated impact can incite and intensify crises.

Corroboration hardens our perspectives, and makes them more brittle. Among people drawn together by very similar perspectives, there is no debate, no deep questioning of personal or collective perspectives, no internal correction of inaccurate assumptions or false narratives. Instead, in a homogeneous group, members' beliefs are validated consistently by the shared perspectives that brought them together, a cycle that is inherently biased.

With persistent confirmation, a homogeneous group and its members lose the ability to imagine or empathize with other viewpoints. Whether from within or outside, diverse voices become unthinkable, intolerable, unbearable, especially to staunch members. This selective deafness distorts and constricts decisions and actions across the group and among its individual members. When crises strike, these deficits and disruptions burn bridges, stalling and shortchanging relationships that are desperately needed to rise above threatening circumstances and uncertainties.

TECHNO-CONVENIENCE IS MAKING US CALLOUS

Crises require difficult conversations. Exceptional uncertainties, urgencies, and losses brought on by crises must be met with cognitive agility and emotional intelligence. Unfortunately, techno-convenience hampers empathic skills. The more we interact with and through technology, the less we relate directly with people. As a consequence, we lose practice listening, tuning in to others and their contexts, and managing our own reactions. When our emotional intelligence withers, we struggle to imagine the gravity of negative impacts that others experience. Even the presence of a phone nearby inhibits how we listen and diminishes our degree of connection and trust.[63]

On the surface, our handy 4IR devices seem to relax the effort, time, and patience needed to build and retain relationships. We can reconnect with long-lost colleagues and friends easily and quickly, for example. Asynchronous information exchanges enable us to avoid time-zone juggling, language barriers, and calendar conflicts. With techno-tools, we can even minimize or avert potentially disagreeable real-time and face-to-face challenges, and skirt unpleasant issues. The overall impact? Techno-mediated interactions seem so much simpler than dealing directly with people.

Thanks to their fast, low-effort, asynchronous features, communication channels like email and texting have long been default choices for many people, even when communicating profound news. But in pursuit of efficiency and ease, terse techno-interactions can nick relationships. Succinct e-swaps can feel blunt, abrupt, personally critical or denigrating, even under normal circumstances, even among cordial correspondents. Feeling snubbed or discounted can cause individuals to feel detached, which can exacerbate raw sensitivity to negative emotions. When trouble is looming, typical sentiments of anger, fear, and sadness make it tougher to rise above setback, mistakes, and threatening circumstances.

Some have become so hooked on techno-gadgets, they find it difficult to carry on a conversation or make eye contact. These impacts are predictable. Faceless techno-connections lack cues and clues of body language. In voiceless links, there are no expressive audibles, like speed, volume, and tone of speech. Over time, without opportunities to practice these as sender or receiver, even basic interpersonal skills atrophy.

We reinforce the cycle when we drift our attention from conversations into our e-gadgets, or disappear in online meetings, substituting our photos for video presence. The techno-interventions occur in person, too, when our eyes flit reflexively to the ping of our phones, even during crucial conversations. At home, we are seduced by our screens, even while relaxing with our partners or playing with our children. And the techno-tariffs are not borne by humans alone. Screen-time is even eroding one of our deepest intraspecies bonds: guidelines for rebuilding eye contact have entered the realm of dog training classes.

4IR tools are even delivering compassion conveniently. The unconditional, rapt attention and responsiveness of sociable robots is gaining ground on distracted humans. Mabu the humanoid health companion, AIBO the robotic dog, and PARO the therapeutic seal-shaped medical device are popular replacements for human care-givers. In response, care recipients are adapting, confiding their deepest human emotions to the robots, as if they were connecting with sentient beings.[64]

The human costs of techno-convenience are profound impairments to crisis detection and response. Steering away from real-time connections dumbs down our insights about crises and their impacts. Frequent techno-intervention diminishes our patience with people, especially through the tougher aspects that erupt during crises, like silence, emotional displays and disclosures, and random ramblings.

As we conveniently dodge or techno-terminate these elements of relating, we debilitate essential human intimacies for handling crises compassionately, effectively. When we relinquish our attention, we forfeit rapport and affinity. When interpersonal cues are inaccessible to us, when we miss priceless signs of the magnitude, urgencies, and impacts of crises, we fall short on individual and organizational responses.[65]

PRACTICAL IMPLICATIONS

To avert or mitigate crises requires careful, creative thinking, collaborative attention, and astute awareness of self and others. Adjustments made now can be invaluable for regaining and safeguarding awareness, attention, and relationships.

Teach and reinforce best practices for virtual teams

- Invest in the beginning. Get acquainted, socialize before working together.
- Keep expectations clear across the team. Keep work and accountability visible.
- Reinforce progress through prompt, detailed feedback.
- Step in when there is a lack of participation. E-silence is not compliance or consensus.
- Encourage and model openness, disclosure.
- Schedule virtual meetings to suit all time zones, rotating preferred times if needed.
- Celebrate accomplishments virtually, across the team.

To think better in 4IR, take back control of your time

Quick hits

- Practice monitoring and managing the rhythm of your work.
- Learn what supports your best performance, while guarding your energy and resilience.
- Get the feel of slowing down when you are deliberating, planning, and preparing.
- Build experience and insights that will help you reserve rapid-fire decision and action for true urgencies.

Evaluate your technology dependence via gadgets, screen-scrolling, internet alerts, and e-feeds

- Separate leisure apps from work-related apps. You might also turn off social app notifications.
- Schedule times to unwind from neuro-stimulated seeking loops.
- Fastidiously sculpt the techno-uses to work for you, then stick to your plan.

Monitor your techno-tendencies now. First, tune into assumptions that you hold about your time on screens. Log your answers.

- Which technologies do you believe save you time or make you more effective? How?
- How much time do you think you spend on your screens every day?
- What is the quality of your screen time? How much of it actually improves your work or personal life?

Next, audit your actual e-habits, using a timer or an app.

- Before engaging with an e-gadget, estimate what you expect to accomplish and how much time it will take you.
- When you have finished, before checking your data, jot down how much time you believe you actually spent, and what you actually gained.
- Compare your estimates to the data.

Then, think very carefully about which of your e-habits are worth your priceless, non-renewable resource: *time*. Build effective time management skills now. As sharply as they are affecting you in normal times, in crisis, they could make the difference between safety and danger, survival and demise.

Get comfortable off devices

Practice using tools deliberately. Work toward these manifestations of control.

- I begin my day with something essential, uplifting, and non-electronic.
- I stick to my schedule, despite e-avalanches.
- I use fixed blocks of limited time for emailing and texting.
- I set a timer before engaging in social media.
- I connect with people and information purposefully, rather than web-surfing, scrolling, and freewheeling.
- I avoid suggestion-based rabbit holes when using my gadgets.
- I shut down my neuro-stimulated seeking loop and push my device out of reach the moment I forget what I was looking for or recognize that I am lost in an e-feed.

Quit multitasking

Stick with one task at a time. Build muscle with important tasks initially, then start to increase your tolerance for uni-tasking with a few mundane tasks, occasionally.

- Do not allow unimportant influences to divert your attention into multitasking.
- Steer clear of alluring distractions. Keep e-gadgets out of reach, and silence them.
- Measure performance improvement, and stress reduction.

Improve deeper thinking

- Give your mind some space.
  - Block unscheduled time daily, to ponder/wonder/imagine, in silence, alone, even just for a few minutes.

- o Exercise. Take a walk. Practice relaxation.
- o Focus on family. Call a friend.
- o Meditate. Practice visualization. Breathe deliberately.
- o Keep a journal.
- o Go deep on a hobby.
- o Identify and practice your preferred ways to disconnect from technology.
- Find or create appealing settings for thinking or working quietly, without interruption, for solo tasks and collaborative efforts.
- Face challenging tasks by taking your time and setting your own pace.
- Attend meetings with a pen and paper, rather than your devices, and make them available at meetings.
- If device distraction during meetings is becoming the norm, read the room, then open a discussion:
  - o What is distracting our attention?
  - o Why are we disappearing into our gadgets?
  - o Who or what is setting this standard for us, and why?

Push back on mind-narrowing homogeneity

Quick hits

- Join groups or affiliations that will expand your thinking.
- Get involved with purposes that are appealing to you, especially those you have never explored.
- Civilly adopt a devil's advocate view during discussions, occasionally.
  - o Observe reactions to your perspective.
  - o Discuss potential values of testing and stretching your views as individuals and as groups.
  - o Aim to discover the reasoning behind diverse lines of thinking.

Greater improvements

- Connect smartly with people whose views and backgrounds differ from your own.
    - Aim to understand the foundations of their perspectives.
    - Get to know them as individuals.
    - Tune into rather than out of dissenting opinions, especially in difficult times.
    - Encourage your subordinates to do the same.
- Implement cross-training or job shadowing to build appreciation for others' jobs and responsibilities.

APPLY CONSCIOUS EFFORT TO RELATE BETTER IN 4IR

When gadgets and people vie for your attention, choose people over devices. Demonstrate that you are doing this conscientiously.

Quick hits

- When you are with people, aim to connect with them solidly.
- When you are bored or restless with people, tune in, not out.
- Audit how your devices help or hinder your bonds with people. Start with your closest relationships.
- If you absolutely cannot give priority to people in the moment, let them know that. Agree on how and when you will talk with them, and fulfill that commitment.
- Practice taking control back from your devices until it becomes automatic.
- Do not interrupt conversations to check your smart phone, watch, or laptop. Kick the impulse to avoid looking like a trained seal.

- If you anticipate an electronic interruption that is unavoidable, let people know that before conversing.
- In conversation, turn your back on your computer, and silence your phone and put it out of sight. Do not let the presence of a phone cause typical losses, such as inhibiting how you listen and diminishing the degree of connection or trust that you and others will feel.[66]

Challenge email as your communication default

Aim to use email only for brief, straight-forward, task-focused messages. Always choose a richer, more personal medium, such as in-person conversation, videoconferencing, or a phone call for all of the following goals:

- Sympathize, apologize, or console.
- Mentor.
- Introduce a major change.
- Provide significant feedback (positive or negative).
- Clear up misunderstandings.

Sharpen emotional and social intelligence to overcome techno-distractions and shortcomings

- When you sense the need to step back from technology, step back.
- Make time to relate personally during breaks or lunch.
- Appreciate the power of pauses and silence. Practice sitting with silence during meetings and conversations. Do not talk or escape into devices to fill the void.
- Master eye contact, including learning, accepting, and practicing cross-cultural variations on norms. Get comfortable with lack of eye-contact from others.
- In e-communications, keep your tone realistically positive to counter negative interpretations, which are common in e-space.

- Tune into cross-cultural variances in e-communications. Pay attention to your correspondents' formal versus familiar tone, and the extent of personal information they share. Where comfortable for you, adapt to recipients' styles in your communications with them.
- Practice relating-by-walking-around. Wander gadget-free. Aim to make eye contact and non-verbally acknowledge anyone you encounter with a quick nod or a smile.
- If you come within closer proximity of someone, say hello.

PAY CONSCIOUS ATTENTION TO THINK BETTER IN 4IR.

Build tolerance for quiet, slower thinking, and broad techno-free connections

Quick hits

- Give people time and space to work out some problems on their own, so that they can develop strong skills with undivided attention and solitude.
- Don't confuse time on task with speed to goal, nor velocity with your destination.
- Discuss when to use and put aside devices during a crisis. Practice and reinforce these distinctions during crisis preparation, planning, and simulations.

Greater improvements

- Build shared experiences without technology at all levels so that individuals can develop comfort and competence undistracted, off devices, and without constant techno-buzz.

PRACTICE DISENGAGING FROM DEVICES

Quick hits

- Emphasize the value of undisturbed attention and thought, especially in crisis.
- Help people devise and practice physical, reflexive reactions the moment they recognize they are caught in a loop. Teach them to tap the close button or toss the gadget out of reach as a reflexive reaction.
- Take meetings off-line. Make them gadget-free. For private conversations, take a walk together while you talk.
- Designate some gadget-free space within your work environment.

PRACTICE TEAM DECISION-MAKING IN THE FACE OF UNPREDICTABILITY

Greater improvements

- Teach, practice, and provide feedback on table-top scenarios to think and experiment quickly and reactively, and discuss when and why that approach is desirable. (See Chapter 17.)
- Do the same with more extensive scenario-based discussions and simulations to think deeply and broadly, and discuss when and why that approach is desirable.
- Model and teach rising above impatience and anxiety when a solution is not obvious.
- Model and teach asking questions with greater curiosity and openness, and with less certainty and advocacy.

PRACTICE BEHAVIORS THAT POWER COLLABORATION

Quick hits

- Stop texting or screen scrolling during conversations, even phone or video conversations. These telltale nonverbal signs extinguish connection and collaboration.
- Review basics of teaming versus delegation: why, when, and how.
- Coach and provide feedback for relationship fundamentals:
  - How to start and end conversations.
  - How to find common ground with others.
  - How to reflect understanding and personal connecting while listening.
  - How to avoid listening blocks, such as rehearsing, daydreaming, and comparing.

Greater improvements

- When hiring and promoting, prioritize candidates' abilities to develop relationships and share power and credit.
- When diverse or complex insights or actions are needed, encourage teamwork.
- Create workplace opportunities for casual, face-to-face conversations. Host lunches or social breaks occasionally, whether in-person or virtual.
- Build tolerance and appreciation for device-free meetings. At first, provide frequent short breaks for device access, then gradually build longer device-free endurance.

———————————— Up Next ————————————

Chapter 15 focuses on how and when to set our habits aside to avert and mitigate crises, how to keep habitual responses from blocking danger signals or exceptional actions that may be needed, and how to recognize and harness habit-based errors to improve individual and organizational crisis capabilities.

15

Our Habits are Dulling Our Insights

We try very hard not to think on our feet.
— James Reason

habit: *an acquired mode of behavior that has become nearly or completely involuntary*[67]

Without habits, we could not function. Our days would be devoured as we weighed the pros and cons of even the simplest decisions, an effort that would guzzle our time and exhaust our thinking. Organizational success depends on the appropriate execution of habits individually and collectively. When we apply habits correctly, we gain efficiency. The predictability of our habits permits us to anticipate others' behaviors to coordinate our efforts. Luckily, habits guide about half our waking hours.[68]

We build habits by repeating behaviors that are reinforced physically and neurologically until they become nearly automatic. In the habit cycle, a cue triggers our behavior to act in a routine way. Cues include people, places, times of day, symbols, sounds, and scents. We sense the cue (arrive at work, return home, reenter our childhood home, hear a siren, smell our favorite cookies) and we react in our usual ways. For habits to stick, the consequence of our behavior must bring an outcome that we desire, or diminish or stop an outcome we wish to avoid. With each repetition of the cycle, the habit deepens.

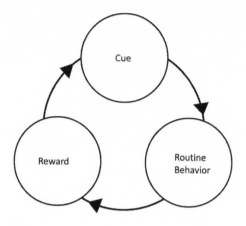

When danger lurks, habits free us to turn our thoughts to emerging hazards. They guide our habitual actions even before we recognize the nature or source of trouble. Effective habits help us summon assistance and take urgent corrective action promptly, with accuracy. We pull an alarm when we smell smoke, look to the source when we hear a loud whistle, and pull over when we hear a siren. Even from childhood, we learned to redirect our attention and brace for danger, responding automatically to words like, "Help!" and "Look out!"

The quality of a habit rests on two criteria: (1) Does the habit fit the circumstance? (2) Is the habit being applied effectively? Ill-chosen and ineffective habits lead to errors, which can cause delays, accidents, and injuries. In the worst cases, using the wrong habits, or applying the right habits in the wrong ways can lead to crises. Understanding that risk is key to averting and handling crises.

THE PERILS OF HABIT

We get into the habit of living before acquiring the habit of thinking.
— Albert Camus

During crises, habits can help us maneuver through danger, or misguide our responses. When normal habit cycles persist despite novel cues or dynamic contexts, rather than solving or preventing crises, patterned behaviors may deepen or escalate them. Leaning on customary actions dims attention and stifles sensitivities to what might have changed.

Habit errors can be caused by using the wrong habit or applying the right habit in the wrong way. When differences are faint, we tend to stick with habits, even when they are dramatically unfitting to new circumstances. Dangerous complications can arise when action guidelines or training are created by people who have never performed the task, or when they assume operators will be able to respond automatically to situations that actually require extraordinary reactions.

Habit errors can be caused by using the wrong habit or applying the right habit in the wrong way. Dangerous complications arise when action guidelines or training are created by people who have never performed the task that they are instructing. Perilous aspects also emerge (1) when designers assume that operators will be able to respond automatically to situations that would require extraordinary reactions, or (2) when designers lack full understanding of how their design could malfunction.

Pilots are trained to make appropriate choices along the fine line between following procedures explicitly, and making extraordinary judgment calls in the spur of the moment, sometimes sealing hundreds of peoples' fates in the balance. When Lion Air Flight 610 plunged nose-first into the Java Sea shortly after takeoff, all 189 passengers and crew were killed. Investigations revealed that the pilots had attempted 20 times to right the Boeing 737 MAX (B737 MAX) airplane, but their actions were overridden by the malfunctioning of the MCAS (Maneuvering Characteristics Augmentation System), the plane's automatic anti-stall software. Less than five months later, a similar accident cost the lives of all 157 passengers and crew aboard Ethiopian Airlines (ETH) Flight 30 when a malfunctioning sensor erroneously indicated that the plane was on the verge of stalling. The MCAS activated automatically, pitching the B737 MAX into an unrecoverable 700 mile per hour dive that formed a crater 30 feet deep.

In both cases, preliminary speculations pinned the accidents on pilot error. However, investigations concluded that the pilots had applied appropriate responses and sound expertise. In both cases, they were applying the right habits in the right ways. The National Transportation Safety Board investigation also concluded that Boeing had underestimated the effect that a malfunction of the MCAS would have on flight crew members, and that pilots could immediately counteract and correct the system.[69]

A trail of latent conditions preceded these accidents. Concerns about the B737 MAX had been raised by Boeing test pilots years before the crashes, and Boeing engineers had proposed that MCAS alert systems be added to the cockpit.[70] After the crises, Boeing was charged with conspiracy to defraud the Federal Aviation Administration, and two of its Flight Technical Pilots for the B737 MAX were charged with criminal misconduct. Attorney Erin Nealy Cox was quoted by the US Department of Justice: "The misleading statements, half-truths, and omissions communicated by Boeing employees to the FAA impeded the government's ability to ensure the safety of the flying public. This case sends a clear message: The Department of Justice will hold manufacturers like Boeing accountable for defrauding regulators—especially in industries where the stakes are this high." Boeing agreed to pay over $2.5 billion, which included criminal penalty and compensation payments to Boeing's 737 MAX customers and the beneficiaries of victims who died in the Lion Air 610 and Ethiopian Airlines 302 crashes.[71] Boeing's former CEO, Dennis Muilenburg, was fired by the Board of Directors.[72]

The details of these extraordinary crises continue to draw global scrutiny from regulators, pilots, passengers, and the media. Opportunities for learning from this situation are extraordinary, regarding all of these stakeholders. Lessons and guidance throughout this book are readily applicable to these Boeing crashes, and should serve as warnings, especially, for organizations that are currently choosing to ignore latent conditions or dramatic warning signals.

Of much broader impact, habits can also inject troubles into mildly challenging decisions and actions. For example, confusion is especially likely to stir danger when adjusting to new contexts or situations, for example, when habit cues *seem* familiar, but are not.

Consider the relatively mundane experience of driving a car in a new location from the opposite side of the road. In the beginning, with keen alertness to differences, we may find the transition easier than anticipated—until we arrive at a congested intersection. Here, new parameters (unfamiliar merging patterns, incomprehensible road signs, uninterpretable nonverbal cues from passing drivers) increase the conflict between our newly successful adaptations for driving on the opposite side of the road and our normal, proven driving habits. We may experience cognitive tunneling, losing our ability to process the relevance of contextual information and respond in time. Behaviorally, we are likely to revert to our familiar muscle-memory habits impulsively, and disregard imminent dangers in doing so.

People also tend to stick with habits whenever tools *seem* similar to those already mastered, but are not. Returning to our roadway situation, if a sudden downpour occurs, we may turn on the headlights, radio, and heater before finding the windshield wipers, reverting to habits based on our own cars' equipment locations. If we happen to be highly trained or deeply experienced drivers, we might be able to adjust quickly, but most individuals will be disoriented. Those wise enough to recognize their lack of control may find a safe route out of traffic to sort things out and diminish the danger.

These examples of adapting driving habits incorporate cognitive, behavioral, and emotional challenges, but they are relatively minor stressors because many standard assumptions and driving practices (cues/behaviors/consequences) do not change. By contrast, crisis parameters often include deep shifts, profound unknowns, and intense time pressures, as experienced by the B737 MAX pilots. Many crisis options may be grim. Reliable habits may fail under new stresses brought on by unfamiliar equipment. The intensity and uncertainty may confound urgent choices and put unthinkable stresses on equipment and people, including decisions about whether to apply, adjust, or abandon habits.

Now, add fundamental interpersonal challenges that arise in crisis, including bewilderment and disagreements. Then, add the pressures to learn collaboration, immediately, ad hoc, often with strangers, under time crunch, with innumerable uncertainties. Mix in diverse, deeply rooted values and preferences that will add ambiguity, confusion, and sometimes hostility to interpreting others' behaviors. It is no wonder that the attention and insight needed to spot, interpret, and alter habit patterns (despite the differing assumptions, norms, and values) will profoundly influence collaboration, and therefore, the evolution of the crisis and effectiveness of responses.

THE HAZARDOUS DEMOCRACY OF HABIT FAILURES

The speed, complexity, and connectivity of today's work environment can launch any employee, at any level, with any quantity or quality of experience or expertise into a vital crisis response role, and they will choose—consciously or not—whether to persevere, adapt, or relinquish habits when novel situations or signals occur. In emergencies, first-responder employees anywhere in an organization may have to make excruciating decisions rapidly, sometimes without access to anyone with greater authority or expertise. They may be forced to creatively concoct alternatives or radically reshape options, without verification or authorization for their choices, which may be further encumbered by dangerous contexts, causes, and impacts.

The democracy of crisis response is one more reason why the common practice of limiting crisis preparations to formal leaders must change. While those at the top may get extensive information and practice, those at the bottom may learn only rote responses, or specific habit sequence adaptations geared exclusively to predictable interruptions of their specific tasks. In some organizations, even under normal conditions, lower level workers who detour from prescribed habits typically encounter criticism or penalties, even if their actions were warranted by exceptional circumstances, inappropriate tools, or lack of accurate information. This norm sets the stage for disaster. Where employees at any level are underprepared, reluctant, unwilling, or unable to adjust or cease unfit habits, the likelihood, dangers and impacts of crisis intensify. When trouble is brewing, individuals and teams that are driven blindly by habit will miss novel warnings, and respond inappropriately, automatically. When ineffective habits kick in, if emerging misfitting signals are met with entrenched passivity, the underlying problems and blind-sightedness can morph into catastrophe.

THE POWER OF JUST ONE (HABITUAL) WORD

It took more than a year for the US National Transportation Safety Board (NTSB) to sort out why and how Avianca flight 052 (AVA052) crashed into a hillside in a wooded residential area of Cove Neck, New York. After deep investigation, the probable cause was determined to be the inability of the crew to manage fuel load, a fundamental vulnerability of flight. Furthermore, as with all crises, the fate of AVA052 was agitated by a deadly layering of intricate problems, the most tragic among them sprang directly from habits missed and misapplied.

Recorded dialogue among AVA 052's flight crew and air traffic controllers (ATC) exposed the lethal impact of inconsistent execution of fundamental cue and response habits. In this particular case, the cue-response cycle was made ineffective by the absence of just one word, and the consequence was fatal.

AVA052 carried a three-person flight crew.

	L. Caviedes-Hoya	M. Klotz	M. Moyano
JOB/TITLE	Captain	Co-pilot	Flight Engineer
AGE	51	28	45
TENURE AT AVA	27 years	3 years	23 years
TOTAL FLT HRS.	16,787	1,837	10,134
B707 FLT HRS.	1,534	64 (as co-pilot)	3,077
NIGHT FLT HRS.	2,435	408	2,986
B707 NIGHT FLT HRS.	478	13	1,062

The verbatim transcript segments below begin as AVA052 enters the airspace of New York's Kennedy Airport (JFK). The plane, which is running out of fuel, is being directed into its third holding pattern of the night. All three members of the flight crew are aware of the fuel shortage.

20:44:43 [time stamps reflect local eastern standard time in 24-hour notation]

Klotz: "Thank you sir. You have any estimates for us?"

ATC: "Avianca 052 expect further clearance time."

Klotz: "Zero five two, well, I think we need priority. We're passing (unintelligible)."

ATC: "Avianca 052, Roger, how long can you hold and what is your alternate [airport]?"

Klotz: "Okay, stand by on that."

Klotz: "Yes sir, we'll be able to hold about five minutes. That's all we can do."

ATC: "Avianca 052 what is your alternate?"

Klotz: "It is Boston, but we can't do it now. We will run out of fuel now."

[AVA 052 is quickly folded into the landing pattern by ATC. Meanwhile, within the cabin, Moyano reads aloud flight manual operating procedures for low fuel emergencies.]

21:19:58

JFK Tower: "Avianca 052...cleared to land."

Klotz: "Slightly below glide slope."

Klotz: "Below glide slope."

[Within the cockpit, altitude alert chimes sound 15 times. The first 11 warnings signal that the plane is below the path of safe descent for landing. The next four alerts warn the flight crew to "pull up" to avoid running into the ground. During warnings, dialogue within the cockpit continues.]

21:22:57

Caviedes: "Where is the runway?

Caviedes: "The runway, where is it?"

Klotz: "I don't see it. I don't see it."

[Flight pattern records show that, at this time, the plane was still 1.3 miles from the approach end of the runway.]

Klotz: [to JFK Tower]: "Executing a missed approach."

JFK Tower: "Avianca 052, Roger. Climb and maintain two thousand turn left heading one eight zero."

21:23:43

Caviedes: "We don't have fue-..."

Caviedes: [to Klotz] "Tell them we are in emergency."

Klotz: [to JFK Tower] "That's right to one eight zero on the heading and we'll try once again. We're running out of fuel."

JFK Tower: "Okay."

Caviedes: "What did he say?"

Caviedes: "Advise him we are emergency."

Caviedes: "Did you tell him?"

Klotz: "Yes sir, I already advised him."

JFK Tower: "Avianca 052, contact approach..."

Klotz: [to Tower]: "Approach Avianca 052, we just missed a missed approach and we're maintaining two thousand..."

JFK Approach: "Avianca 052...climb and maintain three thousand."

21:25:08

Caviedes: "Advise him we don't have fuel."

Klotz: "...Maintain three thousand and we're running out of fuel, sir."

JFK Approach: "Okay, fly heading zero eight zero."

Klotz: "Flying heading zero eight zero climb to three thousand."

21:25:28

Caviedes: [to Klotz] "Did you already advise that we don't have fuel?"

Klotz: "Yes, sir, I already advise him...we are going to maintain three thousand feet and he's going to get back to us."

Caviedes: "Okay."

JFK Approach: "And, Avianca 052 I'm gonna bring you about 15 miles north east and then turn you back onto the approach. Is that fine with you and your fuel?"

Klotz: "I guess so. Thank you very much."

21:29:11

Klotz: [to JFK Approach]: "Can you give us a final now?"

JFK Approach: "Avianca 052, affirmative sir turn left heading...Avianca 052, climb and maintain three thousand."

Klotz: "Negative sir. We just running out of fuel, we okay three thousand now okay."

JFK Approach: "Okay, turn left heading three one zero sir."

21:32:39

Moyano: "Flame out, flame out on engine number four."

[Flameout is the failure of a jet engine because flame in the combustion chamber has been extinguished.]

21:32:43

Moyano: "Flameout engine number three, essential on number two on number one."

Caviedes: "Show me the runway."

Klotz: "Avianca 052, we just, ah, lost two engines and we, ah, need priority please."

JFK Approach: "Avianca 052, turn left heading two five zero…Avianca 052, you're one five miles from outer marker, maintain two thousand until established on the localizer cleared for ILS two two left."

Klotz: "Roger, Avianca."

21:33:22

Caviedes: [to Klotz]: "Did you select the ILS?"

Klotz: "It is ready on two."

*** End of recording from Avianca 052. ***

ATC: "You have, ah, you have enough fuel to make it to the airport?"

Sixty-five passengers (adults and children), and five flight attendants died. All three flight crew members were fatally injured on impact. Eighty additional passengers (adults, children, and infants) and the sole surviving flight attendant suffered severe injuries.

Many questions still linger.[73] At the core are errors of habit, warnings missed and ignored. The fatal failure was the absence of just one word among several possibilities that signal flight crisis universally: "Emergency!" "Mayday!" or "Pan-pan!"

That night, some experts got stuck in their habits, while others did not perform theirs. ATCs missed repeated cues that the plane was "running out of fuel." A highly experienced chief pilot, who persistently and precisely warned "emergency," continued to defer communication to and from the cockpit to his far less-experienced copilot. In-flight safety habits for the cabin were never invoked.

There were no warnings by the captain or copilot to flight attendants or passengers regarding the low fuel, the loss of engines, or the possibility of an emergency landing. No one was alerted to secure seat belts. No one was told to assume brace position, or to brace children and infants, who were catapulted through the cabin on impact. No instructions were given about evacuation. None of these deeply drilled safety habits were executed.

According to survivors, the only signal of trouble before the crash was a few moments of darkness, and quiet.[74] Yet, as conditions worsened during final approaches into JFK, it is clear that the captain, copilot, and flight engineer were aware of life-threatening hazards. According to the surviving flight attendant, when she entered the cockpit to inquire about flight status, shortly before the crash, the engineer covertly signaled disaster by running his hand across his throat.

PRACTICAL IMPLICATIONS

When crisis looms, the first assumption to adjust is that *normal* no longer is. What exists now: (1) is different, (2) is potentially dangerous, (3) may be worsened by customary, firmly established habits that could be dysfunctional, and (4) should be evaluated conspicuously as related to habits honed for extraordinary situations.

Habit agility derives from awareness, training, and practice to catch inappropriate habits, then adapt or dismiss before they act on them. Attention should be directed, promptly, to habits that could lead mindlessly into deeper difficulties. These recommendations improve habit awareness and adaptability personally, and across organizations.

PERSONAL APPROACHES

In a potential threat, first center yourself and sharpen your focus.

Quick hits

- **Build a habit of pausing as soon as you sense trouble.** Insert a brief hesitation to disrupt the cue and your response, providing space for your new desired behavior to replace the habit you do routinely.

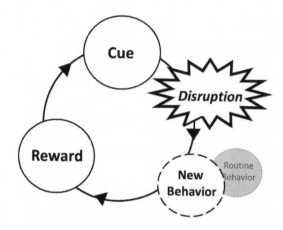

- Build comfort in procrastinating intentionally, practice marking your pause physiologically by taking a deep breath.
  - To engrain the habit, practice hesitating when you encounter lesser obstacles.
- Take actions to collect your thoughts.
  - Take a few deep breaths to slow things down and center your focus.
  - Make notes (mental or written) about what has happened and what lies ahead.
  - List possible next steps.

- o To clear your mind and sharpen your focus, move, walk, drink some water, get some fresh air, or use a focal point to center your thoughts.
- Maintain focus on cues, responses, and potential outcomes.
  - o When you detect signals, tune in, not out.
  - o Do not waste time attempting to attribute or escape blame.
  - o Keep your attention on what you need to do to stop or improve the situation.
- Soak up additional information, solo or with others.
  - o Focus all senses on what is occurring. If possible and safe, watch, touch, taste, smell, and listen for yourself.
  - o Describe or discuss what you see, what you plan to do, what you are taking for granted, and how your assumptions are guiding your plans.

In novel situations, assume differences, rather than defaulting to habitual thoughts or actions

- Focus on how and why the current situation is unlike past challenges.
- Consider how and why normal habit cycles could falter now.
- Consider how and why novel complications could arise from responding as you typically do.
- Before using familiar tools or approaches automatically, determine whether they will match or fail what you are sensing now and how.
- Consider how existing tools or approaches might be used in a new way.
- Consider how new tools or approaches might be needed.

ORGANIZATIONAL APPROACHES

Explore the role of habits during investigations.

Before faulting employees at any level for what may seem like careless errors, explore with them the influence of established habits that proved ill-fitting to the problem or crisis. Delve beyond inappropriate habits and mishandlings to examine how wrong habits and misapplications may have been stirred by the crisis.[75]

Quick hits

- Ask about underlying conditions, contexts, and shifts of situations that arose.
- Determine how goals and reward structures (individual, team or organizational) may have reinforced ineffective habits.
- Learn whether appropriate tools were available and functioning properly.
- Investigate how standard procedures or customary equipment might have led to inappropriate decisions or actions in crisis.

Greater improvements

- Reshape cues, behaviors, and consequence to reflect appropriate adaptations for the future.

Before any crisis occurs, fix habits that tend to slow or stifle response

Quick hits

- **Incorporate users' perspectives to assess and improve habits.**
  - Keep an open mind when users complain or offer suggestions.

o   Rather than pushing back, make "thank you" your immediate response.

o   With genuine curiosity, discuss with employees any guidelines or procedures they avoid and why they cut corners. Then, revise or eliminate unnecessary performance obstructions and reinforce which procedures must be followed, why, and how.

o   Regularly ask task experts to identify potential faults or shortcomings in the procedural habits that drive their performance. Learn about relevant improvements for patterned responses, and implement wherever feasible.

Greater improvements

- **Reduce or eliminate unnecessary barriers to desired habits.**
    o   Build and hone prompt, easily accessible routes to expertise and approval for emergency situations, including 24-hour coverage.
    o   Identify, reevaluate, and improve any procedures that are ignored consistently.
    o   Use strict rules only where actually necessary, for example, to assure safety.
    o   Eliminate unnecessary layers of authorization or sign-offs for doing the right thing.

Teach employees the pros and cons of the habit cycle

Quick hits

- **Help employees understand potential dangers of habits.**
    o   Solicit specifics related to their own responsibilities.
    o   Teach them how to dissect cues and response consequences that can lock in their habitual responses, even when inappropriate or potentially dangerous.

Greater improvements

- **Lead closer examination of specific habit-based procedures.**
  Identify habit cues, behaviors, and consequences that are ineffective,
  unnecessary, gawky or time-consuming, and work together to
  improve them.

Drive crisis detection, reporting, and response habits all the way to the front line, where signs of crises often originate

Quick hits

- **Evaluate your organization's current crisis preparations and
  practice.** Be sure to include front line employees, their supervisors,
  and others who may not be included fully in your crisis approach,
  such as those working from home or at remote international sites.
  To direct your evaluation, consider questions like these:
    o What crisis discussions and training do employees
      receive—or lack?
    o Does their preparation reflect the crisis-relevant roles they
      might have to fill?
    o How can we improve crisis prevention and response
      preparations beyond pure habit-based responses?

Engage champions for crisis preparation at all levels, not just the top.

Quick hits

- Emphasize varied vantage points for understanding and addressing
  questions and concerns of key external stakeholders.
- Increase their opportunities to discuss and provide input, feedback,
  and recommendations for crisis tools, practices, and access.

Greater improvements

- Increase the breadth and depth of information and preparations for front-line employees and supervisors. Add some training and practice with tabletop scenarios and *What if?* thinking, for example.
- Teach and test to verify that they understand the outer bounds of their authority for adjusting and fixing potential dangers. Give them access to resources and expertise for prompt, appropriate decisions and actions under novel threatening circumstances.

Harness the power of crises and near misses to improve habit application in good times and bad

Greater improvements

- Take advantage of the energy and momentum of crises and their aftermath to streamline, sharpen, or extinguish habits. Pinpoint habit-based complications that arose, then learn and teach how to improve them.
- After a crisis or near miss, aim to learn about and replace faulty organizational habits, rather than blaming those who followed them.

——————————— Up Next ———————————

Chapter 16 focuses on another obstacle that can deepen dangers and undermine crisis responses: our biases. We will evaluate personal biases that can lead us to misjudge context, decisions, and actions, intensifying crises, and consider how to identify and reduce our personal blind spots to enhance our insights and actions before, during, and after crises.

16

Our Biases are Blinding Us
Into and Out of Crises

We have met the enemy and he is us.
– Walt Kelly's character Pogo[76]

bias: *a tendency to think, act, or feel in a particular way*[77]

For better and for worse, biases are part of human nature. Without them, we would encounter every experience as if it were brand new. Instead, biases permit us to perceive our world selectively, often by sensing only a fraction of the stimuli that surround us at any time. The biases that we hold reflect and reinforce our narrowed truths, creating a closed loop among (1) our beliefs about how the world operates, (2) the data, information, and evidence that we perceive, and (3) the ways in which we make sense of what we perceive and remember.

We reveal our biases (to others and ourselves) in our opinions, feelings, preferences, and actions. At best, they give us a starting place to help us manage information efficiently. In today's challenging environment, biases can help us ease our way through information overload, enhance our ability to adapt to complexities, and make sense of uncertainties. When accurate and fitting, our biases streamline our thinking and broaden our understanding.

Unfortunately, biases can also stifle and diminish us. They influence our thoughts, feelings, and actions even when they are unreasoned, untrue, or unfair, and even when we are unaware that we are being influenced by them. Biases lead us to misjudge people, situations, causes, and effects, multiplying our potential errors. At worst, when biases cause us to miss the full picture or trap us in familiar perspectives that are no longer valid, they can fuel troubles into crises.[78]

HOW BIASES BOGGLE CRISIS PREPARATION AND RESPONSE

The fatigue, distress, and negative emotions of crises make us more susceptible to inaccurately biased thinking. Our biases can lead us to distort new information, jumble our memories, and suppress our ability to imagine others' perspectives, all of which blind us to crises and block our exit from them. In the crisis context, biases can blur signs of danger, close our minds to essential insights, and divert our attention from effective responses and remedies.

Biases lure us into perceiving what we expect, strengthening the hold of our existing opinions, and hampering our struggles to comprehend or reason through novel, possibly threatening information. When we recede into deep-rooted biases and prevailing frames of mind, we trap ourselves in our troubles. Then we seal the cycle as we reject additional cues or conditions that challenge our perspectives. Consequently, we miss incoming insights, and crush our willingness and ability to imagine, realize, and respond. Also, with or without recognizing it, we send subtle cues to others about what we expect of them. This extends the influence of our biases, guiding their reactions, to further curtail or derail their preparations and responses to crisis.

REMOVING THE BLINDERS OF BIAS

The first step toward reducing the constrictive influences of bias is self-awareness. Recognizing our own biases helps us relax judgment, which can open our minds to understand others' perceptions, values, beliefs, and contexts. The better we understand others, the easier it is to identify common ground and coordinate our efforts, even in dreadful situations. Recognizing and guarding against the limitations of our own biased blind spots[79] even seeds our insight to appreciate how others' biases might limit their thoughts and actions. It is impossible to overstate the importance of addressing biases for effectively analyzing, planning, and responding in crises.

The number of possible biases may be infinite, but those that follow were selected because they can be particularly harmful during crises. As you read these examples, your first reaction could be, "Not me." You may be correct in many cases, but do not miss the irony: dismissing our own inclinations and tendencies is one of the most common biases.

Self-awareness is a great lever for overcoming undesirable bias. Begin your reflection with this short list. Do any describe your own preferred ways of thinking, feeling, and behaving? They should! These perspectives are so widespread, they are considered human nature. Of course, not all biases pertain to everyone, but if you cannot see any of your own tendencies here, try reading the list again, with your less-then-ideal self in mind.

WIDESPREAD BIASES

We believe that we see reality precisely as it is.

We overestimate the accuracy of our knowledge, our perspectives, and our estimates.

We prefer to see the world as we know it, from our own particular perspective.

When we are privileged (more powerful, a leader), we are blinded by that privilege.

We assume that our perspectives are held universally, or that they should be.

When we are non-privileged (less powerful, a follower), we avoid offending those who are privileged.

A wider variety of biases that are likely to influence how we handle crises are grouped below, according to how they affect us. As you read these examples, take the bold step to check the items that resonate with your beliefs about your deeper self. As an immediate payoff, just advancing to this level of self-awareness can help you reduce harmful effects of your biases. To take your perspective a step further, seek candid feedback from people who know you well because, for all of us, our bias blind spots also distort our perceptions about ourselves.

- **How we think**
    - We believe we are more objective and less biased than other people.
    - We believe that rational, smart people will agree with us. We categorize people who oppose our views as uninformed, irrational, lazy, or just plain stupid.
    - We have trouble imagining alternative problems and solutions.
    - We do not like to think about negative, unusual, or unlikely possibilities.
    - We do not like to think about outcomes that have not happened yet.

- **How we gather information and seek advice**
    - We pursue and notice information and advice that fit our perspectives, while retreating from and ignoring information and advice that do not.
    - We search for evidence that confirms our plans. We disregard evidence that suggests that our plans may fail.

- **How we evaluate information**
    - We overestimate our control of our environment.
    - We overvalue available information.
    - We underestimate the impact of chance, and the variety of possibilities that exist.
    - We overvalue information that fits our view. We devalue and resist information that does not, which causes us to defend our view more strongly.
    - We remember choices we have made as being better than they actually were.

- We ignore and devalue information that comes from people we do not like. We interpret their words and behaviors as having hostile intent, even when what they say or do is ambiguous, benign, or well-intended.
- When there is no evidence about why we are wrong, we assume that lack confirms our accuracy.

- **How we make decisions**
  - When we plan, we prefer to focus on what we already know.
  - We do not like to change our decisions, especially if we have invested considerable time, effort, or money in them.
  - When we define extremes, we do not think extreme enough, or we overemphasize the differences.
  - When we work in groups, we spend more time and energy discussing what is already known to the group, and less time and energy discussing what is new to some members.
  - We prefer reducing smaller risks to zero, rather than making larger advances on bigger risks.

- **How we deal with mistakes and trouble**
  - We prefer to ignore negative circumstances, and to limit our involvement when trouble strikes.
  - We ignore the influence that context contributes to errors.
  - We search for scapegoats when trouble occurs.
  - We are quick to accept human error as cause, rather than a symptom or signal of something that needs further explanation.

- **How we treat privilege/power differences**
  when we are privileged
  - We are often unaware of how we treat non-privileged people.

- o Our elevated status keeps us from understanding non-privileged people.
- o Our presence silences non-privileged people.
- o The greater our privileges, the less direct experience we have with the non-privileged, the less attention we pay them, and the more we rely on stereotypes about them.
- o Our privilege trumps expertise, even when non-privileged experts know that we are terribly wrong.
- o Others attribute greater accuracy and influence to our opinions than to the opinions of non-privileged people.
- o Decisions and actions that we champion will prevail, even when the nature of our privilege is irrelevant.
- o The information (news, articles, books, films, broadcasts) that we receive about non-privileged people will usually be filtered through the lenses of the privileged.

- **How we treat privilege/power differences** *when we are non-privileged*
  - o We do what we can to avoid offending privileged people.
  - o We voice our sentiments to privileged people in ways that are more socially acceptable than our true opinions, often even when asked to express our true opinions.
  - o If we voice our concerns, privileged people often ignore them.
  - o If we are pressed to share negative information with the privileged, the information we share is often vague or ambiguous.

PRACTICAL IMPLICATIONS

Many biases curtail individuals and organizations from engaging in the process of crisis management. Some impede our understanding of emerging information. Others obstruct us from amending our thoughts and actions to match new organizational, environmental, and crisis realities.

Now is a great time to corral biases that you wish to change.

If you acknowledged bias-based blind spots on the checklist, you have already completed the essential first step. Next, determine your objectives for reducing or eliminating them. The more specifically you can articulate desired improvements, the more likely you will succeed.

Specific recommendations below are organized into the same categories as those used for the biases above. As you read the suggestions, consider how they could reduce your personal blind spots, then choose a few options that resonate for you. To bring the improvement to life, create a brief description of the person you want to become, one who is less influenced by biases. Having that desired future self in mind will also make difficult choices clearer and simpler.

As you think about best outcomes and your newly desired behavioral boundaries, write or discuss the outcomes relative to your particular circumstances. For example, with whom will you behave differently? How, precisely? In which specific circumstances? How will you know when you are succeeding in reducing or eliminating your bias? Who can help you evaluate your progress and stay on course? These recommendations will give you some practical approaches.

- **To think**
    - Let go of the need to be right. Let others have the last word.
    - Hold your conclusions lightly. Accept other viewpoints more often.
    - When you get stuck sorting your decisions or actions, think carefully about how they might limit the person you want to become. Imagine the alternatives someone you admire greatly would choose.

- **To gather information, seek advice.**
    - Focus on the greatest risks first. Prioritize agendas accordingly.

- o Do not lead others' advice by the way you ask for help or describe a problem.
- o Seek perspectives that differ from your own.
- o Listen carefully to people who disagree with you, and people whom you do not like.
- o Acknowledge others' opinions, even when you disagree with them. Learn why they differ, and how they came to their perspectives.
- o Before you come to important conclusions, ask the tough questions.
- o Read more, read more broadly. Tap diverse sources and genres.
- o Practice these approaches under various circumstances, not just work-related.

- **To evaluate information**
  - o When bad news comes your way, separate the message from the messenger.
  - o For important issues, keep the sources of your information and insights clearly in mind.
  - o Do not use the results that you know now to evaluate prior actions, or to determine how or why prior actions were taken.
  - o Do not assume that silence or other lack of disagreement means agreement.

- **To make decisions**
  - o Do not confuse coincidence and consequence.
  - o Do not accept correlation as cause.
  - o When weighing alternatives, always include at least one wild option, and a few improbable outcomes.
  - o When weighing potential outcomes, always include at least one worst-case scenario.

- **To deal with mistakes**
    - Admit your mistakes promptly. They will be found out anyway, and usually, the sooner you admit mistakes, the easier it is to repair them.
    - Treat mistakes (yours and others') as part of learning, rather than evidence of stupidity, incompetence, or carelessness.
    - Seek to understand what the error was, and aim not to repeat it.
    - Learn to examine your own mistakes as if you were observing someone else's, with clarity and compassion.

- **To counteract barriers of greater privilege**
    - Be civil to everyone, always, no matter who, what, when, where. No exceptions.
    - When information or problems do not make sense to you, ask those closest to the situation what you are missing or misunderstanding.
    - When someone's information seems vague, ambiguous, or inconsistent, consider how power differences between you could be affecting their communication. Maybe you have not even suspected a power difference, or realized how many privileges or advantages you have. Maybe someone you consider to be in an equal or higher position conversely believes that in some way, you have greater privilege, position, influence, or power.
    - Always ask "why?" with genuine curiosity. Listen especially for circumstances over which non-privileged respondents had little or no control, expertise, support, or resources.
    - Do not use questions to demonstrate your superiority, or someone else's inferiority.
    - When you want others' opinions, speak yours last.

Steering away from biases is not an easy adjustment, but the power to do so lies within each of us. Improving crisis readiness and response is a strong motivator. Developing a clearer view under urgent, novel, threatening circumstances provides extraordinary benefits. Unbiased insights can open diverse perspectives of what has happened, why it matters, to whom, and what to do next.

Reducing biases is a never-ending quest. But any improvement will help you and your organization be more aligned with today's work challenges, and improve crisis processes and outcomes. As with habits, your personal commitment to become more aware of your biases and their negative impacts will dramatically improve your ability to embrace a crisis and come out stronger.

 Up Next

The section that follows includes crisis tools and approaches that I have found to be most effective. These approaches have met tests of time and geography, with enduring benefits across decades of applications, in diverse organizations and industries, across pivot points of the crisis cycle, and among leaders and employees from diverse levels, functions, and cultures.

Crisis Tools

How to Use Crisis Tools

Whether occurring as local accidents or a worldwide pandemic, crises and near misses draw interest and attention to the prospect of strengthening existing crisis plans. As the first wave of coronavirus impacts began to subside, for example, a flash survey by Deloitte captured crisis leadership intentions of senior executives, which included improving their crisis approaches, practicing their crisis responses more frequently, and doing a better job of documenting what they had learned from the crisis. About half of the respondents also wished that they had conducted any kind of a crisis exercise the year before the pandemic began.[80]

Crisis tools will help you advance toward your desired preparation and response. They can power your learning and reduce costly mistakes like repeated errors, missed signals, and neglected troubles. The tools considered here expand and deepen appreciation and understanding of the stakes and impacts of crises, and they sharpen awareness and response in alignment with stakeholder expectations and needs. Specifically, these tools will provide frameworks and processes to achieve the following:

- Expand and deepen individual and organizational awareness and competence about crisis preparation, signal recognition, and crisis response.
- Bring attention to your organization's probable and less likely crisis risks and opportunities, constraints and resources.
- Improve insights about your stakeholders' expectations and needs.
- Develop abilities and build habits to scan for unanticipated causes and consequences of near misses and crises.
- Expose errors and omissions in planning and execution.

- Test how your existing preparations will hold up to a range of crisis impacts and evolutions, and how well they will measure up to your core values and crisis objectives.
- Strengthen relationships and processes, improving your corporate culture, goal-setting, collaboration, and productivity throughout the organization—in routine times as well as crises.

Tools presented here incorporate approaches like stretch thinking, tough and appreciative inquiry, and open nonjudgmental discussion, which deepen engagement and trust to elicit and weigh divergent viewpoints, achieving collaborative decision-making. In organizations or teams that function at a reasonable level of performance and employee satisfaction, these tools can improve input, insight, decisions and actions throughout the crisis cycle. Used effectively, they minimize debilitating inclinations and habits, such as dodging responsibility and passing blame. Use them to identify, practice, and enhance best methods for tailoring and applying your crisis frameworks and approaches, while staying true to your organization's core values.

We'll examine each from three perspectives: *What* is it? *Why* use it? *How?*

1. Best-case/Worst-case Framing
2. No-fault Learning
3. Stakeholder Analysis
4. Table-top Scenarios
5. Cases
6. Simulations

1. BEST-CASE/WORST-CASE FRAMING

What?

This approach centers on extreme perspectives of crisis threats, experiences, and impacts. This framing informs decision-making and action by expanding the bases for contemplation and discussion. Two fundamental questions capture the essence of this approach:

1. What would be the *ideal* circumstances and impacts, when your organization is threatened?
2. What would be the *grimmest*?

Perspectives and insights prompted, and the thought process itself are eye-opening, whether planning for potential crises, dealing with actual events, or learning from crisis experiences. The process can be used by individuals and groups. The CLT should develop expertise and agility in this approach.

Why?

Imagining extreme boundaries unlocks creative thinking and enriches discussions. Collaboratively framing both extremes stretches collective and individual awareness of conceivable threats and opportunities. The approach can nudge participants out of complacency, and challenge naïve assumptions that some people may hold, for example regarding their organization's crisis invulnerability.

Focusing candidly on worst cases exposes organizational taboos, the issues that people dare not raise openly. Results can be priceless if participants question critical assumptions that are touted but untested, or reveal dangerous vulnerabilities that are known but ignored. Imaging worst-cases strengthens participants' familiarity with dire realities and, often, their grit for confronting them.

Discussions about best-case views draw attention to insights and approaches that affirm and reinforce your organization's core values and crisis objectives. This perspective is invaluable for retaining alignment with your organization's North Star relative to crises, and helps participants generate broader real-world solutions collectively.

How?

Introduce and build acceptance of this approach by describing its benefits. Then, with input from participants, review your organization's core values and crisis objectives. Move to discussion of alignments and disconnections between (a) the values and crisis objectives that your organization claims to hold, and (b) specific ways in which values and objectives play out in behaviors in your organization. Develop a shared sense of current actions and approaches that exemplify and chafe against your organization's ideals.

Use examples of solid alignments to uncover quantitative and qualitative measures that capture your organization's behavioral preferences. Consider how *best* behaviors are recognized or rewarded. Focus on specific connections to decisions and activities that drive crisis preparation and response. Which critical practices support or oppose the best-case parameters and outcomes? How would performance be affected? Which resources and procedures reinforce your pursuit of values and crisis objectives? What more is needed to build and retain positive momentum? Are we considering enough possibilities?

Then, drill down on potentially dangerous misalignments. Focus on conflicts that could stir crises or spoil your ability to handle them. A common example is a boss at any level who consistently brushes off or punishes messengers of bad news, despite organizational objectives for reporting mistakes and problems promptly. Also, consider how worst and best behaviors are addressed.

Discuss participants' actual experiences with crises and near misses, and their roles in those experiences. What were their best and worst experiences? Why? Where would they conduct themselves in precisely the same way, and where would they wish for a do-over? As a group, reflect on these critical incidents, and how they could have been turning points or contributing factors that led to crisis successes and failures. What were the best and worst examples of signal detection and reporting? How was clear, accurate, timely contact and notification achieved, or what led to glitches in information flow? Where and how were handoffs within your organization smooth, or hazardous? Which tasks and responsibilities during crisis or near misses were appropriate, or excessive? How were experts identified and contacted, or ignored?

Best-case/worst-case framing pays off in the present and the future. Apply it to explore potential impacts of actions in process and proposed approaches. Practice this tool to envision highly beneficial outcomes and practice mitigating deeply destructive threats.

These types of questions can prompt, expand, and inform best/worst-case discussions.

- How do we expect our core values to strengthen and facilitate best-case outcomes?
- What are we confident will occur?
- What are our concerns?
- What responses to crises could devastate our core values and drive us into worst-case situations? How can we safeguard against that possibility?
- How could our core values obstruct crisis preparations or responses? How could they constrain our choices and push us into worst-case circumstances?
- How might trends that we are pursuing affect best/worst-case crisis outcomes?
- How would these best/worst-case circumstances affect our key stakeholders? Which negative outcomes do we avoid talking about? What are the costs and benefits of increasing our emphasis on stakeholder outcomes?

2. NO-FAULT LEARNING

What?

No-fault Learning is a tool to uncover lessons embedded in decision and action mistakes. No-fault learning is *not* a fitting approach for situations involving actual wrong-doing, for example, when employees have knowingly violated policies or broken laws.

"No-fault" refers to the nature of the process, which de-emphasizes blame, prohibits scapegoating, and promotes acceptance of responsibility. At the core, this tool rests on acceptance of error and fallibility as part of human nature.

Why?

To learn optimally from a crisis, a near miss, or a relevant exercise is to look squarely, candidly, not only at what went well, but also at what could have been done better. Reducing the stigma of blame and eliminating fears about telling the whole truth are important steps to admit and discover shortcomings and mistakes.

Silence and blame often characterize fact-finding discussions when it comes to errors and limitations. A legitimate no-fault foundation diminishes fears about risk-taking and punishment, being throttled or chastised. The process reduces resistance to revealing details that are less than optimal, and opens the flow of information to uncover deeper issues, to identify and correct underlying problems and mistakes in judgment and action.

No-fault learning is valuable for recognizing, acknowledging, and bridging divergent perspectives. Using the tool can clarify misunderstandings, improve collective understanding, and reinforce conclusions about why and how errors and mistakes occurred, as well as the types of changes that may be needed.

How?

Trust and courage play fundamental roles in the success of no-fault learning. The tool will not work in organizations that withhold or taint information. The process will also be a waste of time if participants are untrusting or untrustworthy.

To discover root causes, everyone involved must be willing to speak the truth in order to reveal and explore what lies beneath surface problems and what preceded or surrounded last-touch errors. The process often requires speaking truth to power, which only occurs if personal safety is genuine for all involved.

After assembling trustworthy individuals, start with a brief discussion of what went well regarding the crisis, near miss, or exercise under consideration. Begin by recognizing positive outcomes, and solidifying group perspectives regarding best practices. Follow these guidelines to bring participants to common ground, which will ease the discussion of errors.

Introduce no-fault learning using simple crisis exercises, such as a discussion of table-top scenarios. After developing participants' expertise and comfort with the tool, apply it to more challenging situations, progressing from exercises to near miss experiences, and then to actual crisis events.

Build skills and confidence slowly by initially limiting no-fault learning to small groups, to particular levels or departments where communication tends to flow smoothly and trust already exists. As your organization becomes more familiar with no-fault learning, use the process with larger groups representing multiple functions and viewpoints.

3. STAKEHOLDER ANALYSIS

What?

Use this tool to identify stakeholders and prioritize their needs and impacts for crisis preparation and response. Stakeholders include individuals, groups, organizations, and population segments who hold interest in or are affected by your organization's decisions and actions, or who could significantly affect your ability to decide and act. The process is achieved through discussion and data collection. Effective stakeholder analyses can improve crisis planning and response, and post-crisis learning.

Why?

This tool helps organizations align crisis decisions and actions with their stakeholders' expectations, and align their stakeholders' expectations with their crisis preparations and responses. Stakeholder awareness and alignment can improve contact and support as you surface assumptions about your stakeholders, as well as what you believe they assume about you.[81] This can help you think through threats, opportunities, and potential impacts under crisis situations, to identify and reveal solutions.

Stakeholder analysis can be useful to determine, clarify and establish appropriate degrees of access and engagement with particular stakeholders. It can help you think through the types and qualities of expertise and resources that could be shared in either direction, and the appropriate attention to invest in specific stakeholder relationships. Insights can help you determine best communication and operational channels and conduits for better crisis preparation and stronger outcomes.

Lessons and follow-up actions can align key players and their planning to avert dangerous surprises. Not only will you learn more about your internal and external stakeholders, but also those whom you may have neglected or dismissed in planning.

How?

Stakeholder analysis requires participants to think creatively, reason logically, and collect and analyze data fitting to the scope of crises. Expectations are based on participants' experiences, knowledge, and assumptions regarding their influencers' history, reputation, values (both advocated and practiced), and the contexts that they inhabit or control.

First, generate an extensive list of individuals, groups, organizations, and population segments who could affect or be affected by your organization's ability to handle a crisis. This is best achieved as a brainstorming discussion. Some stakeholders will come to mind immediately. To expand the array, encourage participants to think about particular categories of candidates, various functions they fulfill (governing, supplying, or using your organization's products or services), and those at more distant connections (your suppliers' suppliers, your customers' advocacy groups). The graphic below captures a basic array of known, generic, first-level stakeholders who commonly affect or are affected by organizational crises. Think of the relevant players for your organization.

This figure captures the traditional perspectives of stakeholders, as independent agents who would be likely to have direct connection to or from your organization, or in both directions. For decades, this perspective has guided stakeholder analysis for crisis preparation, but it is insufficient now.

Growing availability, ease, and speed of connectivity drives fluid interactions, often among diverse and distant forces, sometimes instantly. Now, even loosely coupled stakeholders can consolidate their information and resources, build strength across industries and geographies, gather data, and exude influence through gateways that were formerly impenetrable.

The depiction below suggests added complexities of ties among contemporary stakeholder relationships. Although the number of stakeholders depicted is identical to the diagram above, the various directions and strengths of their links begin to capture the need to think comprehensively, to imagine a broader, more diverse array of stakeholder connections, whether their conduits or impacts are social, logistical, or technological, for example. The graphic below is limited, and yet the potential scope is daunting. But, additional analytical steps of stakeholder analysis can clarify who matters most and what is at stake.

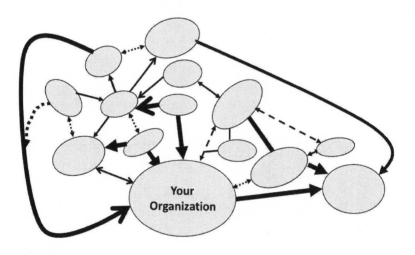

After participants have exhausted reasonable stakeholder candidates, seek wilder suggestions. Instruct them to imagine some candidates whose significant crisis impacts are highly unlikely, still possible (contracted landscapers), but not ludicrous (zombies).

For the next step, help participants reduce the extensive list of stakeholders. Ask them to consolidate the list into clusters according to the ways in which stakeholders might similarly affect or be affected by your organization's ability to handle a crisis. Then, work as a group to identify the primary stakeholders among the clusters, including at least a couple of wild card candidates to stretch their thinking.

Focus collective understanding of each key stakeholder or cluster by discussing questions such as these:

- What do we take for granted about each of these stakeholders/clusters? Why?
- How would we expect each to respond to our crisis?
  - What roles might they play?
  - How might their efforts and impacts change in best-case versus worst-case circumstances?
  - What experiences or observations lead us to these assumptions?
- What do we believe each stakeholder assumes about our organization? What might they misunderstand that could make a significant difference in their responses, and our ability to handle crisis?
- What if our assumptions are dangerously wrong?
- How can we test our beliefs? What more do we need to learn?

The final analytical step is to evaluate and plot selected stakeholders according to their presumed level of influence or power over your organization or environment, and their presumed interest regarding your organization's plans or approaches. To evaluate, think about how much power you attribute to each stakeholder, as well as your assumptions about to what extent and how each could support or oppose your organization. Do not limit your discussions to their direct power. Also consider the added muscle of high-powered influencers who might step up on their behalf, such as consumers who boycott on behalf of abused laborers.

This level of stakeholder analysis should stretch and refine participants' perspectives of the reach and control of key organizational influencers, as well as those who might be outside that immediately recognizable group. To help direct and improve crisis readiness and response, plot key stakeholders and a few wild cards regarding their strength and their interest in your plans and approaches in Matrix A below. Then, overlay Matrix B to broadly guide appropriate approaches for crisis preparation, planning and response relative to specific stakeholders' influence and interest.

Matrix A: Stakeholder Influence x Interest

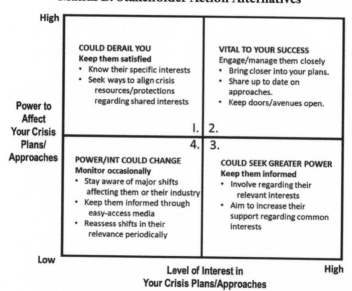

Matrix B: Stakeholder Action Alternatives

Use what you have learned from this process as a basis from which to reflect, reevaluate, and plan regarding your stakeholders. Where mysteries or uncertainties surface, gather additional data. These sample questions are reasonable starting points:

- What can we do now to clarify and improve our understanding of our key stakeholders?
- What can we do to improve their understanding of us?
- How can we align our mutual expectations better?
- Which improvements would bring the greatest positive impact for us?
- Which would be most beneficial for our key stakeholders?
- Is it plausible to work more closely with this stakeholder to improve our crisis planning/response? How could we do that?
- What benefits and costs could come from their engagement?

Take the final step to create an additional tool from this process. Convert your short list of stakeholders into a roster to streamline communication and the coordination of resources in crisis. Include standards like titles, locations, and basic contact information. Note priceless additional data, such as crisis-relevant expertise and supplies that specific stakeholders might be able to access or control. Internally, establish accountability for reviewing and updating the details annually, and whenever significant changes occur to your stakeholders or to your own organization.

4. TABLE-TOP SCENARIOS

What?

Table-top scenarios are popular tools for introducing, expanding, and evaluating perceptions and facts about crises, for example, their causes, decision options, and potential outcomes. Scenario narratives can be built on hypothetical or factual details of crisis circumstances, based on actual events, data-based trends and trajectories, or fantasy. Effective scenarios may resemble your organization in some way, or not at all. Scenarios can be brief, relatively simple summaries, covering just one context of a crisis, requiring only a few minutes of discussion. Or scenarios can span intricate evolutions of crises and stir a great deal more time commitment, follow-up projects, interdepartmental efforts and far more engagement.

Why?

The function of scenarios is to provide context for working through crisis assessments and decisions. They set the stage for "What if?" thinking and conversation, increasing individual and collective insights, collaboration, and buy-in.

Practicing with scenarios can help participants discover and test approaches for managing alignment and disagreement in light of very challenging circumstances. When hypotheticals are used, the inherent distance from actual organizational issues tends to free participants to reveal their inclinations and biases. Participants can build skills for anticipating and managing alignment and disagreement personally and across the group. Scenarios can provide structure to debates about existing plans and potential adjustments. Often, the process leads to new ideas or features that improve crisis preparations.

How?

A particular appealingly characteristic of table-top scenarios is that table-top scenarios are simple to use. They require only four steps.

1. Formulate learning objectives for the exercise.
2. Choose a scenario that will engage your participants (which need not be set in your industry or in an organization similar to your own).
3. Facilitate an open discussion that moves toward your objectives and beyond them.
4. Draw out lessons learned and practical implications for your organization and your contexts.

To optimize the value of a scenario experience, bring the right people to the exercise. Most importantly, select a skilled facilitator who understands and supports your organization's core values and crisis objectives. Participants should include people who are capable of systems thinking and imagining possibilities for your organization and its contexts. To maximize buy-in, aim for ideal timing, soon after a relevant organization or industry (or your own) has dodged or experienced a crisis.

The "Toy Troubles" scenario below, which is loosely based on an actual situation, is a sample of the tool. I have used this scenario successfully in organizations of assorted industries, sizes, and locations, as well as mixed groups of participants who represented highly varied organizations and backgrounds in public, private, and NGOs. I am also including questions that have proven effective in drawing out important crisis preparation and response principles, regardless of the nature of participants' work or their organizations' levels of crisis readiness.

Sample Scenario: Toy Troubles

Your company, Global Zests, is an international food chain that features low-cost traditional entrees from around the world. In recent years, it has grown into a popular niche player, with sites in North and South America, Europe, and Asia. Recently, to attract an additional, younger demographic of consumers, a new kid's menu was added.

Your meeting today begins with the marketing department's glowing view of preliminary data that support their growth projections. The takeaway is that to achieve year-end targets, they must move aggressively to put new plans in place. The Director of Marketing explains that test sampling the kids' menu targeted age group confirms the need for a toy or other non-food premium to capture kids' attention and drive parents' intent to purchase. Investments have already been made, including acquisition of two million "Zesty Zebras," the first premium. The molded plastic zebra is currently being distributed across North American and European regions. The Director seems excited to announce that the new kids' meals campaign will begin airing in two days, with Zesty Zebra as spokesperson.

No one doubts the power of toys to drive sales, but an operations manager asks about additional risks of handling products targeted for children. The Health and Safety Manager assures everyone that Zesty Zebra is similar to other industry premiums, and that it was tested and passed the child choke tube test.

As you glance through the marketing data, you notice customer complaints about the new kids' meal offerings. Food-based gripes seem predictable: not enough product diversity, too few healthy choices for children. Then, among a few summarized complaints about the toy premium, one in particular catches your eye—just three words—"minor surgery needed." You read it to everyone, which prompts debate about the types and intensity of potential dangers if younger children got hold of Zesty Zebra. Someone reminds the group that the toy is only included with kids' meals designed for children six years of age or older, and with that, the conversation drifts to the high costs of the advertising campaign.

Questions to contemplate and discuss:

- What sorts of dangers may be lurking in the Zesty Zebra premium? What possibilities might be taboo or unthinkable, threats that people in the meeting may recognize but be reluctant to discuss openly?

- How would you evaluate whether the potential dangers suggested in this scenario warrant further attention?
- What sorts of worst- and best-case scenarios could evolve from this situation?
- If you were attending this meeting and felt compelled to voice your concerns, how would you frame your argument?
- How could issues and questions embedded in this scenario translate in your own organization's crisis preparations and responses?
- If you were a member of this organization, what responsibility would you step up for? How could your current knowledge or experience be assets in dealing with this situation?

5. CASE STUDIES

What?

Like scenarios, cases are analytical frameworks, real or fictitious, in narrative form. They are generally longer and more detailed than scenarios, often including background data and other exhibits.

Why?

Cases provide common ground for group discussion and application of crisis principles and processes, as well as actual and potential impacts. Cases may exemplify what or what not to do, how or how not to think or behave. As with scenarios, crisis cases provide opportunities to practice problem-solving, analysis, and decision-making, in light of the values, objectives, contexts, and options faced by featured organizations or individuals.

How?

Discussion of case facts and reasoned speculation often centers on what worked and what did not, with details or hints of why and how decisions were made and actions taken. Participants in case discussions are usually encouraged to explore similarities and differences between the case examples and their own experiences, wisdom, and expectations. Lessons are shaped from these comparisons.

Crisis cases often highlight decisions made by assigned and emergent leaders. Sometimes, villains and heroes are part of the narrative. Fine details about specific case characters sharpen learning opportunities, especially when lessons are geared toward improving participants' own thinking styles and behavioral preferences in crisis. Unpredicted circumstances, high-impact uncertainties, tight timeframes, and difficult decisions faced by case stakeholders are powerful prompts for challenging participants to examine their own and others' assumptions and current shortcomings regarding crisis preparation and response.

Although scenarios require four key steps, cases require five. The addition is step #3: to achieve effective outcomes, participants should read and prepare before meeting to discuss the case.

1. Formulate learning objectives for the exercise.
2. Choose a case that would be engaging for your participants, remembering that it need not take place in your industry or in an organization similar to your own.
3. Assign case preparation, including questions to guide participants toward targeted learning objectives.
4. Facilitate an open discussion that moves toward your objectives and beyond them.
5. Draw out lessons learned and practical implications for your organization and your contexts.

The case of the *Train d'Enfer* below describes an actual crisis. I'm including this example because it has proven highly effective for stirring discussion and insights across varied organizations and industries, and with mixed groups. Questions like these can be distributed as preparation to reinforce crisis leadership concepts and shape learning to participants and their organizations:

- Bring emphasis to the learning process by starting and ending discussion with the same fundamental question: Who was to blame for the crisis at Lac-Mégantic?
- Which stakeholders, internal and external, were key to the evolution of the crisis? How might their needs and power (importance and influence) variously affect the core organization, Montreal, Maine and Atlantic Railway (MMA)?
- Which categories of stakeholders were most significant to key outcomes? How does this list compare to categories most likely to influence your organization's success in the event of a crisis?
- How did communication practices of MMA align and contrast with best practices?

- How would you evaluate the MMA leader's crisis management competence? Which of his words and deeds led you to this evaluation? How did context affect the perceived quality of his communication style and content?

Sample Case: *Le Train d'Enfer and the Derailing of Crisis Leadership*[82] *

Within a stone's throw of one the worst train accidents in Canadian history, Edward Burkhardt, the chairman of Montreal, Maine and Atlantic Railway, flouted crisis management imperatives that common sense would have assured. Burkhardt's conferences with the media and grieving townspeople were characterized as "impromptu scrum,"[83] and Burkhardt was promptly cast as "the most hated man in Lac-Mégantic,"[84] the scene of the accident. Using ploys such as finger-pointing (within and outside his own organization) and lamenting his personal financial losses (from a crisis that devastated a town and killed dozens of its residents), Burkhardt managed, single-handedly, to draw media scorn and provoke public rage internationally.

Lac-Mégantic was a tranquil French-Canadian town on the Chaudière River in Québec. The small town was home to about 5,600 people, more than 98% of whom were French-speaking. The town was known as a quiet lakeside vacation spot. But, in the earliest hours of July 6, 2013, the tranquility was decimated by "le train d'enfer," the train from hell.

Just before midnight on July 5, the fire department at the nearby town of Nantes received a 911 call: a locomotive of a train parked at the railway's change point was on fire. Within minutes, firefighters arrived at the freight train, which was running but unmanned. To extinguish the fire, they turned off the power, stopping circulation of fuel into the flames. The firefighters also contacted Montreal, Maine and Atlantic Railway (MMA), the company

---

* Christine M. Pearson. *Le Train d'Enfer and the Derailing of Crisis Leadership.* Thunderbird A15-19-0010. *© 2019 Thunderbird School of Global Management, a unit of the Arizona State University Knowledge Enterprise. Used by permission.*

that owned the train, requesting that a representative inspect the now-doused locomotive. By 12:45 a.m., the responding firefighters and the MMA representative had left the train, unmanned, as they had found it, but with the power off.

Less than half an hour later, at approximately 1:00 a.m. on July 6, the train started rolling from its parking spot on the main line track, 325 feet above the town of Lac-Mégantic. With neither lights nor signals, the runaway train ghosted along seven miles of track into the heart of town. Accelerating during the descent, the train reached a speed of 65 miles per hour. As it neared the Mégantic West turnout, the locomotive successfully hurtled through the curve, but 63 of its 72 tank cars jumped the tracks, landing in a dented, ruptured heap.

More than 1.5 million gallons of what had been labelled petroleum crude oil spewed from the breached tanks. In less than two minutes, the actual product, Bakken crude, ignited and detonated like gasoline. A pool of burning oil surged through Lac-Mégantic. Flames soared 200 feet in the air. Fireballs blasted from sewer drains, manholes, basements, and chimneys. Earthquake-like explosions rocked the town for three hours.

Eighty fire departments responded from Montreal to Maine to assist Lac-Mégantic's volunteer firefighters. For nearly 24 hours, the core of the fire was so hot that it was inaccessible to fire crews. The town burned for two days. "Le train d'enfer" had detonated one of the worst accidents ever to occur in Canada.

Forty-seven townspeople were incinerated. World-class forensic anthropologists had to be summoned to the site to find remains among rubble and ashes. In many cases, positively identifying individual victims was possible only by confirming DNA matches to personal items, such as hair brushes or razors. After five months of search and testing, only 22 of the 37 remains had been identified.

Businesses, houses, and historic buildings burned to the ground. Two thousand residents were forced to evacuate their homes because of fire and toxic fumes. Among the 69 buildings in the downtown area, 30 were destroyed by fires and explosions. Dozens more would be razed eventually because of petroleum contamination.

The Face of Leadership in Crisis

At the time of the crisis, Edward Burkhardt, the chairman of MMA, had more than 50 years' experience in the rail transportation industry. A graduate of Yale who began his career with the Wabash Railroad, Burkhardt was named "Railroader of the Year" in 1999 by *Railway Age,* a trade magazine. Later that same year, he was ousted from CEO/President roles at the head of Wisconsin Central Transportation Corporation, reportedly for financial losses and shareholders' sentiment that he had overreached. In 2003, Burkhardt bought the remaining assets of bankrupted holding company Iron Road Railways and, from them, created MMA.

Under Burkhardt's leadership, MMA developed a reputation as one of the most aggressive cost-cutting rail companies in the industry.[85] Within months of forming the company, Burkhardt initiated the first of three layoffs within five years. Then, he slashed surviving employees' salaries by 40%. In 2010, in a continued effort to cut costs radically, MMA became one of only two railways in Canada to use single-person train crews. With that shift, the original workforce of 350 employees was down to 175.

Then, in the earliest hours of July 6, came the crisis at Lac-Mégantic. Grief engulfed the town. Sympathy flooded across the nation and around the globe. Pauline Marois, the Premier of Québec, arrived on the day of the crisis to express compassion with citizens and confer with the media. On July 7, Canada's Prime Minister, Stephen Harper, toured the devastation and spoke with media and townspeople, describing the scene as a "war zone." On July 8, Queen Elizabeth II expressed shared thoughts and prayers, and "profound sadness" about the tragedy "that has shocked us all." On July 9, Pope Francis conveyed empathy from the Vatican to the victims, their families, and emergency workers, and offered an apostolic blessing to all affected.

It was not until July 10, the fifth day of the crisis, that MMA Chairman Burkhardt arrived in Lac-Mégantic. As the face of MMA, he met with the media and townspeople on a local street near the epicenter of the disaster. Burkhardt spoke in English, without an interpreter and without participation from any other representatives of the railway.

The transcripts that follow are verbatim and in full, as recorded and posted to YouTube by the *Montreal Gazette,*[86] the *Windsor Star,*[87] and *Canadian*

Broadcasting Corporation News,[88] respectively.

Transcription of Video #1

Burkhardt [responding, presumably, to a question about the timing of his arrival in Lac-Mégantic]: "You know, I've been asked that same question about five times. When I got news of this on Saturday morning, I had to think about how we would best use our people in a short period of time. Our entire management team was headed to this location, our chief executive and all of our department heads and everybody that is involved in running the Railway. I felt that I was better trying to deal with insurance companies, contractors, and the press from my office in Chicago, rather than trying to do all of that on a cell phone in Mégantic. And, uh, I knew that when the first responders had the city basically locked down, that all I would do is be able to get within a couple of miles of the place anyway. I didn't think that that was a good way to use my time."

Reporter: "What would you say to the people who have lost people and say you had a train that was unmanned for several hours?"

Burkhardt: "I say that I'm absolutely with them in their tragedy. I understand their tragedy. Feel personally absolutely rotten about it. But, what can you do at this point? You could make the point, especially in the aftermath of this, that that was wrong. But, we were following normal practice. You can go into any province in Canada or any state in the U.S. and find trains parked with no crew on them."

Reporter: [question inaudible]

Burkhardt: "I'm not placing blame on anybody at this point. I'm trying to develop all of the facts that are known. It's still behind police lines. Our inspectors on Saturday, when they first arrived here, had about five minutes to inspect the locomotive. When our people investigated this locomotive, they found the emergency shut-off switch had been pulled on the locomotive and the circuit breakers in the cab had been all moved. They said, 'somebody has done something to this locomotive.' We didn't make guesses. The engine, the locomotive had been tampered with. That is definitely true, and it was the fire people that tampered with it. Now, were they negligent in their tampering? I think not. I understand there's a criminal investigation and, if people, I believe normally it's people that have criminal investigations against, uh, and if there is sufficient evidence, uh, to charge people criminally, they should be charged."

Reporter: "But, you don't accept full responsibility for this?"

Burkhardt: "I didn't say that. You see, you see, people are always putting words in my mouth. Please. I did not say that. We think we have plenty of responsibility here. Whether we have total responsibility is, uh, yet to be determined. We have plenty of it. We're going to try to help out everything that we can with this community, working through the city and the Red Cross, to do our best to meet our obligations to make repairs, and put people back in homes, and things like that."

Transcription of Video #2

Burkhardt: "Don't. Please don't tell me I've not been here when we're standing right here, as close as we can get."

Reporter: "But, this is the first day you've been here."

Burkhardt: "I think I explained earlier that I didn't think that there would be any use for me wandering around on the edge of town until the first responders had an opportunity to do their work. You can see, people are always putting words in my mouth."

Reporter: "But, you're talking about the fire department. You're talking about the track manager."

Burkhardt: "I'm looking at a series of causes, a series of events that occurred, because while we gather those facts, it doesn't mean that we're not accepting responsibility. Those are two different subjects."

Reporter: "Do you think that there's any responsibility that you take?"

Burkhardt: "I'm absolutely appalled that you would say that. If you've been listening to what's been going on here, listening to my..."

Reporter: "That's what people are saying in the town."

Burkhardt: "We think we have plenty of responsibility here. Whether we have total responsibility is yet to be determined. We have plenty of it. I think the Nantes fire department played a role in it. And that's the facts. This is facts. That doesn't mean that we're holding these people out to dry and saying the guys have caused the accident. You always look at any accident and you say, 'how could we have done better?' And, for the future, we and I think, probably, the rest of the industry, aren't going to be leaving these trains unmanned."

Transcription of Video #3

Burkhardt: "Am I a compassionate person? I feel absolutely awful about this. I'm devastated about what has occurred in this community. We are making an abject apology to the people in this town. It has my utmost sympathy and, personally, I'm devastated by what happened here. I would feel the same if something like this happened in my community. Beyond that, I don't know what to say."

Reporter: "Did you sleep well last night?"

Burkhardt: "If you are tired enough, you'll sleep well anywhere."

Burkhardt [presumably, regarding the actions of the train's engineer]: "We think he applied some handbrakes. The question is, did he apply enough of them? He told us that he applied eleven handbrakes and, our general feeling now is that that is not true."

Voiceover by news commentator: "He says Harding [the engineer] has been suspended."

Reporter: "Why has he been suspended?"

Burkhardt: "Because for right now, for investigation, the fact is that he is under the police control. He is not, as I understand, he is not in jail, but the police have talked about prosecuting him and they want him staying where he is."

Reporter: "How much are you worth?"

Burkhardt: "How much am I worth? A whole lot less than I was on Saturday."

Burkhardt was whisked from the scene by police, reportedly, for questioning. After the press conferences, in an exclusive interview with CNN,[89] Burkhardt expressed surprise at the anger directed at him for not arriving until the fifth day of the crisis: "I'd been told about it. But it was worse than I thought. I thought people would respond to my willingness to come there.

Maybe I didn't present my case very well, but I'm not a communications professional. I'm a manager."

Months later, in December 2013, Burkhardt reflected about the reaction of the townspeople to his presence in Lac-Megantic after the accident occurred. Speaking with the Canadian Press, he said, "They had every reason to be very upset with what had occurred. But what they didn't know was that I was equally upset and I was a victim of this whole thing."[90]

The Aftermath of the Inferno

Benzene contaminated the disaster site, seeping several meters into the soil. Lake Mégantic and the Chaudière River were contaminated by 26,000 gallons of crude oil. Hydrocarbons polluted the waterfront. Early estimates projected the costs of clean-up at more than $400 million.

Within days of the catastrophe, the Transportation Safety Board of Canada (TSB) and Sûreté de Québec (the provincial police force) announced, independently, that they would be investigating the derailment. Both organizations confirmed that they were anticipating that their investigations would consider the possibility of criminal negligence.

Turning points in the aftermath include the following actions of key stakeholders:

- July 15, 2013: In Canada and in the U.S., residents of Lac-Mégantic filed class action and individual lawsuits against MMA, as well as a list of additional rail carriers and oil companies.
- August 7, 2013: MMA filed for bankruptcy protection in the U.S. under Chapter 11 and in Canada under the Canadian Companies Creditors Arrangement Act. They cited debts to more than 200 creditors, along with pending lawsuits and anticipated clean-up costs.
- May 12, 2014: Sûreté de Québec arrested three former employees of MMA: the train's engineer, the manager of train operations, and the railway traffic controller.

- May 13, 2013: Prosecutors filed charges of criminal negligence causing death against MMA and its former employees who had been arrested.
- June 14, 2014: The government of Québec filed a claim against MMA for more than $400 million for clean-up costs and damages.
- August 19, 2014: The Transportation Safety Board of Canada (TSB) issued the report of their findings regarding the incident, *Railway Investigation Report R13D0054*.[91] In Section 3.1, "Findings as to Causes and Contributing Factors," TSB identified eighteen distinct factors.

Items particularly relevant to this case are listed here, verbatim and numbered as in the TSB report:

- Item #1: MMA-002 was parked unattended on the main line, on a descending grade, with the securement of the train reliant on a locomotive that was not in proper operating condition.
- Item #12: Montreal, Maine & Atlantic Railway did not provide effective training or oversight to ensure that crews understood and complied with rules governing train securement.
- Item #13: When making significant operational changes on its network, Montreal, Maine & Atlantic Railway did not thoroughly identify and manage the risks to ensure safe operations.
- Item #14: Montreal, Maine & Atlantic Railway's safety management system was missing key processes, and others were not being effectively used. As a result, Montreal, Maine & Atlantic Railway did not have a fully functioning safety management system to effectively manage risk.
- Item #15: Montreal, Maine & Atlantic Railway's weak safety culture contributed to the continuation of unsafe conditions and unsafe practices, and compromised Montreal, Maine & Atlantic Railway's ability to effectively manage safety.
- Item #18: The limited number and scope of safety management system audits that were conducted by Transport Canada Québec

Region, and the absence of a follow-up procedure to ensure Montreal, Maine & Atlantic Railway's corrective action plans had been implemented, contributed to the systemic weaknesses in Montreal, Maine & Atlantic Railway's safety management system remaining unaddressed.

The following additional findings that are particularly relevant to this case are listed below, verbatim, from Section 3.2, "Other Findings" of the TSB report:

- Item #3: The Nantes Fire Department had to shut down the locomotive to stop the flow of oil, which was feeding the fire. Their actions were consistent with railway instructions.
- Item #5: Despite the challenges of responding to a major disaster not specifically covered by many firefighters' practical training, the emergency response was conducted in a well-coordinated and effective manner.
- June 9, 2015: The families of victims of the disaster agreed to a settlement package totaling more than $430 million. More than half the settlement was designated to reimburse legal fees, as well as municipal, provincial, and national government expenditures. Distributions to victims' families would range from $400,000 to $5 million dollars, depending on losses.
- January 19, 2018: After nine days of deliberation by the jury, each of the three former employees of MMA were acquitted of all charges.

Four years after the tragedy, despite criminal investigation and acquittal of MMA's employees, as well as the TSB's conclusion that the company's safety culture was a cause of the accident, Burkhardt continued to blame the tragedy on his former employees. As Burkhardt told a reporter from the *Journal de Montreal,* "It was caused by a violation of operational rules…If we can ensure that employees follow the rules more strictly, then we could reduce the risks."[92]

6. SIMULATIONS

What?

Simulations are the most sophisticated of crisis tools. Powerful simulations convey a sense of the intensity and chaos of crises. Think of them as rehearsals for testing, evaluating, and improving crisis plans, and enhancing participants' knowledge and skills for handling crises and dealing with stakeholders.

Some types of organizations are required by state, regional or national regulation to perform crisis simulations. For example, schools in many locations must conduct fire and lockdown drills to make emergency responses systematic, habitual and rapid, while food manufacturers in some regions must run mock product recalls to verify that retrieval of unsafe foods could be achieved thoroughly, accurately, and within a specified time limit.

To customize this tool for your organization, take a look at your crisis road map. Consider which threats could be reduced by preparing, practicing and learning from a coordinated, organization-wide response. Start with a simple simulation as a drill—cybercrime, spills, accidents, or whatever your organizational needs may be—to reassure participants that preparing and practicing are safe and beneficial, and to make improvements through lessons learned.

The scope of simulations varies widely. Simplest versions take place in-house, with a limited group of employees who have already been well prepared to deal with crises. Common examples of this scope might include senior executives or the Crisis Leadership Team (CLT) only, or a combination of these groups. Starting with skilled, top level participants is an excellent beginning, but the limitations miss some of the greatest benefits of this tool.

Other versions of in-house options can broaden crisis readiness. These roll-outs may include additional leaders at varying levels, with representatives from simulation-relevant functions. Threats of cybercrime might include not only info-tech experts, but also legal and financial experts, internal and external. In-house options can involve employees at just one site, across multiple locations, or organization-wide.

Realism grows when external stakeholders take part in simulation exercises. Externals can be portrayed by actors, or by representatives selected among your actual, trustworthy stakeholders. Diverse ensembles may come together through industry affiliations, local crisis responders (firefighters, EMTs), or shared concerns about threats. Actual external stakeholders can be enticed by potential improvements to their own crisis readiness and by opportunities to expand or strengthen ties with others engaged in the exercise. Diverse representation is invaluable for aligning expectations and objectives, and building stronger ties through hands-on collaboration and shared learning, but it complicates design and coordination.

Why?

Simulations expose participants to a range of crisis possibilities, from identifying and interpreting early warning signals and underlying causes, to handling potential impacts, consequences and repercussions. Simulation practice increases understanding of crises, including what works and what does not, and why. Even in simulated format, facing into crises can improve essential interpersonal techniques for crises, such as appreciative questioning, adept listening, and no-fault learning. Through open discussions and feedback, unforeseen strengths and vulnerabilities may become obvious. Expectations may collide or prove inaccurate when put to the test of simulation. Real time face-offs sometimes occur regarding who will be in charge. Incompatibilities may surface, such as misfits of shared equipment. Solving such tensions through simulation can save the day when actual crises loom.

How?

Simulations are the most sophisticated crisis tool and also the most challenging to plan and lead. Effective simulations have an intricate story line, revealing twists and turns as the event and participant responses evolve. Those taking part should feel constriction of time, pressures of grave uncertainty, and emotional impacts of dealing with stakeholders under the influence of (simulated) crises.

To optimize outcomes when the exercise is fictional, not a regulated drill, everyone involved should be encouraged to experiment astutely with new roles and demands, to innovate approaches where fitting prescribed options do not exist, and to take calculated risks as they attempt to make their best responses. This does not imply that mistakes will be ignored. To the contrary, highest impact lessons evolve from deep, candid, collective analysis and honest self-reflection, especially regarding errors and issues missed. Achieving these results requires free flowing information, in the context of no-fault learning.

Orchestrating a simulation event is much like setting the stage and feeding rich cues for an improv theater production. Generally, details of excellent simulations include unpredicted challenges, unthinkable outcomes, and unforeseen stakeholder needs and responses. Like improvisation, many circumstances of powerful simulations must be dealt with extemporaneously.

For the most part, crisis simulations lean into worst-case circumstances. Many details regard things that go wrong, issues and threats that emerge or evolve in unanticipated ways. Often, glitches impair execution, snags tie up resources and cloud guidance. Information at hand may be inadequate intentionally, or the exchange of information may falter during execution. Dangerous turning points may be signaled implicitly, and the intensity of threats may heat up very slowly, at first. The process is complex, which makes simulations invaluable tools to energize preparation, enhance individual and team engagement in crisis thinking and action, set course for improvements, and foster some unforgettable lessons for all involved.

Simulation Example: Kenaco

For a closer view into the dynamics of simulations, glimpses and excerpts here come from simulations that I designed, orchestrated, debriefed, and evaluated with diverse types and sizes of organizations and mixed groups. These are simply guidelines, samples of the types of information that bring the tool to life. In application, keep the information that you provide concise and mostly relevant to the specific crisis at hand. Aim to keep participants engaged and to stretch their thinking and skills with creative, challenging details.

Generic Storyline Briefings

Share background facts with all participants. For this level of briefing, only one overview perspective is necessary, which should include basic information about the organization of focus. Summaries can include any of the following: organizational history, industry, products and services, competitiveness and financial standing, reputation, customer and site locations, strategy, core values, major competitors.

This excerpt is drawn from the opening paragraphs of a simulation regarding Kenaco, a fictitious chemical manufacturer.

> The wealth of opportunities that are currently available in the global chemical industry stress the need for Kenaco to become a valued partner in all targeted regions of the world. Beyond the limited developmental possibilities in its home country, Kenaco is targeting future regional expansion opportunities in Eastern Europe and the Pacific Rim, and plans to evaluate prospects in South America soon.
>
> Kenaco's product line includes fertilizers and agricultural additives, plastics, and artificial fibers. The company's strong presence in the worldwide production of fertilizers, plastics, and artificial fibers provides a gross revenue of US$7.6 billion.
>
> News has just broken that Kenaco has experienced a leak in one of its ammonium hydroxide tanks at its Andrews Plant, located near Rahway, New Jersey (a suburb west of New York City). Initial modeling of the projected gas plume indicates a very slight chance that Overview Hills Estates or Rahway City Hall could lie within the path of the leak, if gas escapes the plant. At this point, the leak has been contained within the plant.

Briefings Customized to Participant Groups

External roles played to enhance simulations often include the media, customers, and other representatives of the public who might be affected by the crisis. For each category of stakeholder portrayed, customize information to their specific role and distribute only to them. Provide enough information to get started, as well as any desired guidance about how best to play the role for the simulation. Encourage participants to stick to their role throughout the simulation, and to respond accordingly as context and circumstances evolve.

These excerpts are from briefings written for members of the media (actual or actors):

- *At a minimum, attempt to probe:*
  - *details of the crisis*
  - *the organization's responses to this point, and future plans*
  - *threats that still linger*
  - *reasons why responses were not quicker or better*
- *Lean toward attempting to guide and push respondents to make the interaction as lively as could be realistic. Please do be at least somewhat responsive to answers that seem effective, but step up to question or counter glaring errors of judgment.*
- *Feel free to create and add a few rumors into your questions, for example, blemishes on the organization's safety record, or employee actions alleged as causes of the crisis.*

Briefings Customized to Individual Characters

Briefings are also useful for individuals playing specific stakeholders. Here, characters' notes introduce new details. For any simulation, there is an unlimited array of specific roles that could be portrayed. Think creatively to help bring the simulation to life.

Mark Egan, Rahway fireman. *"What is that stink?" Your Chief has asked you to call to determine the latest information regarding the possibility of evacuation or fire hazards. You want to know whether you need to bring HazMat suits and how many would be needed by city officials.*

Dr. Elizabeth Drucker, M.D., Head of Emergency Medicine at the hospital closest to the plant. *You have heard that there may be toxic fumes coming from the plant. "What is the status?" Yours is a small hospital and you are short-staffed today. You're trying to determine how widespread the impacts will be, and whether additional patients will need to be transferred to City General Hospital.*

Frank Hogan, principal of Helen Keller Elementary School, about two miles from the plant. *Some parents have called his office, concerned about their children. "Is it true that there's a poisonous gas cloud heading for the school, and that it might explode?" Does he need to evacuate the school or should they shelter in place? Should he alert the fire department or police for more information? Who is going to assist us with transportation since the fumes are dangerous and our students are vision and hearing impaired?*

Background Detailing

Sometimes, to get things rolling smoothly, initial tasks are recommended for specific stakeholders. In this case, deeper background details and preliminary guidance were provided to members of the Crisis Leadership Team.

> *The plant management has closed the spill control gates in an effort to restrain any additional leakage that could occur. Preliminary notification has been phoned to government agencies, Kenaco's corporate-level health and safety leadership, and local emergency responders.*

> *The initial task for the CLT is to discuss the situation, including identifying and preparing a list of decisions and actions that might be anticipated based on what you know so far about the crisis and the Kenaco organization. Determine and record initial plans for responding to the current and projected challenges in ways relevant to Kenaco's core values.*

Scenario Updates

Have new information and revisions to scenario details ready for distribution throughout the simulation. Create some that are appropriate for all participants; give others to select roles only. Use a variety of communication channels.

Be prepared to create updates ad hoc as the simulation unfolds. Use these to support, refute, or complicate information, insights and approaches that have emerged from perspectives and behaviors of participants during the simulation. Sources of this hypothetical information might be personnel files, shifts in weather forecasts, public records, or anonymous tips, as represented below.

Anonymous Tip

A background check on the forklift driver whose carelessness is believed to have caused the original rupture in the storage tank indicates that they have been employed by Kenaco for nearly a decade. Their "above average" performance evaluations led to lateral transfers through four Kenaco plants. Their personnel file includes summary information about two charges of sexual harassment, which were overturned by senior executives. An additional document in their file, dated last year, states that they were reprimanded and sent home for the day after threatening a supervisor during an argument.

Where To Learn More

How to Maximize Your Research Time

I challenge and encourage my clients and graduate students to read a book a week, devoting about one hour to the task. Most business books can be read in an hour if you read in a focused way, looking for answers to particular questions and challenges. I call this Leader-level Reading, and here is how to do it:

- Read with your brain turned on.
- Eliminate two habits: subvocalizing and highlighting.
- Remember: this approach is for business trade books, not textbooks, professional manuals or novels you read to grasp or enjoy every detail.
- Set a timer for each stage.
- If the book isn't giving you what you need, read faster, jump ahead, or find a better book.

1) First 3 minutes

- Goal: Consider what this book might mean to or for you.
- Task: Soak up context before you start reading (or buying/borrowing the book).
  - o Review the title, jacket (flaps, back, publisher, date of publication, other books by author) table of contents, and index.
- Stop & Reflect:
  - o How is this book likely to fulfill your goal?
  - o How might it relate to issues important to you now?

2) Next 10 minutes

- Goal: Consider basic message/focus/structure, how it might be useful to you now.
- Task: Skim introduction and early chapters, focus on structure and your interests.
- Stop & Reflect:
  - What's the basic message of the book?
  - What do you want from the book?
  - What do you need from the book?
  - How might it relate to issues important to you now?

3) Next 20 minutes

- Goal: Catch key concepts and spark new thoughts of your own.
- Task: Skim opening paragraph, flip to and through chapters that grab your interest and skim them quickly, fold pages, make quick notes, as desired.
- Stop & Reflect:
  - What are key concepts for you?

4) Final 15 – 20 minutes

- Repeat step 3 as desired for chapters that grab your interest.
- Stop & Reflect:
  - How do these ideas apply to you and your work now?
  - What can you glean for issues important to you?
  - Will you return to this book as a reference for further reflection and application? Will you recommend it to someone? Who could really benefit from reading it?

If it seems worth your time, schedule your next session with this book on your calendar.

I hope this book you are reading now will be one of those helpful companions and references worth returning to and recommending to others as you embrace crisis, plan, prepare and learn, to come out stronger.

Notes

Front Matter

[1] **Crisis definition.** Christine M. Pearson and Judy A. Clair, "Reframing crisis management," Academy of Management Review, 23.1 (January 1998), 59-78.

BEFORE

Chapter 1: Why Not Just Wing It?

[2] **Normal accidents.** Charles Perrow, *Normal Accidents: Living with High Risk Technologies* (New York: Basic Books, 1984).

[3] **Board members unaware of crisis management preparations. One half had no action plans for crisis management.** Deloitte, "A Crisis of Confidence," 2016. http://www.deloitte.com/acrisisofconfidence.

   Only one-fourth had tested their plans. Deloitte, "Stronger, fitter, better: Crisis management for the resilient enterprise." 2018. https://www2.deloitte.com/content/dam/insights/us/articles/GLOB305_Crisis-management-survey/DI_Crisis-Management-Survey.pdf

[4] **Problem-solving.** Richard O. Mason and Ian I. Mitroff, *Challenging Strategic Planning Assumptions* (New York: John Wiley & Sons, 1981).

[5] **Reacting without conscious thought.** James Reason, *A Life in Error* (Burlington, VT: Ashgate Publishing Company, 2013).

[6] **Satisficing to solve problems.** James G. Marsh and Herbert A. Simon, *Organizations*, 2nd ed (New York: Wiley, 1993).

[7] **"Safe dangerous."** Steve Larese, "Ready, set, scream! Verruckt open for business," *USA Today*, July 9, 2014. https://www.usatoday.com/story/travel/destinations/2014/07/09/verruckt-water-slide-schlitterbahn-park/12411769/.

[8] **Verrückt case.** Christine M. Pearson, "Verrückt: Insane Design, Testing, Construction, and Operation." Thunderbird Case Series A15-20-0019 (Phoenix, AZ: Thunderbird School of Global Management, 2020). https://thunderbird.asu.edu/faculty-and-research/case-series/id/a15-20-0019.

[9] **Frequency of corporate crisis experiences.** Deloitte, "Stronger, fitter, better: Crisis management for the resilient enterprise." 2018. https://www2.deloitte.com/content/dam/insights/us/articles/GLOB305_Crisis-management-survey/DI_Crisis-Management-Survey.pdf.

[10] **Grace period measured in minutes.** Davia Termin, "You Have 15 Minutes To Respond To A Crisis: A Checklist of Dos And Don'ts," *Forbes*, Aug 6, 2015. https://www.forbes.com/sites/daviatemin/2015/08/06/you-have-15-minutes-to-respond-to-a-crisis-a-checklist-of-dos-and-donts/?sh=7289104250a8.

Chapter 2: Behave Like Adept Crisis Leaders, Embrace their Perspectives

[11] **Fukushima as man-made disaster.** Najmedin Meshkati, "Fukushima Nuclear Accident: Lessons Learned for U.S. Nuclear Power Plants," *Viterabi*, Spring 2015. https://magazine.viterbi.usc.edu/spring-2015-2/editorial/fukushima-nuclear-accident/

[12] **Fukushima II leadership.** Ranjay Gulati, Charles Casto, and Charlotte Krontiris, "How the Other Fukushima Plant Survived," *Harvard Business Review*, July-August 2014. https://hbr.org/2014/07/how-the-other-fukushima-plant-survived

[13] **Asking better questions.** Edgar H Schein, *Humble Inquiry: The Gentle Art of Asking Instead of Telling* (San Francisco: Berrett-Koehler, 2013).

[14] **Improving investigations.** Todd Conklin, *Pre-Accident Investigations: Better Questions - An Applied Approach to Operational Learning* (Boca Raton, FL: CBC Press, 2016).

[15] **Hayward's emotional remarks.** Monica Langley, "Hayward defends tenure, BP's spill response," *The Wall Street Journal*, July 30, 2010. https://www.wsj.com/articles/SB10001424052748703578104575397483256188088.

[16] **Safety is not our business model.** Jack Kelly, "When A Company Prioritizes Profit Over People: Boeing CEO Tells Congress That Safety Is 'Not Our Business Model'," *Forbes*, Oct. 30, 2019. https://www.forbes.com/sites/jackkelly/2019/10/30/when-companies-prioritize-profits-over-employee-and-consumer-safety-after-fatal-boeing-737-max-crashes-ceo-tells-congress-that-safety-is-not-our-business-model/.

[17] **Responding to negative emotions at work.** Christine M Pearson, "The Smart Way to Respond to Negative Emotions at Work," *Sloan Management Review*, March 13, 2017. https://sloanreview.mit.edu/article/the-smart-way-to-respond-to-negative-emotions-at-work/.

[18] **Leading from all levels.** Scott Berinato, "You have to lead from everywhere," *Harvard Business Review*, Nov. 2010. https://hbr.org/2010/11/you-have-to-lead-from-everywhere.

[19] **Fukushima II leadership.** Gulati, 2014.

[20] **Fukushima II leadership.** Gulati, 2014.

Chapter 3: Establish Your Foundation

[21] **James Burke of J&J on Fortune's list.** Jim Collins, "The 10 Greatest CEOs of All Time: What these extraordinary leaders can teach today's troubled executives," *Fortune*, July 21, 2003.
https://archive.fortune.com/magazines/fortune/fortune_archive/2003/07/21/346095/index.htm.

[22] **J&J Credo.** "Our Credo," Johnson & Johnson website.
https://ourstory.jnj.com/living-our-credo#our-credo-ch-4-1].

[23] **J&J Credo.**

Chapter 4: Create a Superb Crisis Leadership Team

[24] **Exceptional crisis teaming.** Erika Hayes James and Lynn Perry Wooten, *Leading Under Pressure* (New York: Taylor and Francis Group, 2010).
George B. Graen and Joan A. Graen, editors, *Management of Team Leadership in Extreme Contexts* (Charlotte, NC: Information Age Publishing, 2013).

[25] **IDEO's creative approaches.** IDEO website.
https://designthinking.ideo.com/resources. IDEO's Shopping Cart Design Process: https://www.youtube.com/watch?v=izjhx17NuSE.
Tom Kelly and Dave Kelly, *Creative Confidence: Unleashing the Creative Potential Within Us All* (Redfern, Australia: Currency Press, 2015).

[26] **Mike Tyson's famous response.** When asked by a reporter about his concerns regarding his upcoming bout with Evander Holyfield, Tyson replied, "Everybody has a plan until they get punched in the mouth."

Chapter 5: Map Your Crisis Plans

27 **Working in creative bursts:** Austin Kleon, *Steal Like an Artist.* (New York: Workman Publishing, 2012).

28 **Suspending simplification:** Karl E. Weick and Kathleen M. Sutcliffe, *Managing the Unexpected,* 3rd ed. (Hoboken, NJ: Wiley, 2015).

Chapter 6: Take Your Crisis Roadmap on a Test Drive

29 Jane E. Dutton, *Energize Your Workplace: How to Create and Sustain High-quality Connections at Work* (San Francisco: Jossey-Bass, 2003).
    Edgar H. Schein, *Humble Inquiry: The Gentle Art of Asking Instead of Telling* (San Francisco: Berrett-Koehler, 2013).

Chapter 7: Build Strength Organization-wide

30 **Advanced crisis preparation and practices at H-E-B.** Dan Solomon and Paula Forbes, "Inside the Story of How H-E-B Planned for the Pandemic," *Texas Monthly*, March 26, 2020. https://www.texasmonthly.com/food/heb-prepared-coronavirus-pandemic/

Chapter 8: Amplify Signal Detection

31 **NASA organizational causes of Columbia Accident.** NASA, "Report of the Columbia Accident Investigation Board, Volume 1," Aug. 26, 2003. https://www.nasa.gov/columbia/home/CAIB_Vol1.html.

32 **NASA organizational causes of Challenger Accident.** NASA, "Report of the Presidential Commission on the Space Shuttle Challenger Accident, Chapter V: The Contributing Cause of The Accident," July 14, 1986. https://history.nasa.gov/rogersrep/v1ch5.htm.

[33] **"When a Manager Whitewashes" case.** Christine M. Pearson, "Crisis Management, Signal Detection, and Organizational Destruction: When a Manager Whitewashes, Buries, and Demolishes the Evidence," Thunderbird Case Series A05-21-0001 (Phoenix, AZ: Thunderbird School of Global Management, 2021). https://thunderbird.asu.edu/faculty-and-research/case-series/id/a05-21-0001.

[34] **Rewarding signal notification.** Chris Clearfield and András Tilcsik, "How to prepare for a crisis you couldn't possibly predict," *Harvard Business Review*, March 16, 2018. https://hbr.org/2018/03/how-to-prepare-for-a-crisis-you-couldnt-possibly-predict.

Chris Clearfield and András Tilcsik, *Meltdown: What Plane Crashes, Oil Spills, and Dumb Business Decisions Can Teach Us About How to Succeed at Home and Work* (New York: Penguin Random House, 2018).

[35] **Avoiding detection blocks.** Margaret Heffernan, *Willful Blindness* (New York: Bloomsbury, 2011).

Matthew McKay, Martha Davis, and Patrick Fanning *Messages: The Communication Skills Handbook.* (Oakland, CA: New Harbinger Publications, 2009).

DURING AND AFTER

Chapter 9: Reinforce the Crisis Response Cycle

[36] **Tour de France case.** Christine M. Pearson, "COVID and Crisis Management: How the Tour de France Averted Ultimate Super-spreader Status," Thunderbird Case Series. A15-21-0002 (Phoenix, AZ: Thunderbird School of Global Management, 2021). https://thunderbird.asu.edu/faculty-and-research/case-series/id/a15-21-0002.

[37] **Explosion at Lac Megantic case.** Christine M. Pearson, "Le Train d'Enfer and the Derailing of Crisis Leadership Lac Mégantic," Thunderbird Case Series A15-19-0010 (Phoenix, AZ: Thunderbird School of Global Management, 2019). https://thunderbird.asu.edu/faculty-and-research/case-series/id/a15-19-0010.

[38] **Burkhardt's insensitive comments.** Aaron Hutchins, "Breakfast with the most hated man in Lac-Mégantic: In conversation with Rail World Inc. president Edward Burkhardt," *Maclean's*, July 11, 2013. https://www.macleans.ca/politics/breakfast-with-the-most-hated-man-in-lac-megantic/.

[29] **Burkhardt continued.** Andy Blatchford and Paola Loriggio, "Railway boss Edward Burkhardt arrives in Lac-Mégantic as death toll rises," *Vancouver Sun*: July 10, 2013. https://vancouversun.com/News/National/railway-boss-edward-burkhardt-arrives-in-lac-mégantic-as-death-toll-rises?r.

[40] **Developing a meditation practice.** Pema Chodron, *How to Meditate: A Practical Guide for Making Friends with Your Mind* (Louisville, CO: Sounds True, 2013).

Jon Kabat-Zinn, *Wherever You Go, There You Are: Mindful Mediation in Everyday Life,* (New York: Hatchette Books, 2005).

Meditation apps are a popular way to learn the practice, including (at the time of publication) Headspace, Insight Timer, Calm, Ten Percent Happier, and many more.

Chapter 10: Learn, Improve, Sustain

[41] **Learning from crises.** Chris Argyris, *Teaching Smart People How to Learn* (Boston: Harvard Business School Press, 2008).

[42] **Double-loop learning.** Chris Argyris and Donald A. Schön, *Organizational Learning II: Theory, Method and Practice* (Reading, MA: Addison-Wesley, 1996).

[43] **Triple-loop learning.** Wietska Medema, Arjen Wals, and Jan Adamowski, "Multi-Loop Social Learning for Sustainable Land and Water Governance: Towards a Research Agenda on the Potential of Virtual Learning Platforms," *Journal of Life Sciences* 69 (2014): 23-38.

Ase Johannessen, Asa Gerger Swartling, et al. "Transforming urban water governance through social (triple-loop) learning," *Environmental Policy Governance* 29.11 (January 2019). https://doi.org/10.1002/eet.1843.

[44] **Especially for smart people**. Chris Argyris, *Teaching Smart People How to Learn* (Boston: Harvard Business School Press, 2008).

[45] **Resilience.** Kathleen Tierney, *The Social Roots of Resilience* (Stanford, CA: Stanford University Press. 2014).

[46] **Playing to your strengths.** Laura Mitchell Roberts, Gretchen Spreitzer, Jane E. Dutton, Robert E. Quinn, Emily D. Heaphy, and Brianna Barker, "How to play to your strengths," *Harvard Business Review*: January 2005. https://hbr.org/2005/01/how-to-play-to-your-strengths.

[47] **Crucibles.** Warren Bennis and Robert .J. Thomas, "Crucibles of leadership," *Harvard Business Review, 80.9* (September 2002), 39-45. https://hbr.org/2002/09/crucibles-of-leadership.

[48] **Coping.** Glenys Parry, *Coping with Crises* (London: Routledge, 1992).

[49] **Tragedies.** Jon Kabat-Zinn, *Full Catastrophe Living.* (New York: Bantam Books, 2013).

TODAY'S CRISIS ACCELERATORS

Chapter 11: Running on Fumes, Relentlessly

[50] **Crisis costs.** IBM Security, "Cost of a Data Breach Report 2020." https://www.ibm.com/security/digital-assets/cost-data-breach-report/#/.

[51] **CrazyBusy.** Edward M. Hallowell, MD, *CrazyBusy: Overstretched, Overbooked, and About to Snap! Strategies for Handling Your Fast-Paced Life* (New York: Ballantine Books, 2007).

[52] **Four ingredients of empowerment.** David E. Bowen and Edward E. Lawler III, "Empowering Service Employees," *Sloan Management Review,* July 15, 1995. https://sloanreview.mit.edu/article/empowering-service-employees/.

Chapter 12: Nowhere Left to Hide

[53] **Expansion exacerbates exposure.** N. Anand and Jean-Louis Barsoux, *Quest: Leading Global Transformations* (Lausanne, Switzerland: IMD, 2014).

[54] **Classic perspective of culture.** Adapted from Edgar H. Schein, *Organizational Culture and Leadership* (San Francisco: Jossey-Bass, 1990), p. 14.

[55] **Cultural implications.** Erin Meyer, *Culture Map: Breaking Through the Invisible Boundaries of Global Business* (Philadelphia: Perseus, 2014).
David A. Thomas and Kerr Inkson, *Cultural Intelligence: Surviving and Thriving in the Global Village,* 3rd ed. (Oakland, CA: Berrett-Koehler, 2017).
Robert J. House, Paul J. Hanges, Mansour Javidan, Peter W. Dorfman, Vpin Gupta, et. al., *Culture, Leadership, and Organizations: The GLOBE Study of 62 Societies* (Thousand Oaks, CA: Sage Publications, 2004).

[56] **Cultural self-assessment tools.** Cultural Orientations Indicator (COI). https://www.berlitz.com/en-es/business-services/culture-training.

Hofstede Insights Culture Compass. https://www.hofstede-insights.com/product/compare-countries/.

Erin Meyers Country Mapping Tool: https://www.erinmeyer.com/tools/culture-map-premium/.

[57] See Cultural implications and Culture tools above.

Chapter 13: Privacy and the Grace Period are Vanishing

[58] **Impacts and implications of the Fourth Industrial Revolution.** Chris R. Groscurth, *Future-Ready Leadership: Strategies for the Fourth Industrial Revolution* (Santa Barbara: Praeger, 2018).

Klaus Schwab, *The Fourth Industrial Revolution* (New York: Currency, 2016).

Klaus Schwab, *Shaping the Fourth Industrial Revolution* (Geneva: World Economic Forum, 2018).

[59] **15 minutes to respond to a crisis.** Davia Termin, "You Have 15 Minutes To Respond To A Crisis: A Checklist of Dos And Don'ts." *Forbes,* Aug 6, 2015. https://www.forbes.com/sites/daviatemin/2015/08/06/you-have-15-minutes-to-respond-to-a-crisis-a-checklist-of-dos-and-donts/?sh=7289104250a8.

[60] **Siemens China refrigerator repair.** Holmes Report, "The Top 12 Crises Of 2012: Part 2," Feb 3. 2013. https://www.provokemedia.com/long-reads/article/the-top-12-crises-of-2012-part-2.

[61] **Techno-fused Hall of Shame.** Tom Simonite, "Don't End Up in This Artificial Intelligence Hall of Shame," Wired, June 3, 2021. https://www.wired.com/story/artificial-intelligence-hall-shame/

Chapter 14: Our Attention has Been Seized, Our Empathy is Hardening

[62] **Devices impairing attention.** Sherry Turkle, *Reclaiming Conversation: The Power of Talk in a Digital Age,* (New York: Penguin Random House, 2015), pp. 358-360.

[63] **Presence of a phone inhibits how we listen and diminishes the degree of connection or trust**: Andrew K. Przybylski and Netta Weinstein, "Can you connect with me now? How the presence of mobile communication technology influences face-to-face conversation quality," *Journal of Social and Personal Relationships,* 30.3 (2010): 237-246. https://journals.sagepub.com/doi/full/10.1177/0265407512453827.

[64] **Connecting with devices as if connecting with sentient beings.** Turkle.

[65] **Safeguarding our attention.** Adam Alter, *Irresistible: The Rise of Addictive Technology and the Business of Keeping Us Hooked,* (New York: Penguin Press, 2017).
   Maggie Jackson, *Distracted: The Erosion of Attention and the Coming Dark Age,* (Amherst, NY: Prometheus, 2008).

[66] **Not confusing time on task with speed to goal.** Jeff Hunter, "Embracing Confusion." Interview with Shane Parrish. *Farnam Street: Knowledge Network.* Podcast audio. January 20, 2020. https://podcasts.apple.com/us/podcast/74-jeff-hunter-embracing-confusion/id990149481?i=1000463242851.

Chapter 15: Our Habits are Dulling Our Insights

[67] **Habit definition.** "Habit," *Merriam Webster Dictionary.* https://www.merriam-webster.com/dictionary/habit
   Charles Duhigg, *The Power of Habit: Why We Do What We Do in Life and Business,* (New York: Random House, 2012).

[68] **Habits control nearly half our waking hours.** *David T. Neal, Wendy Wood, and Jeffrey M. Quinn*, "Habits—A Repeat Performance," *Current Directions in Psychological Research*, 15.4 (August 2006): 198-202. https://journals.sagepub.com/doi/10.1111/j.1467-8721.2006.00435.x.

[69] **NTSB on Boeing 737 Max design.** David Gelles, "Boeing 737 Max: What's Happened After the 2 Deadly Crashes," *The New York Times*, updated October 28, 2019. https://www.nytimes.com/interactive/2019/business/boeing-737-crashes.html.

[70] **Boeing engineer urged addition of alert system.** Natalie Kitroeff, David Gelles and Jack Nicas, "Boeing 737 Max Safety System Was Vetoed, Engineer Says," *The New York Times*, October 2, 2019, updated October 29, 2019. https://www.nytimes.com/2019/10/02/business/boeing-737-max-crashes.html.

[71] **Boeing criminal charges and agreement.** The United States Department of Justice, *"Boeing Charged with 737 Max Fraud Conspiracy and Agrees to Pay over $2.5 Billion,"* January 7, 2021. https://www.justice.gov/opa/pr/boeing-charged-737-max-fraud-conspiracy-and-agrees-pay-over-25-billion.

[72] **Muilenburg fired.** Ankit Ajmera and Tim Hepher, "Boeing fires CEO Muilenburg to restore confidence amid 737 crisis," *Reuters,* December 23, 2019. https://www.reuters.com/article/us-boeing-737-max-ceo/boeing-fires-ceo-muilenburg-to-restore-confidence-amid-737-crisis-idUSKBN1YR1FL.

[73] **Questions linger about AVA052.** NTSB (National Transportation Safety Board), "Aircraft Accident Report: Avianca the Airline of Columbia, Boeing 707-321B, HK 2016, Fuel Exhaustion, Cove Neck, New York, January 25, 1990." Adopted April 30, 1991. https://www.ntsb.gov/investigations/AccidentReports/Reports/AAR9104.pdf.
AVA 052 case. Christine M. Pearson, "Slighting Urgency: A Cross-Cultural Reexamination of the Crash of Avianca Flight 052," Thunderbird

Case Series A05-19-0005 (Phoenix, AZ: Thunderbird School of Global Management, 2019). https://thunderbird.asu.edu/faculty-and-research/case-series/id/a05-19-0005.

[74] **A few moments of darkness and quiet.** John H. Cushman, Jr., "Avianca Flight 52: The Delays That Ended in Disaster," *The New York Times,* February 5, 1990, B1, B6. https://www.nytimes.com/1990/02/05/nyregion/avianca-flight-52-the-delays-that-ended-in-disaster.html.

    See NTSB incident report, p. 73.

[75] **Eliminating error.** Jan U. Hagen, *Confronting Mistakes: Lessons from the Aviation Industry When Dealing with Error.* (New York: Palgrave Macmillan, 2013).

    James Reason, *Managing the Risks of Organizational Accidents* (Burlington, VT: Ashgate Publishing, 1997).

    James Reason, *A Life in Error* (Burlington, VT: Ashgate Publishing, 2013).

Chapter 16: Our Biases Are Blinding Us Into and Out of Crises

[76] **Pogo.** "We Have Met the Enemy and He Is Us." Billy Ireland Cartoon Library & Museum at The Ohio State University. https://library.osu.edu/site/40stories/2020/01/05/we-have-met-the-enemy/.

[77] **Bias definition.** Pamela A. Hays, *Addressing Cultural Complexities in Practice,* 3rd ed. (Washington, DC: American Psychological Association, 2016).

[78] **Outsmart your own biases.** Jack B. Soll, Katherine L. Milkman, and John W. Payne, "Outsmart Your Biases: How to broaden your thinking and make better decisions," *Harvard Business Review*, May 2015.

https://hbr.org/2015/05/outsmart-your-own-biases.

Caroll Tavris and Elliot Aronson. *Mistakes Were Made (but Not by Me): Why We Justify Foolish Beliefs, Bad Decisions, and Hurtful Acts*, 3rd ed. (New York: Houghton Mifflin Harcourt, 2020).

[79] **Correcting blind spots.** Mahzarin R. Banaji and Anthony R. Greenwald, *Blindspot: Hidden Biases of Good People* (New York: Bantam, 2016).

Jennifer L. Eberhardt, *Biased: Uncovering the Hidden Prejudice that Shapes What We See, Think, and Do* (NY: Penguin, 2020).

Pamela Hays, *Connecting Across Cultures* (Thousand Oaks, CA: SAGE Publications, 2013).

See Soll, Milkman, and Payne, "Outsmart Your Biases" above.

CRISIS TOOLS

How to Use Crisis Tools

[80] **Executives wish they had prepared.** Deloitte, "Confronting the crisis: How financial services firms are responding to and learning from COVID-19." https://www2.deloitte.com/content/dam/insights/us/articles/6738_confronting-the-crisis/DI_Confronting-the-crisis.pdf.

Stakeholder Analysis

[81] For a classic, definitive view of stakeholder analysis and its application, see Richard O. Mason and Ian I. Mitroff, *Challenging Strategic Planning Assumptions: Theory, Cases and Techniques* (NY: Wiley, 1981).

Case Studies

[82] **Le Train d'Enfer case.** Christine M. Pearson, *Le Train d'Enfer and the Derailing of Crisis Leadership*. Thunderbird A15-19-0010. (Phoenix:

Thunderbird School of Global Management, 2019).
https://thunderbird.asu.edu/faculty-and-research/case-series/id/a15-19-0010
© *2019 Thunderbird School of Global Management, a unit of the Arizona State University Knowledge Enterprise. Used by permission.*

[83] Although the shipping documents were officially labelled "petroleum crude oil," after testing, it was later determined that the product being transported was "Bakken Formation crude oil," a substance of much higher flammability.

[84] Grant Robertson, "Ten-second procedure might have averted Lac-Mégantic disaster." *Globe and Mail*, March 7, 2016.
https://www.theglobeandmail.com/news/national/new-info-shows-backup-brake-may-have-averted-lac-megantic-disaster/article29044518/.

[85] Jessica McDiarmid, "Head of MMA railway has reputation for cost-cutting." *The Star.* July 11, 2013.
https://www.thestar.com/news/canada/2013/07/10/head_of_mma_railway_has_reputation_for_costcutting.

[86] "Rage and frustration during Burkhardt Lac-Mégantic visit." *Montreal Gazette*: https://www.youtube.com/watch?v=WfULxhsPm3Y.

[87] "Lac-Megantic residents angry with train company execs." *Windsor Star*: https://www.youtube.com/watch?v=UTxSj0wemdU.

[88] "RAW: Railway Chairman faces press, angry residents in Lac-Mégantic." *Canadian Broadcast Corporation News*:
https://www.cbc.ca/player/play/2396305048.

[89] Andy Blatchford, Head of railway at centre of Lac-Mégantic disaster: 'I was also a victim'." The Canadian Press. Dec 26, 2013, updated June 16, 2014. https://financialpost.com/business/head-of-railway-at-centre-of-lac-megantic-disaster-i-was-also-a-victim/.

[90] The Canadian Press, "Head of railway in Lac-Mégantic disaster says he's 'also a victim'." https://www.cbc.ca/news/business/head-of-railway-in-lac-m%C3%A9gantic-disaster-says-he-s-also-a-victim-1.2477242.

[91] Transportation Safety Board of Canada (TSB), "Runaway and main-track derailment, Montreal, Maine & Atlantic Railway, Freight train MMA-002, Mile 0.23, Sherbrooke Subdivision, Lac-Mégantic, Quebec, 06 July 2013." https://www.tsb.gc.ca/eng/rapports-reports/rail/2013/r13d0054/r13d0054.html.

[92] Vincent Larin "Burkhardt met la faute sur ses ex-employés," *Le Journal de Montreal*, January 20, 2018. https://www.journaldemontreal.com/2018/01/20/burkhardt-met-la-faute-sur-ses-ex-employes.

Acknowledgments

I'm delighted to have the opportunity to express appreciation to the many people who have helped me move this book forward, even as its development took considerable turns. Thanks to Chris Breon, Jeff Mask, and Peter Hanson for welcoming my requests for feedback on early versions, and for graciously emphasizing the possibilities in their comments. I also appreciate the inspiration and energy brought by the curiosity, open minds, thoughtful questions, and deep global roots among my EMGM, MALM, MGM, and MOOC students. To our Dean and Director General, Sanjeev Khagram, and to our innovative, conscientious staff at all levels, thank you for reigniting the joy of being a T-bird, making truly global expansion a reality, catapulting the School into 4IR, and reinforcing my teaching and service.

For decades, I have had the joy of working with deep thinkers who have broadened and improved concepts and practice of crisis leadership. In particular, thank you, Judy Clair, Amy Sommer, Christophe Roux-Dufort, and Synnove Nesse for always leading with your best ideas and with warm engagement. At the top of this list is Ian Mitroff, to whom I am indebted for profound influences, from fortifying my ability and will to think unconventionally, to opening priceless opportunities for conceptual framebreaking and cutting-edge crisis management experiences. From our earliest endeavors at the University of Southern California's Center for Crisis Management, I am also extremely grateful to the countless executives, managers, supervisors, line employees, volunteers, and emergency responders with whom I have collaborated in thought and action.

As this book took shape, some of its shifts and pivots were inspired by insights developed in other fields, by experts I have not yet met. Prominent among these influencers are James Reason, Pamela A. Hays, Jan Hagen, Sherry Turkle, Erin Meyer, and Klaus Schwab. Thanks to each of you for exceptional blends of rigor, practicality, and substance.

At a more personal level, thank you, Gwyn Nichols, for being the most engaged editor I have ever worked with, and for exceeding your commitments at every turn. I anticipated you would bring meticulous feedback and rich suggestions, as you did. But, I had no idea that you would provide oxygen, too. I am immensely grateful.

Tracy Steen, *Coach Extraordinaire*, your wisdom and guidance have helped me flourish through some of life's great challenges, celebrate progress, and appreciate each aspect of this journey. Thank you for stirring new insights and habits to clear bottom line and stretch hurdles, and for bringing exceptional perceptiveness and kindness always.

I am blessed with four soul sisters, Joan, Maurine, Caren, and Karen, who have fundamentally influenced who I am for five, four, three and (nearly) two decades, respectively. I appreciate your checking in regularly and supportively on my writing, and never grimacing as I rationalized drifting deadlines, repeatedly. I treasure that our relationships are rooted in the best and the worst of times and that, regardless of the circumstances we share, we always aim to help each other come out stronger.

To my son, John, your perspectives transformed this book. With each round of feedback, you added practical insights, stretched and reshaped my thinking. I am touched that, somehow, despite being the embodiment of crazybusy, you created time whenever I asked. Your practical scrutiny and insightful, clever recommendations will benefit every reader.

To my husband, Bryan, thank you for mustering unflinching support, even as my targeted timeframe tripled. This book wouldn't exist without you. Thanks for tolerating my distracted attention and for picking up slack at home for the five plus years that it has taken to write it, and for helping schlep manuscripts across four continents, even as we attempted vacations. I'm grateful you were always my first reader (of too many drafts), who found ways to support my planned paths and occasional rerouting. You are the anchor and the lift that helps me embrace life's most difficult challenges to, eventually, emerge stronger.

About the Author

Christine M. Pearson, Ph.D., has built a global reputation as an expert on leading through the dark aspects at work. An architect of the field of organizational crisis management, for more than three decades, she has guided leaders at all levels in corporations, non-profits, and government entities across five continents to plan for, respond, learn from, and appreciate the extraordinary impacts of crises. She is an award-winning Professor of Global Leadership at the Thunderbird School of Global Management (at ASU), whose research has been featured in practical outlets such as, *Harvard Business Review*, *Sloan Management Review*, *Financial Times*, *The Wall Street Journal*, *The New York Times*, *Fortune*, *Forbes*, *Fast Company*, and *Conference Board Review*, and in more than 600 newspapers and magazines. *Come Out Stronger* is her sixth book.

Made in the USA
Middletown, DE
24 December 2023

45288102R00182